आ नो भद्राः क्रतवो यन्तु विश्वतः ।

Let noble thoughts come to us from every side

—**Rigveda, I-89-i**

BHAVAN'S BOOK UNIVERSITY

ŚRI VIṢṆUSAHASRANĀMA STOTRAM

With English Translation of the Commentary by
Sri Sankara Bhagavatpada

by

P. SANKARANARAYANAN

BHAVAN'S BOOK UNIVERSITY

ŚRI VIṢṆUSAHASRANĀMA STOTRAM

With English Translation of the Commentary by
ŚRI ŚANKARA BHAGAVATPĀDA

Translated by

P.SANKARANARAYANA

Foreword by

N. RAGHUNATHAN

2015

BHARATIYA VIDYA BHAVAN
Kulapati K. M. Munshi Marg
Mumbai - 400 007

1st Edition - 1978

2nd Edition - 1996

3rd Edition - 2007

4th Edition - 2015

Price : ₹. 150.00

PRINTED IN INDIA

By Atul Goradia at Siddhi Printers, 13/14, Bhabha Building,
13th Khetwadi Lane, Mumbai - 400 004, and
Published by P. V. Sankarankutty, Joint Director,
for the Bharatiya Vidya Bhavan,
Kulapati Munshi Marg, Mumbai - 400 007.
E-Mail : bhavan@bhavans.info
Web-site : www.bhavans.info

।।श्रीः।।

यस्मिन्नेतद् विभातं यत इदयभवद् येन चेदं य एतद्
योऽस्मादुत्तीर्णरूपः खलु सकलमिदं भासितं यस्य भासा।
यो वाचां दूरदूरे पुनरपि मनसां यस्य देवा मुनीन्द्रा
नो विद्युस्तत्त्वरूपं किमु पुनरपरे कृष्ण तस्मै नमस्ते ।।

He Who is the Ground on Which this world manifestation appears; Who is both the material and the efficient cause of it; into Whom it dissolves; Who manifests as all the world but none-the-less transcends them all and forms the light of Consciousness by Which, and to Which, they are revealed; Who is far beyond the scope of exact description by words and conception by mind; Whose true nature neither the Devas nor the sages have known, much less others—to that Krishna my salutations!

नो तिर्यञ्चं न मर्त्यं न च सुरमसुरं न स्त्रियं नो पुमांसं
न द्रव्यं कर्म जातिं गुणमपि सदसद्वापि ते रूपमाहुः।
शिष्टं यत् स्यान्निषेधे सति निगमशतैः लक्षणावृत्तितस्तत्
कृच्छ्रेणावेद्यमानं परमसुखमयं भाति तस्मै नमस्ते ।।

The wise describe Thee by a series of negations—as neither human nor non-human; as neither divine nor demoniacal; as neither male nor female; as neither existent nor non-existent; and as without any of the descriptive specifications of the world of objects like substance, attribute, function, and species. Residual after all such negations, and described with great difficulty by the Upanishads through implied references, is that Pure Blissful Awareness that Thou art. To that Being my salutations!

(Nārāyaṇīyam, Canto 98, ślokas 1 and 3 Eng. translation by Swami Tapasyananda).

KULAPATI'S PREFACE

THE Bharatiya Vidya Bhavan—that Institute of Indian Culture in Bombay—needed a Book University, a series of books which, if read, would serve the purpose of providing higher education. Particular emphasis, however, was to be put on such literature as revealed the deeper impulsions of India. As a first step, it was decided to bring out in English 100 books, 50 of which were to be taken in hand almost at once.

It is our intention to publish the books we select, not only in English, but also in the following Indian languages: Hindi, Bengali, Gujarati, Marathi, Tamil, Telugu, Kannada and Malayalam.

This scheme, involving the publication of 900 volumes, requires ample funds and an all-India organisation. The Bhavan is exerting itself to the utmost to supply them.

The objectives for which the Bhavan stands are the reintegration of Indian culture in the light of modern knowledge and to suit our present-day needs and the resuscitation of its fundamental values in their pristine vigour.

Let me make our goal more explicit:

We seek the dignity of man, which necessarily implies the creation of social conditions that allow him freedom to evolve along the lines of his own temperament and capacities; we seek the harmony of individual efforts and social relations, not in any makeshift way, but within the frame-work of the Moral Order; we seek the creative art of life, by the alchemy of which human limitations are progressively transmuted, so that man may become the instrument of God, and is able to see Him in all and all in Him.

The world, we feel, is too much with us. Nothing would uplift or inspire us so much as the beauty and aspiration which such books can teach.

In this series, therefore, the literature of India, ancient and modern, will be published in a form easily accessible to all. Books in other literatures of the world, if they illustrate the principles we stand for, will also be included.

This common pool of literature, it is hoped, will enable the reader, eastern or western, to understand and appreciate currents of world thought, as also the movements of the Indian mind, which, though they flow through different linguistic channels, have a common urge and aspiration.

Fittingly, the Book University's first venture is the *Mahabharata,* summarised by one of the greatest living Indians, C. Rajagopalachari; the second work is on a section of it, the *Gita,* by H. V. Divatia, an eminent jurist and a student of philosophy. Centuries ago, it was proclaimed of the *Mahabharata:* "What is not in it, is nowhere." After twenty-five centuries, we can use the same words about it. He who knows it not, knows not the heights and depths of the soul; he misses the trials and tragedy and the beauty and grandeur of life.

The *Mahabharata* is not a mere epic; it is a romance, telling the tale of heroic men and women and some who were divine; it is a whole literature in itself, containing a code of life, a philosophy of social and ethical relations, and speculative thought on human problems that is hard to rival; but, above all, it has for its core the *Gita*, which is, as the world is beginning to find out, the noblest of scriptures and the grandest of sagas in which the climax is reached in the wondrous Apocalypse in the Eleventh Canto.

Through such books alone, the harmonies underlying true culture, I am convinced, will one day reconcile the disorders of modern life.

I thank all those who have helped to make this new branch of the Bhavan's activity successful.

New Delhi.
1, Queen Victoria Road,
October 3, 1951.

K. M. MUNSHI

स्मारकम्

"भूयाः दीर्घसुमङ्गली"त्यभिदधुः यां कामकोटीश्वराः
या नित्यं सहधर्मनिर्वहणकार्येऽभून्ममालम्बनम् ।
या मे निर्गतसारजीवनवनीवासन्तसञ्जीवनी
याऽऽरूढा परमं पदं जनमिमं निक्षिप्य दुःखाम्बुधौ ॥

तस्या मे धर्मपत्न्या निरुपमभगवद्भक्तिनिष्ठानुभूतेः
सत्पुत्रायाः शुभायाः पतिचरणसरोजातसेवैकतृप्तेः ।
पट्टम्बायाः पवित्रप्रियमधुरमतेः स्मारकत्वेन जीयात्
श्रीविष्णोः नामसाहस्रविवरणकृतेः सोऽयमांग्लानुवादः ॥

IN MEMORIAM

This English translation of Śrī Śaṅkara's Bhāṣya

on

Śrī Viṣṇusahasranāma Stotra

is inscribed to the memory of

my wife Śrimati Pattammal

who was my *sahadharmacāriṇī* for sixty-two years

in fair weather and foul.

FOREWORD

The redeeming power of the Divine Name is an article of faith with the mystics of all religions. It is hedged in with awful mystery. And Sanatana Dharma with its roots in the Veda has given *Nama-japa* a very high place in the practice of religion. The Ṛgveda, which proclaims the *Ekam Sat,* also breathes the spirit of loving devotions in such hymns as the Varuṇa Sūktas of which Vasiṣṭha is the seer. And it affirms the potency of the Divine-Name in such verses as the following of Dīrghatamas:

Āsya jānanto Nama-chid-viviktana
mahaste Viṣṇoḥ sumatim bhajāmahe

(Ṛg.V.I. 15b. 3)

which means, "O ye who wish to gain realization of the supreme truth, utter the name of Viṣṇu at least once in the steadfast faith that it will lead you to such realization".

It is this Vedic insight that has led to the proliferation of the vast body of prayers and hymns of praise down the ages and has been responsible for the development of a whole cult, that of the Nāma-siddhānta. The *Sahasranāmas* of which we have quite a few devoted to the various aspects of the Godhead, Viṣṇu, Śiva, Ambā and so on, provide the textual base for this mode of religious practice. To mention two of the most famous, we have the *Lalitā Sahasranāma* and the *Śiva Sahasranāma* in the Ānuśāsanika Parva of the Mahābhārata, which Śrī Kriṣna Himself gives out at Bhīṣma's instance, as taught Him by Upamanyu when He wanted to propitiate Śiva. But the distinction of the Viṣṇu Sahasranāma lies in this, that it has a commentary by Śrī Śankara Bhagavadpāda, which Nīlakantha, the famous commentator of the Mahābhārata considered so authoritative that he himself refrained from commenting on it.

The distinctive feature of the Viṣṇu-Sahasranāma, as Śrī Śankara interprets it, may be gathered from his commentary on verses 9 and 10. It emphasises that the Object of adoration of this hymn is that Supreme Deity, the Light that lights up all existences, the Inner Ruler Immortal, the Author of the creation, preservation and destruction of the worlds and the Redeemer who terminates the bondage of Karma by imparting the saving knowledge. In other words, it is the Kārya Brahma (Saguṇa Brahma) Who is posited in the very first of the *Brahma* Sūtras, Whose grace may be gained by singing His manifold glories, which the Sahasranāma tries to indicate by those descriptive names which the great *ṛṣis* have garnered from the entire corpus of Vedic and Purāṇic literature, as Bhīṣma suggests. In the thousand Names, there are to be found many that are familiarly associated with one or other member of the Trinity as well as with those of other aspects or incarnations of the Godhead. But Śrī Śankara insists (*vide* his comment on the name *Śarva*) that all the names refer only to Nārāyaṇa. He maintains that this Saguṇa-Brahma-upāsanā will logically find its fulfilment in the realization of the Nirguṇa through the dawn of the supreme knowledge by the grace of Īśvara.

The Bhakti Śāstra has, in the course of centuries, been developed with extreme acuteness and subtlety by many schools of devotion with their distinctive metaphysics. But it is worth noting that Śrī Śankara's *Bhāṣya* on the Viṣṇu Sahasranāma deals with all the main arguments on which the Nāma-Siddhānta rests and anticipates and refutes the objections raised by its critics.

Just one or two points may be touched upon here by way of illustration. It might be asked, "when the Vedas prescribe the offering of costly and difficult sacrifices for the propitiation of the Lord, how can mere praise, which comes easy and costs no money, fill the bill". The Ācārya points out that the very ease with which the praise of the Lord may be sung is a point in its favour. Its superiority to other modes of propitiation lies in the fact that is causes no harm to others, it does not need the service of another person, it requires no object (not even a leaf or a flower), and it is not dependent on suitable times and places. But it does require the fulfilment of two other conditions. It is the Lord Vāsudeva Who shines in the heart-lotus that the devotee must exalt by singing His numerous qualities, impelled to do so by the whole-hearted love and exclusive devotion that he feels towards Him.

Lakṣmīdhara in his *Bhagavan-Nāma-Kaumudi* interprets this 'bhakti' as 'rati' (love). *Śrīmad-Bhāgavatam* traces the growth of this active love in this manner. 'A man goes on pilgrimages. There he happens to meet the saintly and hear them sing the praises of the Lord. Hearing those praises repeatedly, he falls so much in love with the Lord Who is thus glorified, that he joins in the singing. The result is described by Lakṣmīdhara as a progressive spiritual growth. 'Singing the Lord's praises leads to the elimination of sin; constant repetition of the same strengthens the impulses that make for love for the Lord and that lead to the eradication of the tendencies to sin; he devotes himself more and more to the service of the saintly; and from that is generated unshakable love and devotion to the Lord, which results in the uprooting of all causes of grief and misery, the enhancement of *sattva,* and as a natural culmination, *tattva-sākṣātkāra* and *mukti.*' The fundamental pre-requisite is *śraddhā* (faith).

This might seem to be contradicted by such stories as that of Ajāmiḷa in the Sixth Skandha of *Śrīmad Bhāgavatam,* where a life-long sinner was rescued from Yama's messengers by the attendants of Viṣṇu, because he had inadvertantly uttered the name of Nārāyaṇa in calling his child. This signal proof of the God's Grace brings him repentance and that results in liberation. The famous verse in the *Bhāgavatam,* which supports this thesis runs as follows: 'Men of old have known that all sins are destroyed by the uttering of the Name of the Lord of Vaikuṇṭha even casually — in calling somebody by his name, or in jest, or as a meaningless vocuble, to sustain a chant or a melody, or in light-hearted badinage.' Lakṣmīdhara, after an elaborate consideration of the matter, concludes that it is the man who is at the point of death that is saved by the utterance of the Lord's Name even unintentionally. Even that involuntary utterance (which is itself the result of *vāsanās* of former births) invites the Lord's attention to his plight ('yatas-tad-viṣayā matiḥ'), and the infinite Fountain of mercy offers him instant succour.

There are two ways of glorifying the Lord: (1) by singing the litany of His thousand Names or (2) by chanting the Name of one's *Iṣṭa devatā.* The Names that make up the Sahasranāma are all descriptive (gauṇāni) of His excellences, exploits and glorious attributes. Being the sum of the best qualities the human mind can conceive of as inherent in God, this prayer, by constant and devout recitation, builds up in the devotee's heart, (little detail by details) the image of the Lord that evokes his adoration. Śrī Śankara's *Bhāṣya* is intended to help in the process of identification of the worshipper, in self-forgetful love with the Object of his devotion, and it does that very convincingly. It is of course possible to differ as to the signification of particular Names. Śrī Parāśara Bhaṭṭa, in his valuable *Bhāṣya,* offers alternative explanations to many of the Names. Take the name of 'Vyāḷa' (monster or serpent) for instance. Śrī Śankara says that the suggestion is that the Lord is as elusive and slippery as the serpent. Bhaṭṭa says it means, 'He who grapples His devotees to Himself with hoops of steel'. The reader may or may not agree with either. But he should be glad to have the benefit of the insight of both expounders. For the infinity of God may contain contradictions which do not cancel out each other, but enhance the richness of the whole.

Prof. P. Sankaranarayanan has done a valuable service to the *āstika* public by giving us a faithful, almost word-for-word translation of Śrī Śankara's *Bhaṣya* on the *Vishnu Sahasranāma* with its wealth of Vedic and other scriptural quotations that support his view that the Sahasranāma is no sectarian document and that it can be a great support for Advaita Bhakti. At the same time he explains lucidly the terse statements that are to be met with occasionally in the *Bhaṣya.* This book comes as a fitting sequel to his English rendering of the Commentary, by the saintly pontiff of a Śankarācārya Pīṭha, the late Śrī Candrasekhara Bhārati of Sringeri on *Sankara's Vivekacūḍāmaṇi;* which, of all the Ācārya's *Prakaraṇa-granthas,* is the one that most persuasively introduces the devout student to the heart of Advaita Vedānta.

Bangalore:

Sankara Jayanti, 1978. N. RAGHUNATHAN

TRANSLATOR'S PREFACE

Some years ago, when I had the privilege of darśan of Śrī Periyavāḷ, His Holiness Śrī Candraśekharendra Saraswatī Śrīcaraṇas, the 68th *adhipati* of Kāñci Kāmakoṭi Pīṭha, with my good friend Sri T. V. Viśwanatha Aiyar at Tenambakkam, His Holiness desired me at that time to translate into English Śrī Śaṅkara Bhagavatpāda's *bhāṣya* on the following verse of the Viṣṇusahasranāma Stotra:

पवित्राणां पवित्रं यो मङ्गलानां च मङ्गलम् ।
दैवतं दैवतानां च भूतानां योऽव्ययः पिता ॥

Pavitrāṇām pavitram yo maṅgalānām ca maṅgalam ।
daivataṁ daivatānām ca bhūtānām yo'vyayaḥ pitā ॥

and distribute it widely among the *āstikas*. I wondered at the time why His Holiness was so particular of the *bhāṣya* on this verse being translated and made known widely. I came home and looked into the *bhāṣya* on this śloka and found that it dealt at length with the truth of Advaita and the concept of *Śiva Viṣṇu abheda,* non-difference between Śiva and Viṣṇu, they being manifestations of one and the same Divinity. The propagation of this cardinal feature of Hindu philosophy and theology has engaged the energies of His Holiness for long. The *Tiruppāvai-Tiruvembāvai* movement initiated by him and which is so popular in South India is one of the means by which sectarian fanaticism in our religion is sought to be overcome. In fact, a careful study of the *bhāṣya* will show that for the most part, the God extolled in the hymn is not a sectarian Deity appropriated exclusively as their own by the votaries of Viṣṇu.

It then occurred to me to translate not only the *bhāṣya* on this śloka, but the entire *bhāṣya* on the whole stotra as well. This I have done in the following pages. In doing this, I have had the benefit of the translation by late Sri R. Anantakrishna Sastrigal brought out by the Theosophical Publishing House, Adyar, which, I am told by them, is now out of print. It is not, however, quite exhaustive. I have also pressed into service the very able Tamil translation by my esteemed friend the late Sri V. Narayanan, a Kāmakoṭi Kośasthān publication. But, it does not provide the explanation of the Upaniṣadic and other scriptural passages and the grammatical authorities in the *bhāṣya* relied on by Śrī Śaṅkara while explaining certain Nāmas, but is content with merely transliterating them into Tamil. In my translation, not only have such scriptural passages been transliterated in English, their meanings also have been given. The Pāṇinian rules relied on by the venerable author of the *bhāṣya* have been separately listed in the Appendix I against the concerned Nāmas giving reference to the śloka where they occur in the stotra and explained. Because to understand these rules requires a working knowledge of Vyākaraṇa, and unless trained in it, one cannot have that equipment, I have grouped them separately in the Appendix with their explanation. For this I am indebted to my valued friend Dr. M. Narasimhachary, Reader in Sanskrit, University of Madras, who very kindly wrote this Section of the book for me. I also owe to him the Invocatory ślokas for the success of my undertaking and the ślokas inscribing the translation of the *bhāṣya* to the memory of my wife who passed away when the translation was being written, embodying my ideas in the two cases. I have listed separately in Appendix II such Nāmas as occur more than once in the stotra and the numbers of the ślokas where they occur.

I had the benefit of reading the *bhāṣya* with Brahmaśrī Vazhuthūr Rājagopāla Śarma who, out of consideration for my physical disability impeding my movement, was kind enough to come to my residence almost daily for four months to explain the *bhāṣya* to me and to three respected gentlemen* who were interested to read it, in consonance with the maxim: "Meditate alone, but study in company." It was a great service for which I am beholden to Śrī Śarma, who found the time to render it in the midst of his tight schedule of daily engagements in furtherance of the cause of Śāstraic and literary knowledge in Sanskrit among the young and the not-so-young who go to him for instruction.

I have lifted from Śrī V. Narayanan's Tamil translation the reference to the sources of the authorities quoted by Śrī Śaṅkara in the course of the *bhāṣya* which bespeak Śrī Narayanan's deep knowledge of the wide range of our classical lore. The Kāmakoṭi Kośasthān has kindly accorded me permission to do so and I am thankful to them for it.

I must not forget to acknowledge the great prestige that Śrī N. Raghunatha Aiyar, formerly of the "Hindu"

* Śrī K. Balasubrahmanya Aiyar of the L.I.C., Śrī K. Ramacandra Aiyar of the Railways and Śrī Tyagaraja Aiyar of the Postal Department.

who has made a monumental translation into English of "Śrīmad Bhāgavata", and who combines in himself a rare mastery of English and a deep scholarship of the Sanskrit classics, has conferred on this book by introducing it to the āstika world with his valued Foreword. For, as the poet Kālidāsa would have it, *ā paritoṣāt viduṣām na sādhu manye prayogavijñānam*: 'No literary work deserves to be called good until it is commended by those who know.'

I am grateful to the Bharatīya Vidyā Bhavan, Bombay, for so kindly taking on itself the printing and publication of this book and to its Production Manager, Sri C. K. Venkataraman, for seeing it through the press.

I must not forget to thank profusely my friend Śrī S. K. Anantanarayanan for typing for me my clumsy and badly written manuscript.

The *Viṣṇusahasranāma Stotra* has come down to us from the hoary past having been told by *Bhīṣma* from his bed of arrows to Yudhiṣṭhira in the presence of Bhagavān Śrī Kṛṣṇa Himself. It has gained currency down the ages in every nook and corner of our puṇyabhūmi. In fact, the word *Sahasranāma* has come to mean the *Viṣṇusahasranāma* only in the tongues of the devout in the first instance, even as mention of the word *Gītā* calls to mind only the *Bhagavad Gītā* though there are many other Gītās. Other Sahasranāmas in vogue among us are referred to with their appropriate adjectives as *Lalitā* Sahasranāma, *Lakṣmī* Sahasranāma and *Śiva* Sahasranāma etc. But when Sahasranāma alone is uttered, it refers only to *Viṣṇu* Sahasranāma. There are no restrictions of place or time, sex or age for reciting the stotra. It cuts across sectarian divisions of the Hindus and is held in great reverence by all denominations among us. It is practically the first lesson in our hymnology and is a matter of daily recital by every devout Hindu. It embodies the Nāma Sankīrtana of the Lord which is a potent means of spiritual benefit in this decadent age.

There is a tradition that when Śrī Śaṅkara desired one of his *śiṣyas* in Vārāṇasi to pull out at random any one of his *śiṣyas* in Vārāṇasī to pull out at random any philosophy for writing a *bhāṣya* on it, the *Viṣṇusahasranāma Stotra* came to the śiṣya's hand. It would appear that the Master told him to do likewise again for a second time and yet again for a third time. Repeatedly, the same volume came to his hand. It is said that, feeling that his writing the *bhāṣya* on it was divinely ordained as the first of the commentaries that he should write on our sacred books, Śrī Śaṅkara started with it.

It is not for me, less than a novice, to hold the candle to the sun and expatiate on the excellence of Śrī Śaṅkara's *bhāṣya*. I can only invite the reader to the original of this translation which, such as it is, is intended only for those who have unfortunately denied themselves access to Śrī Bhagavatpāda's euphonious language.

To most of us the daily recital of this stotra has become a habit, and like all habits, it has been tended to be mechanical. The meanings of many Nāmas are not clear, especially when they occur more than once in different parts of the Stotra. The Chāndogya Śruti says:

> *"yadeva vidyayā karoti śraddhayopaniṣadā tadeva vīryavattaram bhavati"*

'Whatever is done with knowledge of the meaning of the mantras with an earnestness born of faith and insight into it acquires added efficacy more than what is done without these accompaniments.' It is to help to achieve this object that I have attempted to translate this *bhāṣya* on this widely popular hymn for the benefit of those who may prefer to understand it through the medium of English. And, in the process, if my attempt receives, in ever so little a measure, the commendation of His Holiness of Kānchi, I shall feel extremely blessed and amply rewarded.

I have a small request to make to the indulgent reader. In the page in which there appears Śrī Śaṅkara's invocation, in line sixteen, the word 'are' may kindly be altered to 'is'.

Mylapore, P. SANKARANARAYANAN
Madras-4.
April 2, 1978.

ABBREVIATIONS

Ait. Up.	Aitareya Upaniṣad
Bṛh. Up.	Bṛhadāraṇyaka Upaniṣad
B.S.	Brahma Sūtras
Ch. Up.	Chāndogya Upaniṣad
G.P.	Garuḍa Purāṇa
Kaṭha	Kaṭha Upaniṣad
M.Bh.	Mahā Bhārata
M. Bh. Anu.	„ Anuśāsana Parvan
Muṇḍ. Up.	Muṇḍaka Upaniṣad
Rk. Sam.	Ṛk Samhitā
Varāha	Varāha Purāṇa
Viṣ. Pu.	Viṣṇu Purāṇa

The rest are self-explanatory.

SCHEME OF TRANSLITERATION

अ	a	ञ	na
आ	ā	ट	ta
इ	i	ठ	tha
ई	ī	ड	da
उ	u	ढ	ḍha
ऊ	ū	ण	ṇa
ऋ	ṛ	त	ta
ॠ	ṝ	थ	tha
ऌ	ḷ	द	da
ए	e	ध	dha
ऐ	ai	न	na
ओ	o	प	pa
औ	au	फ	pha
ं	ṁ	ब	ba
:	(visarga) ḥ	भ	bha
ऽ	(avagraha)'	म	ma
क	ka	य	ya
ख	kha	र	ra
ग	ga	ल	la
घ	gha	व	va
ङ	ṅa	श	śa
च	ca	ष	ṣa
छ	cha	स	sa
ज	ja	ह	ha
झ	jha	क्ष	ksa

॥ श्रीः ॥

INVOCATION BY THE TRANSLATOR

प्रार्थना

प्रणतजनविधेयं पार्वतीभागधेयं
गणपतिमुपतिष्ठे स्कन्दपूर्वं गजास्यम् ।
श्रवणचलनजातैः यस्य वातूलजातैः
प्रचलितदृढमूलाः तूलतां यान्ति विघ्नाः ॥

त्रिजगदुदयरक्षाभङ्गमोक्षैकलीलं
निखिलनिगममूलं मेघमालाविनीलम् ।
सकलवचनलक्ष्यं पुण्डरीकायताक्षं
परमपदचरिष्णुं श्रीमहाविष्णुमीडे ॥

श्रुतिशिखरविहारं सुप्रसन्नं गभीरं
विरचितबहुभाष्यं दिक्षु सङ्क्रान्तशिष्यम् ।
यतिपरिबृढमाद्यं नौम्यहं शङ्करं तं
विमलतरतदुक्तीः अन्यवाचा (आङ्गलवाचा) वितन्वन् ॥

मुनिपतिरिह काञ्चीकामकोटीपदस्थः
कलिहरणसमर्थः चन्द्रकोटीरनामा ।
कियदपि चिरजीवं शीतलैः मामपाङ्गैः
सकरुणमनुगृह्णात्वासमाप्ति क्रियायाः ॥

TRANSLATION OF THE INVOCATION

1. I adore the elephant-faced Lord Gaṇeśa, the obedient servant of his devotees the supreme blessing of goddess Pārvatī and the elder brother of Skanda, by the winds produced through the flapping of whose ears even deep-rooted impediments get uprooted and become (as light as) cotton.

2. Praise be unto the lotus-eyed Lord Viṣṇu the consort of Śrī, Whose sport it is to create, protect, dissolve and emancipate the three worlds. He is the source of all Vedic lore, dark blue in colour like a chain of (rainy) clouds, the ultimate import of all speech, and is the One that moves in the Highest Abode.

3. Before rendering his pure and clear words into another language (English), I prostrate before the gracious and solemn Śrī Ādi Śaṅkara, the King of ascetics who sports on the crown of the Vedas (Upaniṣads), composed many commentaries and whose disciples have spread in all directions (of the world).

4. May His Holiness Śrī Candraśekharendra Sarasvatī Svāmigal of Kānchi Kāmakoṭi Peetha, the master of sages, who can remove the evils of the Kali age, favour me through his cool and compassionate glances with some more lease of life till I finish the work undertaken.

CONTENTS

॥ श्रीः ॥

श्रीविष्णुसहस्रनामस्तोत्रम्

श्रीमच्छंकरभगवत्पादविरचितेन भाष्येण सहितम् ।

सच्चिदानन्दरूपाय कृष्णायाक्लिष्टकारिणे ।
नमो वेदान्तवेद्याय गुरवे बुद्धिसाक्षिणे ॥

कृष्णद्वैपायनं व्यासं सर्वभूतहिते रतम् ।
वेदाब्जभास्करं वन्दे शमादिनिलयं मुनिम् ॥

सहस्रमूर्तेः पुरुषोत्तमस्य
सहस्रनेत्राननपादबाहोः ।
सहस्रनाम्नां स्तवनं प्रशस्तं
निरुच्यते जन्मजरादिशान्त्यै ॥

ŚRĪ GURUBHYO NAMAḤ

VIṢṆU SAHASRANĀMA STOTRAM

with

The Commentary of Śrī Śankara Bhagavatpāda.

Invocation by Śrī Śankara:

Obeisance to the Guru (Preceptor)[1] who is of the form of Sat, Cit and Ānanda, of the name of Kṛṣṇa, who effects actions with ease, who is known by Vedānta and is the witness of the intellect.

I bow to the sage Kṛṣṇadvaipāyana Vyāsa[2] who is intent on the good of all creatures, who is the sun before which the lotus of Vedānta blossoms and who is the repository of śama (self-control) and other qualities.

The meritorious chanting of the thousand Names of the Supreme Person who has a thousand eyes, faces, feet and hands are explained for allaying the effects of birth, old age, etc.

वैशम्पायन उवाच :

श्रुत्वा धर्मानशेषेण पावनानि च सर्वशः ।
युधिष्ठिरः शान्तनवं पुनरेवाभ्यभाषत ।। १ ।।

Vaiśampāyana said:-
Śrutvā dharmānaśeṣeṇa pāvanāni ca sarvaśaḥ /
Yudhiṣṭhiraḥ Śāntanavam
punarevabhyabhāṣata // 1

Having heard completely in different forms all the

---

1. A preceptor is called a *guru* as he is the dispeller of the darkness of ignorance. *gu* stands for ignorance and *ru* for its being dispelled.
2. Vyāsa is so called as he classified the Vedas, Vyāsa is the classifier. He is Kṛṣṇa or dark, and Dvaipāyana, born in a dvīpa or island.

dharmas which are purifying, Yudhiṣṭhira questioned Bhiṣma, the son of Śantanu.

Śri Vaiśampāyana addressed Janamejaya and said:-

dharmān: those prescriptions which are in the form of commands and which are the cause of worldly welfare and spiritual benefit.

aśeṣeṇa: completely.

pāvanāni: which wear away the sins and which are the secrets of dharma.

sarvaśaḥ: In all ways (having heard).

Yudhiṣṭhiraḥ: Dharmaputra.

Sāntanavam: Śantanu's son, Bhiṣma.

Considering that what secures all the meritorious objectives of all human endeavour i.e., *dharma, artha, kāma* and *mokṣa:* (righteousness, wealth, worldly desire and liberation) which can be easily secured with minimum effort but with maximum effect has not been conveyed so far, Dharmaputra questioned again.

abhyabhāṣata: questioned again.

युधिष्ठिर उवाच :

किमेकं दैवतं लोके किं वाप्येकं परायणम् ।
स्तुवन्तः कं कमर्चन्तः प्राप्नुयुर्मानवाः शुभम् ॥ २ ॥

Yudhiṣṭhira said:

Kimekam daivatam loke kim vāpyekam parāyaṇam /
stuvantaḥ kam kamarcantaḥ
prāpnyurmānavāḥ subham // 2

In all the śāstras who is extolled as the one God? What is the sole ultimate goal? By praising whom and worshipping whom will men acquire all that is auspicious?

daivatam means *devam;* for, the suffix *ta* is added to a word when reference is to itself.

loke: in what is the cause of looking, inquiring, among all *vidyas* or subjects of knowledge.

Who is celebrated as the one God? is the first question.

kim vāpyekam parāyaṇam: in that world, which is the one supreme goal? *parāyaṇam=param ayanam* the ultimate that has to be attained. (The ultimate is explained). That by Whose command everything acts, when, Which is known, the knots of the heart are rent asunder. *vide* the śruti. *bhidyate hṛdaya granthiḥ cidyante sarvasamśayāh. kṣīyante cāsya karmāṇi tasmin dṛṣte parāvare.* (Mund: 2.2.8). 'The knots of the heart are broken, all doubts are resolved and all actions are liquidated (without producing any fruits) when That which is the infinite and the infinitisemal is seen (known). (Again), by merely knowing (realising) Which, liberation which is the nature of bliss is secured, the knower (one who has realised) of Which does not fear anything from any quarter, for whom who has entered (become one with) Which there is no re-birth, by knowing (realising) Which one becomes That itself: *vide* the śruti: *brahmaveda brahmaivabhavati* (Mund: 3.2.9): 'The knower of Brahman becomes Brahman Itself; than Which there is no other path (to liberation) for mortals, *vide* the sruti: *nānyaḥ panthā vidyate' yanāya.* (Sveta: 3.8): 'There is no other path to the supreme abode.' Hence it is said *ekam parāyaṇam:* the only ultimate goal. What is that (goal) declared in all the vidyas? is the second question.

kam: Whom among all Gods.

stuvantaḥ: uttering the (divine) qualities.

kam: Whom among all Gods.

arcantaḥ: adoring in various ways externally and internally.

mānavāḥ: the sons of Manu (men).

subham: what is auspicious, the fruits of celestial habitation, mokṣa or liberation from the bonds of samsāra.

prāpnyuḥ: will acquire.

These are two further questions.

को धर्मः सर्वधर्माणां भवतः परमो मतः ।
किं जपन्मुच्यते जन्तुर्जन्मसंसारबन्धनात् ॥ ३ ॥

ko dharmaḥ sarvadharmāṇām bhavataḥ paramo mataḥ /
kim japan mucyate jantuḥ janmasamsārabandhanāt // 3

Of all dharmas, which is considered by you as most superior, by repeated muttering which is one that is born released from the bondage of samsāra (the cycle of birth and death)?

ko dharmaḥ: Of the aforesaid nature, which among all the dharmas?

bhavataḥ: by you.

paramaḥ: most superior (dharma).

mataḥ: is considered.

is the fifth question.

kim japan: by muttering which (loudly, lowly or silently) (three ways of doing japa).

jantuḥ: what has the quality of being born. By the use of the word 'jantu' is indicated the qualification of all creatures according to their capacity to mutter the name or adore or praise (the Lord).

janmasamśārabandhanāt: janma stands for all actions that arise from ajñāna; that bondage which arises from *janma* and samsāra; from that

mucyate: becomes one freed.

This is the sixth question.

"*janma samsārabandhanāt*" is indicative of other fruits as well (like health, wealth and progeny). Those two bonds are specifically mentioned to show their primacy.

Six questions were asked. Among them, the last which related to the subject of japa is answered by the following śloka:—

भीष्म उवाच :

जगत्प्रभुं देवदेवमनन्तं पुरुषोत्तम् ।

स्तुवन्नामसहस्रेण पुरुषः सततोत्थितः ॥ ४ ॥

Śri Bhīṣma said:-

jagatprabhum devadevam anantam
puruṣottamam /
stuvan nāma sahasreṇa puruṣaḥ satatotthitaḥ // 4

A man (jīva) being always alert praising by the thousand Names the Lord of the universe, the God who is the Puruṣottama.

Bhīṣmaḥ: the cause of fear to all enemies, internal and external (to a man). (The internal enemies of man are *kāma, krodha, mada, moha, lobha* and *mātsarya*: desire, anger, arrogance, delusion, covetousness and jealousy). He is all-knowing who expounds mokṣa-dharma, etc.,

jagatprabhum: jagat: what is of the form of the moving and unmoving. *prabhu:* svāmi or the owner: the owner or Lord of the universe.

devadevam: the God of Brahma and others.

anantam : who is not limited by space, time or objects.

puruṣottamam: who is superlatively eminent among the decaying and undying, among effects and causes.

nāmasahasreṇa: by thousand Names.

stuvan: doing utterance of the (divine) qualities.[2a]

satatotthitaḥ: always alert.

puruṣaḥ: a man (jīva) so called because he lies in or is embodied in the *pura,* the vesture of the body, or, he is full, pūrṇa.

(*sarvaduhkādhigobhavet* in sl. 6 must be connected everywhere.)

By the next śloka the fourth question is answered.

तमेव चार्चयन्नित्यं भक्त्या पुरुषमव्ययम् –
ध्यायन्स्तुवन्नमस्यंश्च यजमानस्तमेव च ॥ ५ ॥

tameva cārcayannityam bhaktyā puruṣamavyayam /
dhyāyan stuvannamasyamsca
yajamānastameva ca // 5

Adoring (with flowers) always that undecaying puruṣa who is indestructible and unchanging, with devotion, meditating on Him, praising Him and prostrating before Him only, the worshipper......

tameva ca arcayan: doing external adoration with flowers.

nityam: at all times.

bhaktyā: bhakti: worship as the Supreme; by it, i.e., with devotion (considering Him as the Supreme).

avyayam: devoid of destruction or change.

(tam eva) dhyāyan: adoring Him only internally (meditating on Him only).

stuvan: uttering His (auspicious) qualities.

2a. *guṇaniṣṭha guṇābhidānam stutiḥ.* stuti is the utterance of (good) qualities of one endowed with them.

namasyan ca: making prostration with devotion as said earlier.

The two, stuti and namaskāra are limbs of aforesaid pūja or worship.

yajamānaḥ: the worshipper who derives the fruit of worship.

Or, by saying *arcayan,* the two kinds of arcana (external and internal) are meant. By saying *dhyāyan, stuvan* and *namasyan,* the reference is to worship by mind, speech and body.

By the succeeding three quarters of the śloka, the third question is answered.

अनादिनिधनं विष्णुं सर्वलोकमहेश्वरम् ।
लोकाध्यक्षं स्तुवन्नित्यं सर्वदुःखातिगो भवेत् ॥ ६ ॥

anādinidhanam Viṣṇum sarvalokamaheśvaram /
lokādhyakṣam stuvannityam
sarvaduhkātigobhavet // 6

By always praising Viṣṇu who has no beginning or end, who is the Supreme Lord of all worlds and who is the direct witness of the world, one gets over all sorrows:

anādinidhanam: Him who is devoid of the six forms of change (i.e., birth, existence for a time, growth, change, decay and death known as *ṣaḍvikāras*).

Viṣṇum: Him Who is all-pervasive.

sarvalokamaheśvaram: loka, *sarvasya lokyate:* is seen by all. Whatever is seen is lokaḥ. Being the Lord of all that control and direct the loka, viz., Brahma and others, He is *sarvalokamaheśvara.*

lokādhyakṣam: Him Who sees the *loka* or the collection of perceivable objects directly by His own intelligence.

(tam) *nityam stuvan: praising* Him without intermission

sarvadhukādhigobhavet: will overcome all griefs.

duhkādhigaḥ: one who gets over ādhyātmika and other (ādibhautika and ādidaivika) griefs. This is the fruit of all the three, japa, stuti and arcana.

bhavet: will be.

Again he elucidates Him who is the object of praise.

ब्रह्मण्यं सर्वधर्मज्ञं लोकानां कीर्तिवर्धनम् ।
लोकनाथं महद्भूतं सर्वभूतभवोद्भवम् ॥ ७ ॥

brahmaṇyam sarva dharmajñam lokānām
kīrtivardhanam |
lokanātham mahadbhūtam
sarvabhūtabhavodbhavam // 7

Him Who is dear to Brahman, Who knows all dharmas, Who enhances the renown of creatures of all worlds, Who is the Lord of the worlds, Who is great, Who is the Truth and Who causes the samsāra of all creatures.

brahmaṇyam: Him who is dear to (1) Brahma or to (2) the superior Brāhmaṇa, to (3) tapas, to (4) śruti.

sarvadharmajñam: Him who knows all dharmas.

lokānām: of all creatures.

kīrtivardhanam: Him who enchances the glory of all creatures by the infusion of His own power into them.

lokanātham: 1. *lokaiḥ nāthyate:* is implored by men. 2. *lokānupatapati:* Him who afflicts men for their transgressions. 3. *āśāste:* desires, blesses. 4. *īṣte:* controls.

mahat: Brahma, being superior to the entire universe.

bhūtam: the transcendental Truth.

sarvabhūtabhavodbhavam: Him from Whom the samsāra (bhava) of all creatures arises.

He answers the fifth question—

एष मे सर्वधर्माणां धर्मोऽधिकतमो मतः ।
यद्भक्त्या पुण्डरीकाक्षं स्तवैरर्चेन्नरः सदा ॥ ८ ॥

eṣa me sarvadharamāṇām dharmodhikatamo mataḥ |
yadbhaktyā puṇḍarīkākṣam stavairacennaraḥ sadā // 8

This is considered by me to be the superior dharma of all prescribed dharmas whereby a man always adores the Puṇḍarikākṣa with praises uttered with devotion.

eṣah: this (dharma) which I am going to declare.

Of all dharmas (which are of the nature of commands (of prescriptions and prohibitions), this dharma which I am going to declare is considered by me as the most superior. *matah:* considered.

yad: that is

bhaktyā: by being oriented to Him whole and entire with devotion.

pundarīkākṣam: Him who shines in the lotus of the heart, Vāsudeva.

stavaiḥ: by hymns which are of the nature of utterance of His (auspicious) qualities.

sadā: always

arcet: adores with reverence

naraḥ: man

eṣa dharmaḥ: 'this dharma' is to be applied to the context.

What is the reason for the superiority of this adoration in the form of hymns? It is replied: The superiority is because of its not causing harm to others, or its not requiring another person or object, or its not being determined by considerations of place or time.

Vide: Viṣṇu Purāṇa 6-12-17, 'Whatever one obtains in Kṛta yuga by meditation, by sacrifice in Tretā yuga and by external adoration in Dvāpara yuga, one gets in the Kali yuga by uttering the praises of Keśava.' Manu in 2.87 says: 'Whether one does or does not do otherwise, one becomes a Brāhmaṇa by the mere mutterance of God's Names. See the example of Maitra who became a Brāhmaṇa.' In the *Mahābhārata* it is said: "Japa is said to be the most supreme of all dharmas. Japayajña is adopted as it does not cause any injury to any creature." In the *Gītā* 10.25 Bhagavān said: "Of all yajñas, I am japayajña." With all this in mind, it is said 'this is thought to be superior to all dharmas.'

The second question is answered:

परमं यो महत्तेजः परमं यो महत्तपः ।
परमं यो महद्ब्रह्म परमं यः परायणम् ॥ ९ ॥

paramam yo mahat tejaḥ paramam yo mahat tapaḥ /
paramam yo mahat brahma paramam yat
parayaṇam // 9

He Who is the most superior lustre, He Who is the most superior ruler, He Who is the most superior Truth, He Who is the most superior goal.

paramam: superior

mahat: big

tejaḥ: Of the nature of caitanya, intelligence, illuminating all.

vide the śrutis: yena sūryastapati tejaseddaḥ: 'That by which the sun illumines' (Taitt. Bṛh 3-12-97); *yo devo jyotiṣām jyotiḥ:* 'That shining One is the lustre of lights'. (Bṛh 4.4.16) *na tatra sūryo bhāti na candratārakam:* 'The sun does not shine there, not the moon or the stars'. (Mund. 2-2-10). And the smṛti: *yadātyagatam tejaḥ:*

'That Which is the effulgence in the sūrya'. (B.G. 5.12)

paramam tapaḥ: tapati: ājñāpayati: orders, directs. *vide: ya imam ca lokam param ca lokam sarvāṇica bhūtāni yontaro yamayati:* 'He Who directs from inside this and other worlds and all creatures' (*Antarāyami Brāhmaṇa* of *Bṛh* 3.7.1) *bhīṣāsmāt vātaḥ pavate.* 'by fear of Him the wind blows' etc., (Taitt.2.8.1).

Or, *tapati* means *īṣte:* rules over.

mahat: big, because His Lordship is unlimited. *vide: eṣa sarveśvaraḥ.* 'He is the Lord of all.'(Mand.6) and other śrutis.

paramam: of the nature of satya etc., (etc., includes jñānam and ānandam). *param Brahma,* transcendental Brahma, worshipful, so *mahat.*

paramam parayāṇam: param: superior, without doubt of returning again. *parāyaṇam: paramam ayanam:* the supreme goal.

By the adjective *paramam* everywhere, the lower or inferior tejas, aditya in very case is excluded. In all places, *yo devaḥ* is the qualified. That *deva* Who is *paramam tapaḥ paramam brahma, paramam parāyaṇam,* that One is the ultimate goal of all creatures. That is the meaning of the sentence.

The answer to the first question is given:—

पवित्राणां पवित्रं यो मङ्गलानां च मङ्गलम् ।
दैवतंदेवतानां च भूतानां योऽव्ययः पिता ।। १० ।।

pavitrāṇām pavitram yo mangalānām ca mangalam /
daivatam daivatānām ca bhūtānām yo'vyayaḥ pitā // 10

He Who is the pure of all that is pure, the auspicious of all that is auspicious, the God of all gods and the Father (creator) of all beings.

pavitrāṇām pavitram: the pure of all waters (and sacred places). When the supreme Puruṣa is thought of, praised, adored with fervour remembered, prostrated to, He uproots all sins. Hence He is *pavitrāṇām pavitram.* Or, by (bestowing) proper knowledge of the true nature of the ātman, He entirely destroys the actions (karmas) of the nature of puṇya and its opposite, and ajñāna, their cause. So, called *pavitrāṇām pavitram. vide*:

Hari, who is giver of salvation, bestows, if He is meditated on, a good form, health, wealth, pleasures and other incidental benefits.

Why is not that Acyuta thought of abandoning all other thoughts, Who if thought on, brings about the destruction of all evils?

Let one think of the Supreme God, Nārāyaṇa, in all actions including purifying bath. The śruti says that He is the expiator of all evil actions. (Garuda Purāṇa 1.228.28)

Let a man be released (even by) hearing the Viṣṇu mantra, Kṛṣna, which is the only medicine for one who lies motionless being bitten by the serpent of samsāra.

Even if a man be an excessive sinner, if he thinks of Acyuta even for a moment, he becomes holy capable of purifying people about him (by his mere presence).

Studying (churning) all sāśtras and reflecting again and again, this is the one conclusion arrived at, that Narāyaṇa is to be thought of always. (M.B.Anu 186-11).

When that which is both the Infinte and the infinitisemal is seen (realised), the knots of the heart are rent asunder, all doubts are resolved and all karmas are liquidated, (*Muṇd.* 2.2.8)

'The utterance of that holy Name O! Maitreya! with

devotion makes for the disappearance of all sins as impurities before a fire. (Viṣ. Pu. 6.8.20).

'Even if that Name is uttered in spite of oneself, a man is released at once from all sins like stags threatened by a lion. (Viṣ. Pu. 16-8-19).

'What one obtains by meditation in Kṛta yuga, by sacrifice in Tretā yuga and by adoration *(arcana)* in Dvāpara yuga, one obtains in Kali yuga by uttering the Name of Keśava. (Viṣ. Pu. 6.12.17).

'If remembered even by evil-minded persons, Hari destroys (their) sins. For, if fire is touched even unconsciously, it does not fail to scald (one's fingers).

'Whether done consciously or unconsciously, by the utterance of the Name of Vāsudeva, all that (sin) disappears like salt in water.

'By steadfastly resting the mind on Whom one does not go to hell, by thought of Whom even Heaven appears as an obstacle, by resting the mind on Whom Brahmaloka too appears very inferior, that Acyuta (Who never decays) gives mukti (liberation) to those who enshrine Him in the mind. What is the wonder (in this) that all sins disappear from the mind when that holy Name is uttered (with devotion)? (Viṣ. Pu. 6.8.16).

Water is enough to extinguish a fire; sunrise dispels the darkness. In the Kali Age, uttering the Name of Hari quiets (makes ineffective) the collection of sins.

The mainstay of my life is the Name of Hari alone, that Name alone, that Name alone. In Kali there is no other way, none, none at all.

'By merely hearing (with devotion) the Name of Viṣṇu, who is called Vāsudeva, a man becomes free of all sins. By adoring (performing pūja to) Him daily all sins get destroyed.

'For those in whose hearts Bhagavān Hari Who is the abode of everything auspicious resides always while performing all actions, nothing inauspicious will happen. (M.Bh. Śanti.46-113-4).

'If Hari is thought in the mind (with devotion), dies away that sin which is washed away by a bath in the Ganga a thousand times and a bath in the Puṣkara a crore of times. (G.P. 1.228.187)

'One who thinks of the faultless Nārāyaṇa for just a moment, even he attains siddhi (liberation). What needs be said of him who is ever intent on Him? (M.Bh. 186.13.7)

'Mental recitation of the Name of Kṛṣṇa is complete expiation, tapas and good action. (Vis. Pu. 2.6.37)

'Where (when) Kṛṣṇa is remembered with devotion, the most foul Kali which hurls men into the abyss of hell disappears immediately. (Viṣ. Pu. 6.8.21)

'If Govinda's Name is thought just once, sins committed by men in hundreds of life-terms are burnt surely like fire burning away bales of cotton.

'Even as fire with upward shooting tongues of flame aided by a strong wind burns away a bush, so Viṣṇu lodged in the heart of a yogi burns away all sins. (Viṣ. Pu. 6.7.74)

'One should wail aloud piteously as if purloined by thieves even if a minute is wasted devoid of thought (of God).

'O! great sage! Ever meditating on Janārdana, the Lord of creatures, the World Teacher, one gets over all griefs and fulfils all the purposes that one desires.

'Thus intently remembering Madhusūdhana with an one-pointed mind, one crosses the ocean of samsāra infested with crocodiles of birth and death.

'Even in this Kali abounding in evils, persons attracted by pleasures of sense objects become pure by thought of Govinda though they have committed all kinds of sins.

'O! Maitreya! To him whose mind rests in Vāsudeva in his japa, homa and arcana etc., (muttering, oblation in fire and adoration), the fruit of being Devendra is an obstacle (to his spiritual progress). (Viṣṇu Pu. 1.6.41)

'The sins committed in other life-periods of thousands of spans are quickly destroyed by making obeisance a little to (by bowing to) mighty Viṣṅu who is the Lord of the three worlds and of peerless excellence.

'Even one prostration done with devotion to Kṛṣṇa is equal to the avabhṛta baths (at the end) after ten horse sacrifices. One who has performed ten horse sacrifices is born again (on the expiry of his merit). But one who has made his prostration to Kṛṣṇa is not born again. (M.Bh. 46.122)

'To those who bow to Govinda whose colour is that of a linseed flower, to Acyuta clad in yellow robes, there is no fear. (M.Bh. 40.122)

'Even for one who indulges in make-believe, prostration is ordained to Cakrapāṇi; for, He is the destroyer of the source of samsāra.'

Thus from the sayings of śruti, smṛti, itihāsa and purāṇa *Pavitram Pavitrāṇam* is explained.

Next *mangalānām ca mangalam* etc., is explained.

mangalam: sukham joy or *sukhasādhanam* the means of joy, *tat jñāpakam ca* and what reminds one of joy.

mangaḷānām mangalam: the joy superior to all

earthly or heavenly joys. For, He stands pre-eminent over all lustrous things.

daivatam devatānām ca: devanām *devaḥ*: the God of gods.

bhūtānām yo avyayaḥ pitā: avyayaḥ: not decaying. *pitā*: janakaḥ: generator. The indestructible generator of all beings.

He is the only God in the world is the meaning here.

This truth is reinforced by reference to the following śrutis.

'One God (*deva:* shining One) hidden in all beings, permeating all, the indwelling Ātmā of all beings, the over-seeing witness of all actions, the effulgent cit, the lone and qualitiless.' (Sv. Up. 6.11)

'I, who yearn for liberation take refuge in Him Who at first generated Brahma, Who made the Vedas dawn on Him and Who is the shining One and Who dowers all jīvas with brightness.' (Sv. Up. 6.18)

Thus it has been declared in the Svetāsvatara Upaniṣad. In the Chāndogya it is said: *seyam devataikṣata*: 'that this deva determined,' *ekamevadvitiyam*: 'one only without a second.'

Objection: How can it be said *ekodevaḥ*, only one God when there is difference between the jīva and Paramātman?

Answer: No. The śrutis say *tat sṛṣṭvā tadevānuprāviśat*: 'having created it (the world), It entered into it'. (Taitt. Up. 2.6)

sa eva iha praviṣtha ānakhābhyaḥ: 'He alone here entered (into it) from (the hairs of the head) to the nails (of the toes)'. (Bṛh. Up. 1.4.7)

So, by this, it is clear as Brahman entered into buddhi and is the witness of its modifications. So, there is non-difference (between It and the jīva).

Objection: How can there be identity when those into which It has entered are mutually different?

Answer: Not so. By the śrutis *eko devobahudhā sanniviṣṭaḥ: (Taitt. Āraṇ* 3.14) 'the one God has entered in various forms', *ekaḥ san bahudhā vicāraḥ* (Taitt. Āraṇ 3.11): 'being one, He behaves in various ways'. *tvamekosi bahūnanaupraviṣṭhaḥ* (Taitt. Pu. 3.14): 'You are one who has entered into many', there is no difference between the Supreme and those into which It has entered. In Taittiriya Upaniṣad (Taitt-Samhita. 4.1.8) there are eight mantras which talk of *kasmaidevāya.* In saying *kasmai* "e" 'ए' (ekasmai), meaning 'to one God' has been dropped. They also indicate that the reference is to *one* God.

In the Kaṭha Valli it is said (2.2.9-13):

'As the air which has entered into material things takes many shapes according to the things it has entered into, so the One Who is internal ātmā of all things is outwardly of many forms.'

'As the sun who is the eye of the entire world is not tainted by the external defects of the eye, so the One Who is the internal ātmā of all things is not tainted by the outward griefs of the world.'

'Those brave (wise) men who realise the One, powerful, the inner ātmān of all beings Who makes His one form into the manifold as resident in (their) ātman, to them is bliss, not to others.'

'Those brave (wise) men who realise the (transcentally) eternal among the empirically seeming-permanent things, the supreme Caitanya (Intelligence) of intelligences, the One among the many Who fulfils all desires, to them is permanent peace, not to others.'

The Bṛhdāraṇyaka Upaniṣad says:

brahma vā idam agra āsīt tadekam sat na vyabhavat: 'Brahman was in the beginning (before creation) It was one. It was not produced.' (1.4.11)

nānyo'to'sti dṛṣtā: 'there is no seer other than this' 3.37.22)

The Īśavasyopaniṣad says:

anejamekam manaso javīyaḥ .... tatra ko mohaḥ kaḥ śoka ekatvamanupaśyataḥ: 'It did not shake, One (only) speedier than the mind; what delusion, what grief is there for him who sees oneness?' (7)

The Ṛg Veda says:—

sarveṣām bhutānām antaraḥ puruṣaḥ sama ātmeti vidyāt: (Āraṇyaka 3.3.10) 'Inside all creatures the Puruṣa is the same; He is to be known as their ātmā.'

ātmā vā idameka evāgra āsinnatyāt kincana: The Ātman was one, It was in the beginning, nothing else. (Ait. Up. 1.1)

ekam sat viprā bahudhā vadanti: that which exists is one; the sages speak of it variously. (Ṛk. Sam. 1.164.46)

ekam santam bahudhā kalpayanti: 'What exists as one is made to appear variously'. (Ṛk. Sam. 10.114.5)

eko vimame tribhirltpadebhiḥ: 'The One measured (this universe) by His three feet' (Ṛk. Sam. 1.154.5)

eko dadhāra bhuvanāni viśvā: 'The One held (in position) all the worlds'. (Ṛk. Sam. 1.154.3)

eko evāgnirbahudha samiddaḥ: 'One fire puts out different tongues of flame.' (Ṛk. Sam. 154.4)

The Chāndogya Upaniṣad says:—

sadevaidamagra āsit ekameva advitīyam: 'Existence alone was in the beginning, one only without a second'. (6.2.1)

Śrimad Bhagavad Gīta says:—

'He who, established in oneness, worships Me abiding in all beings, that yogi lives in Me, whatever may be his mode of living'. (6.32)

'Men of Self-knowledge are same-sighted (look with an equal eye) on a Brāhmaṇa imbued with learning and humility, a cow, an elephant, a dog and an outcast.' (5.18)

'I am the Self, O Gudākeśa! seated in the heart of all beings. I am the beginning, the middle and also the end of all beings'. (10.20)

'When he realizes the whole variety of beings as resting on the One, and as the evolution from that One alone, then he becomes Brahman.' (13.30)

'As the one sun illumines the whole world, so does the Lord of the Kṣetra illumine the whole kṣetra,[3] O! Bharata'. (13.33)

'Renouncing all thy dharmas, take refuge in Me. I shall liberate you from all sins, grieve not'. (18.66)

The Harivamśa says:

'By you established in sattva guṇa, Hari alone (as the one Lord) should always be meditated on. Ye, Brahmaṇas! speak and think of Keśava by the syllable Om.' (3.89.8-9)

'What a wonder! Thou art the (great) One among shining ones (devas) Puruṣottama! O! mighty armed! Thou art truly great. In the world there is no other (great) as Thou.'

Manu also said:—

'The ātmayāji (one who makes the sacrifice of (merges) his ātman in the Paramātman, realising the

3. Kṣetra the field comprising the animate and the inanimate including their doership and enjoyership.

ātman in all beings and all beings in his ātman, attains (spiritual) autonomy.' (12.91)

The Viṣṇu Purāṇa says:—

'Bhagavān who is known as Janārdana is one only. He gets different Names by His actions of creation, preservation and dissolution as Brahma, Viṣṇu and Śiva'. (1.2.60)

'Therefore, there is nothing, anywhere or at any time other than Intelligence. O! thou dvija (twice born)! Due to differences of Its actions, the one Intelligence is differently perceived by different minds.

Intelligence entire, pure, free from dross, free from grief, completely detached from all taints like greed etc., the One, always one, the Supreme, the highest Lord is Vāsudeva. There is not another than Him'. (2.12.43, 44)

'When the one Person dwells in all bodies, then the talk of you, he and I is futile.' (2.3.91)

'As the one sky is seen differently as dark and white, so too by people of deluded vision, the one Ātman is spoken of as different.

" 'All that is here is One. That is Acyuta. There is nothing higher than He. He is I. He is you; He is all this which is of the form of the Ātman. Give up the delusion of difference'. Thus instructed acquiring transcendental insight, the great King gave up (all thought of) difference." (2.16.22-24)

" 'All this and I are Vāsudeva. The Supreme Puruṣa and the highest Lord is He, the One'. If this unshakable determination is in the heart respecting Ananta, go far away from them."[4] (3.7.32)

4. Yama's words to his servants.

'Whatever Vasudhā said, all that is the absolute truth, O! devas! I, Śiva and You are all compacted of Nārāyaṇa.'[5]

'Whatever glories pertain to Him, they belong to each other. They appear more or less on account of differences of limitations.' (5.1.29-30)

'O! Universal Ātman! You are I. The reason for our appearing differently is for the purpose of the world.' (5.9.32)

'Whatever assurance of freedom from fear has been promised by You is vouchsafed by Me too. O! Śankara, You should see Yourself as non-different from Me.'[6]

'He is I; He is Thou; and all this world with all the devas, asuras and men is He. People under the delusion of nescience see difference (between all this).' (5.33.47-49)

Śri Maheśvara said in Baviṣyat Purāṇa:—

'The fools who perceive Me and Brahma as other than Viṣṇu are men of perverse thought. At the end (of their lives) they are tortured in hell.'

Maheśvara said in 'Kailāsa Yātra' in Harivamśa:—

'You are the origin of all creatures, similarly the middle and the end (i.e. the creator, preserver and the destroyer). From You the whole universe began and in You everything merges.'

'O! omnipresent Deva, I am You. O! Janārdana! You are I alone. There is no difference between us in name or reference.'

'O! Govinda! whatever eminent Names are current for You in the world, they are My Names too. No doubt need be entertained about this'.

---

5. Śiva to Brahma.
6. Viṣṇu to Śankara.

'O! Janārdana! let worship of You be Mine too, Gopāla, He who hates You is a hater of Me. There is no doubt of this.'

'I am called Bhūtapati as I am Your expansiveness. There is nothing devoid of You.'

'Of whatever was, is and will be, O' Lord of the Universe! You are the Lord; There is nothing without You.' (3.88.59-64)

Further, by the statement, *ātmeti tūpagacchanti grāhayanti ca*: 'but the Upaniṣads acknowledge (Brahman) as the Self and cause It to be so understood'. (B.S. iv.1-3), it should be understood that the ātmā is the Paramātmā thus referred to in the śāstras. It is thus that in the context of the Paramātman Jābālas understand Him: *tvam vā ahamasmi bhagavo deva aham vai tvamasi*: 'Verily You are I, shining One, I am verily You'. (Varāha Up. 34). Similarly in another text: *yadeveha tadamutra yadamutra tadanviha*: 'that which is here is yonder; what is yonder that is here'. (Kaṭha Up. 2.1.10) *sa yascāyam puruṣe yascāsau āditye sa ekaḥ*: 'He who is in this jīva and in this sun, He is one'. (Taitt. 2.8.12) *tadātmānam evavedaham brahmāsmiti*: 'I knew this ātman itself that I am Brahman. (Bṛh. Up. 1.4.10) *tadetad brahma apūrvam anaparam anantaraṃ abahyam ayam ātmā brahma*: ;'this Brahma has no source, no end, no interval, and fearless; this ātman is Brahman'. (Bṛh. Up. 2.5.19) *sa vā eṣa mahānaja ātmājaro'maro'mṛto'bhayo brahma*: 'this great unborn ātma is without old age, without death, immortal, without fear (it is) Brahman'. (Bṛh. Up. 4.4.25) These and other texts are in point here with reference to that. It (Brahman) should be apprehended as the ātman.

grāhayanti means 'teach'. The Vedānta texts teach Īśvara as the ātman. *eṣa ta ātmāntaryamyamṛtaḥ*: 'this, your ātma is the inner controller, immortal'. (Bṛh. 3.7.28) *yan manasā na manute yenāhur manomatam*: 'that which does not think by the mind, that by which they say the mind thinks'. *tadeva brahmatvam viddhi nedam yadidam. upāsate*: 'understand that to be Brahman, not this which you worship'. (Kena Up. 1.5) *tat satyam sa ātmā tattvamasi*: 'that is the Truth, that is the ātmā, That thou art'. (Ch. 6.8.16). These and other texts are to be noted.

Objection: This text: *ātmeti tūpagacchanti grāhayanti ca* should be understood symbolically in the same way as a symbol (like a sāligrāma) is used for representing Viṣṇu. This is not proper. Because, it substitutes the subsidiary for the primary meaning and also because it (the sentence) is differently framed. Where the symbolic reference is meant, then, mention will be made of it only once as in *manobrahma, ādityobrahma*: 'the mind is Brahma, the sun is Brahma.' (Ch. 3.18.1 and 3.19.1). But here it is said *tvamahamasmi aham vai tvamasi*: 'You are I, I am verily You'. As the text is differently framed, non-difference alone is meant. And, the perception of difference is condemned. Similarly are the following: *atha yo'nyām devatāmupaśte anyo'sāvanyo'hamasmīti na sa veda yathā paśuḥ*: 'he who worships another devatā with the idea, He is another, I am another, he does not know like an animal'. (Bṛḥ. Up. 1.4.10) *mṛtyoḥ sa mṛtyumāpnoti ya iha nāneva paśyati*: 'he who sees as many, goes from death to death.' (i.e., goes through a succession of births and deaths, does not attain immortality). (Bṛḥ. 4.4.19) *yathodakam durgepraviṣṭam parvateṣu vidhāvati / evam dharmān pṛthak paśyan tānevānudhāvati / /*: 'as water falling on inaccessible places flows in torrents along mountains, so one who sees the beings as separate (from the Ātman) runs after them only'. (Kaṭha. Up. 3.1.14) *dvitiyāt vai bhayam bhavati*: 'verily fear arises from a second'. (Bṛh. 1.4.2) *yada hyevaiṣa etasminnudaramantaram kurute / atha tasya bhayam bhavati / tattveva bhayam viduṣo manvānasya /* : when he makes even a little difference in this, then there is fear (of mortality) for him who thinks himself to be learned.' (Taitt. Up. 2.7) *sarvam tu parādādyonyatrāmanaḥ sarvam veda*: 'him who thinks that all is different from the ātman, everything excludes'. (Bṛh. Up. 2.4.6) These and other texts again and again speak against the attribution of difference. So too, *ātmaivedam sarvam*: 'all this is the ātman: (Ch. Up. 7.25.2) *ātmani vijñāte sarvamidam vijñātam*: 'When the ātman is known, all this is known'; *idam sarvam yadayamatmā*: 'all that is this is the ātman'. (Bṛh. Up. 2.4.6) *brahmaivedam sarvam*: 'all this is Brahman'. (Muṇd. Up. 2.2.11) are the śruti texts. So the smṛti too: *yajñātvā na punarmoham evam yāsyasi pāṇdava / yena bhutānyaśeṣena drakṣaysyātmanyatho mayi //* : 'Knowing this, O! Pāṇdava! you will not again fall into this confusion, by this you will see the whole of creation in yourself and in Me.' (B.G. 4.35) The meaning of this is that you will see the identity of *kṣetrajña* (the jivātman) and the *Īśvara* which is celebrated in the Upaniṣads. The Lord too has said (in the Bhagavad Gīta) *sarvabhūteṣu enaikam bhāvamavyayamīkṣate / avibhaktam vibhakteṣu tadjñānam vidhdi sāttvikam / /* : 'that knowledge by which the one Imperishable Being is seen in all existences, undivided in the divided, know that that knowledge is sāttvika'.

(B.G. 18.20) Thus, the Lord Himself has declared that advaita ātma jñāna is right knowledge. Therefore vest the mind in the Ātman that is Īśvara.

Further *ātma ca paramātmā ca tvamekaḥ pancadhā stithaḥ*: 'You are the one that is both ātmā and Paramātmā, You stand five-fold.[7] (Viṣṇu Pu. 5.18-50) And again,

athavā bahunaikena kim jñātena tavārjuna /
viṣṭabhyahamidam kṛtsnamekāmśena sthito jagat //

'But what is there, O! Arjuna! For this detailed knowledge? I stand supporting the whole universe by a single fragment of Myself'. (B.G. 10.42)

There are authoritative statements also for the view that the appearance of the world is the result of avidyā.

eka eva mahānātmā so'hamkaro'bhidhīyate /
sa jīvaḥ so'ntarātmeti jīyate tattvacintakaiḥ //

'The ātma who is supreme is one only; that is called ahaṁkāra (the ego), that is (then known as) the jīva; it is said to be the antarātmā (pratyagātmā) by those who reflect on the Truth.'

Similarly in the Viṣṇu Purāṇa—

vibhedajanake jñāne nāśamātyantikamgate /
ātmanobrahmaṇobhedam asantam kaḥ karisyati //

'When the neiscience which produces the sense of difference completely vanishes, who will make the non-existent difference between the ātman and Brahman?' (6.7.96)

paratmāno manuṣyendra vibhāgo'jñānakalpitaḥ /
kṣaye tasyātmaparayorvibhāgo'bhāga evahi //

'O! King! this distinction between the Paramātman and the jivātman is the creation of neiscience. When

---

7. As five elements, or five prāṇas (breaths), five kośas (sheaths) etc.

that vanishes, the difference between the jīva and Brahman becomes non-existent.'

In the Viṣṇu Dharma—

yathaikasmin ghatākāse rajodhūmādibhiryute /
nānye malinatām yanti dūrasthāḥ kutracitkvacit //
tathā dvandvairanekaistu jīve ca maline kṛte /
ekasminnapare jīvā malināḥ santi kutracit / /

'When a particular ether enclosed in a pot appears fouled with dust and smoke, others (open or enclosed in another pot) which are at a distance from it do not get foul, anything or anywhere. So too, when by a number of dualities, the jīva gets impure in a particular case, the other jīvas do not get impure anywhere'.

In the Brahma Yājñavalkya—

ākāsamekam hi yathā ghatādiṣu pṛtagbhaveṭ /
tathāpyātmaiko'pyanekeṣu jalādhāreṣvivamśumān //

'As the same ether appears many and separate in a jar (and other receptacles) and as the sun appears many and different in different reservoirs of water, so the one and the same ātman appears different in many limiting media.' (Upādhis)

The Svetāśvatara says: *kṣaratmānānvīśate deva akaḥ*: 'the one Deva rules over the body and the ātma' (1.10). In the Chāndogya it is said *sa ekadhā bhavati, etc.* It is as one (7.26.2); *sa tatra paryeti*: It pervades there' *sa eṣa etena daivena cakṣuṣā manasaitān kāmān paśyan ramate*: 'this ātman sees these things of desire by Its mind and delights' (8.12.5). *paro'vikṛta evātmā svātmāyam jīvaḥ*: 'the ātman is the Supreme unmodified, this jīva is the ātman'. *sa eva iha praviṣṭaḥ*: 'this is pervasive here'. (Bṛḥ. Up. 1.4.7). *ātmetyevopāsīta; tadedat brahmāpūrvam*: 'let one worship it as the ātman; this is the Brahma without beginning' (Bṛḥ. 2.5.19) etc., *nānyo'tosti draṣṭa nānyo'tosti vijñātā*: 'there is no other seer; there is no other knower'. (Bṛh. Up. 3.7.23)

sa va eṣa mahānaja ātma yo'yam vijñānamayaḥ: 'that ātma is great, unborn, this which is compacted of vijñāna (superior intelligence' (Bṛh. 24.4.22). *atha yo' nyām devatāmupāste*: 'those who worship as another deva' (Bṛh. Up. 1.4.10). *aitadātmyamidam sarvam*: 'all this is identical with It' (Ch. Up. 6.8.7) and *ksetrajñam cāpi mām viddhi*: 'Know Me to be the knower of the kṣetra' (the field of beings in the world) B.G. 13.3).

In the Yogayājñavalkya—

niscaranti yathā lohapindāttaptātspulingakāḥ /
sakāśadātmanastadvat prabhavanti jaganti hi //

'Like sparks of fire go out from a heated ball of iron, the worlds go out from the ātman.'

ajah śarīragrahaṇāt sa jātc iti kīrtyate: 'the Unborn is spoken of as born as It acquires a body', says the Brahma-purāṇa.

sarpavadrajjukhaṇdastu niśāyām veśmamadhyagaḥ /
eko candro dvau vyomni timirāhata caksuṣaḥ //
ābhāti paramātmā ca sarvopādhiṣu samsthitaḥ /
nityoditaḥ svayam jyotiḥ sarvagah puruṣaḥ paraḥ //

'In the twilight inside the house, a bit of rope appears as a serpent; to the eye afflicted by purblindness, the one moon appears in the sky as two. So does the Paramātmā shine limited by all upādhis though it is the ever-present, self-effulgent, omnipresent Supreme Puruṣa.'

ahankārāvivekena kartāhamiti manyate: 'by his egoism and want of discrimination, he considers himself as the doer'.

evamevāyam puruṣaḥ prājnenātmanā: 'this puruṣa (enveloped) by the prajñānatman etc.' (Bṛh. Up. 4.3.21) and *satā somya tadā sampanno bhavati*: 'then, dear one! he becomes endowed with Sat'. (Ch. Up. 6.8.1)

svamāyayā svamātmānam mohayandvaitamāyayā /
guṇāhatam svamātmānam labhate ca svayam
hariḥ //

'Deluding Himself by His māyā of duality, Hari obtains His nature affected by the guṇas' (i.e., Brahman constricts Itself as the jīva in the mould of the guṇas).

The following texts too have to be noticed in this connection.

utkrāmantam sthitam vāpi bhunjānam vā guṇan-
vitam /
vimuḍhā nānupaśyanti paśyanti jñāna cukṣuṣaḥ //

'The deluded do not see Him who departs, stays and enjoys who is conjoined with the guṇas, but they see who possess the eye of wisdom' (B.G. 15.10).

ajñānenāvṛtam jñānam tena muhyanti jantavaḥ: 'Wisdom is veiled by nescience; mortals are thereby deluded'. (B.G. 5.15)

avyaktādi viśeṣāntam avidyā lakṣaṇam smṛtam: 'Everything beginning with the unmanifested (Prakṛti) and ending with the qualities of objects is signified by avidyā; *āsididam tamobhūtam*: 'all this was enveloped by the darkness' (of nescience).

vacārambaṇam etc., 'all these modifications depend on speech' (Ch. 6.1.4). *yatrahi dvaitamiva bhavati taditara itaram paśyati / yatra tvasya sarvamātmaivābhūt tat kena kam paśyet tatkena kam jighret //* : 'where one perceives duality as it were, then one sees another; where however for this one all things were the ātman, then what will be seen by what? What will be smelt by what?' (Bṛh. Up. 2.4.14) *tatra komohaḥ kaḥ śokah ekatvam anupaśyataḥ*: 'there what is (whence arises) the delusion, what is the sorrow for one who sees unity?' (Īś. Up. 7).

yatra nānyat paśyati nānyat vijānāti etc.: 'where one does not see another, does not know another etc.,' (Chānd. Up. 7.24.1). *bhedo'yam ajnānanibandhanah neha nānāstikincana*: 'this difference is founded on nescience; there is no manifold here' (Kaṭha. Up. 2.1.1). *mṛtyoh sa mṛtyumāpnoti ya iha nāneva paśyati*: 'he who sees all this as manifold goes from death to death'. (Kaṭh. Up. 2.1.10). *viśvataḥ caksuḥ*: 'having eyes everywhere' (Svet. Up. 3.3). *yo yonim adhitiṣtatyeka viśvāni rūpāṇi yonisca sarvāḥ*: 'he who was the prime cause of all causes and forms'. *ajāmekam lohitasukla kṛṣṇām*: 'the unborn one which is of the colour of red, white and black' (signifying the beginningless māyā which is compacted of the three guṇas). *ajoheyeko juṣamāno'nuśete.*, 'He who is unborn who loves her and lies by her (Svet. Up. 4.5). *devātmaśaktim vidadhe*: 'It created Its own power'; *na tu tat dvitīyamasti tato'nyat vibhaktam yat paśyet etc.*: 'Other than It there is no second, he who sees it as divided' (Bṛḥ. Up. 4.3.23). *eka eva rudro na dvitiyāya tasthe*: 'the Supreme is One only; it does not stand as two (Svet. Up. 3.2).

The Gaudapāda Kārika says:—

'This, which is anything that is moving or unmoving is what has blossomed out of the mind when the mind rests on the ātman, as there is no duality.

'Whatever appears dual should be annulled by the mind. Duality is the result of the activity of the mind. Advaita is the supreme truth.

'Even as in dream, there is appearance of duality by the activity of the mind, so too is the appearance of duality in the waking state due to the activity of the mind.

'By reasoning too the fact of the world being the work of the mind can be established as all beings are objects of perception like objects appearing in the dream.'[8]

The following śruti texts should be noted:

dvitīyādvai bhayam bhavati: 'Verily from a second there is fear' (Bṛh. Up. 1.4.27); *jñāte tvātmani nāstyet kāryakāraṇatātmanaḥ: eko devaḥ sarva bhūteṣu gūdhaḥ*: 'When the ātman is known, there is no talk of cause and effect; the One shining One is hidden in all beings.' (Śvet. Up.6-11) *asango hyayam puruṣaḥ*: 'this Puruṣa is unattached' (Bṛh. Up. 4, 3.15).

The Viṣṇu Purāṇa says:—

'All this universe is the expression of Viṣṇu who is the all. Therefore it is to be seen as one's own ātman, as non-different by the wise.' (1.17.84)[9]

'Ye! Asuras! attain(ing) equality of outlook everywhere; perception of equality is worship of Acyuta.' (1.17.90)[9]

'Dear One! when the Paramātman that is Govinda who is all this world and is the Lord of the Universe has taken the form of all beings, how can there be any talk of (distinction of) friend or foe?' (1.19.37)[9]

The śruti texts: *tattvamasi*, 'That thou art' (Chānd. Up. 6.6.3), *ahambrahmāsmi*: 'I am Brahman' (Bṛh. Up. 1.4.10). *idam sarvam yadayamātma*: 'All this is the ātman' (Bṛh. Up. 2.4.6). *ayamātma brahma*: this ātman is Brahman' (Bṛh. Up. 2.5.19). *tarati śokamātmavit*: 'the knower of the ātman transcends sorrow' (Chānd. Up. 7-

8. If it is said that whatever is seen while we are awake is real, then objects and actions appearing in the dream will also have to be considered real, because they too are seen.
9. Prahalāda's words to the asuras.

1-3). *tatra ko mohaḥ kaḥ śokah ekatvamanupaśyatah*: 'What delusion or sorrow is there for one who sees unity?' (Īś. Up. 7). From these and others, from smṛtis, Itihāsas and purāṇas and other secular texts one learns that the whole universe is of the nature of the ātman, that there is non-difference between the jīva and Brahman, and among Its several manifestations.

The authoritativeness must be accepted even in respect of existing things (in respect of which there is not the Mimāmsaka reference to command of the form of prescriptions and prohibitions contrary to the Mimāmsaka dictum that the meaningfulness of the Vedas lies in their instigation to action). It has been said of old: *svapakṣasādhanairakāryamarṭhā jātamāha cet / taṭha paro'pi veda çet śrutiḥ parātmadṛk na kim*: 'If a letter or word acquires meaning only in the context of another letter or word, then it will not be connected only with inducements to action. In that case eulogistic sentences (arthavāda) will not prompt to action. The meaning signified by them is action and not merely praise. For instance, the śruti: *vāyavyam śvetāmālabheta bhūtīkāmo vāyur vaikṣepiṣṭhā devatā*: Desire alone prompts to action, not a command. The śruti also says:

atho kalvāhuḥ kāmamaya evāyam purusaḥ iti sa
yathākāmo bhavati tatkratur bhavati
yatkraturbhavati tatkarma kurute yatkarma
tadbhisampadyate:

Therefore, it is said that this jīva obeys the directions of desire.' Whatever desire he has, he purposes action accordingly; whatever his purpose, he does the action determined by it; whatever the action, he attains its result.' The smṛti too is to the same effect. *akāmataḥ kriyā kācit dṛśyate neha kasyacit / yadyaddi kurute karma tat kāmasya ceṣṭitam* // : 'Nobody is seen to act without a desire (kāma); whatever action he does is wrought by desire (Manu 2.4 and) and *kāma eṣa krodha eṣa:* 'this is desire, this is anger' (B.G.3.37)The authoritativeness of Vedic texts which have another meaning must be accepted. By saying they are unauthoritative, Nahuṣa was cursed to assume a serpent body. How was that?

(Nahuṣa performed a hundred yāgas and had qualified for the position of Indra. Out of his haughtiness he asked the Ṛṣis to carry him in a palanquin (to Devendraloka). Carrying him, the palanquin bearers who included high souled Ṛṣis, Devarṣis and Brahmarṣis who were all perfectly taintless were very tired carrying the naughty king. They asked the evil-minded King Nahuṣa to solve a doubt.

'Are these words of the mantra that have been uttered (in the sacrifice) valid? Do you accept their authority or no, O! Vāsava'. Nahuṣa immediately said 'No', his mind enveloped by folly.

The Ṛṣis said:

'You have embarked on adharma (unrighteousness), you abandon dharma. This is authority for us as declared earlier by mahṛṣis.

Agastya said:-

'Then disputed by the Ṛṣis, the King, in the grip of adharma kicked me on the head with his foot. Due to that Indra's (here Nahuṣa's) mind was afflicted and he lost his prosperity; then I told him who was afflicted in mind and trembling with fear: 'Because you have fouled the ordained pure faith followed by the mahṛṣis, because you kick them on the head with your foot, and because you have made these unapproachable (by their eminence) ṛṣis who are like unto Brahma your palanquin bearers, O! King!, you shall fall from svarga losing all your lustre degraded by your sins and you shall be condemned to inhabit the earth in the form of a serpent for ten thousand years. At the end of that period, beholding a descendant of your line known as Yudhiṣṭhira, you shall obtain Heaven."

(M.B. Udyoga 18.8.18)

Therefore one should have religious faith in ātmajñāna (knowledge of the self). The Lord said in the Gīta: *asraddadhānāḥ puruṣā dharmasyāsya parantapa / aprāpya mam nivartante mṛtyusamsāra vartmani //* : 'Men devoid of sradda for this dharma do not attain Me, O! Oppressor of foes! but return to the path of the mortal world (marked by death and samsāra.) In the Aitareya Upaniṣad it is said: *esa panthā etat karma, etat brahma, etat satyam tasmānna paramādye na hyatiyāyan pūrve ye'tayāms te parābabhūvaḥ*: 'this is the way, this is the action, this is Brahman, this is the Truth; therefore let not one be negligent, those who went before did not transgress; those who transgressed were discomfited.' So it was said by a Ṛṣi (R.V.8.101.4) *prajā hatiśro atyayamīyurnanyā akarmabhito viviśre / bṛhadda tasthau bhuvaneṣvantaḥ pavamāno harita aviveśa:* which means: 'Three classes of people transgressed, others settled down round about the venerable Agni, the great Sun stood in the midst of the worlds, the blowing Vāyu entered the Harits (the downs or ends of the earth). The Śruti says: *praja ha tisro atyayamīyuriti yā vai tā imāḥ prajāḥ tisro' atyayamiyas tammani vayāmsi vangā vagadhascerapādāḥ:* when he says: "Three classes of people transgressed, they are what we see here (on earth born again) as birds, trees, herbs and serpents." *vanagāḥ* means trees, *vagadhāḥ* means vegetable kingdom; *irapādaḥ* or *urapādaḥ* are serpents and other crawling creatures. So also in the Īśavasya is a mantra that censures one who has no (spiritual) knowledge: *asūrya nāma te lokā andhena tamasā vṛtāḥ / tāmste pretyabhigacchanti ye ke cātmahano janāḥ //*. 'Those worlds peopled by asuras enveloped by blinding darkness are reached after death by such people who commit suicide of the soul.' In the Taittirīya we have *asanneva sa bhavati asad brahmeti veda cet*: 'he who thinks that Brahman is not, becomes himself-non-existent.' (2.6.1). Similarly in the Śakuntalopakhyāna: *yo'nyathā santam-ātmānam anyathā pratipadayate / kimtena na kṛtam pāpam corenātmāpahāriṇā //* 'What sin has not been committed by the thief who makes away with his ātman, who understands that which is of one (true) nature as of another (untrue) nature?' That is enough by way of explanation.

The mental bath of sahasranāma japa is elucidated: The Mahābhārata says: 'One will become immortal on bathing in those mental waters in which all devas and Vedas acquire their purity. He who bathes in the mental waters constituted of the pond of spiritual knowledge which removes attachment and aversion attains the highest. Bathing in the Triveṇi of Sarasvati whose waters are red, in the Yamunā, which is black and in the Ganga that is white, who do not reach the nirguṇa Brahman? The Ātmā is the river flowing with water of control; the ponds are of Truth; good conduct are its banks, compassion is its waves. O! Pāṇḍu's son! take a plunge in it. The inner ātman is not purified by mere physical waters.' *The Viṣṇu Smṛti says: mānasam snānam Viṣṇucintanam.* 'The meditation on Viṣṇu is mental bath.' *Manu says: japyenaivatu samsidhyet brāhmaṇo nātra samśayaḥ / kuryādanyaḥ na vā kuryāt maitro brahmaṇa ucyate //* : 'No doubt, one becomes Brahman purely by meditation, whatever he does or does not do. Maitra who did like this is said to be a Brāhmaṇa.' Again it has been said *japastu sarvadharmebhyaḥ paramo dharma ucyate*: 'Japa is said to be supreme among all dharmas.' *ahimsaya ca bhūtānām japa yajñāaḥ pravartate*: 'non-injury to beings precedes japayajña' *yajñānam japayajñosmi*: 'I am the japayajña of yajñas' says the Gita (10.15) *apavitrah pavitrova sarvāvasthām gatopivā yaḥ smaret puṇdarīkakṣam sa bāhyabhyantara suciḥ*: 'Whether impure or pure in body, whatever may be one's state, he who thinks of Puṇdarikāṣa is pure outside and inside (physically and mentally).'

Now the marks of That Supreme praised as the one God are given.

यतः सर्वाणि भूतानि भवन्त्यादियुगागमे ।
यस्मिश्च प्रलयं यान्ति पुनरेव युगक्षये ।। ११ ।।

yataḥ sarvāṇi bhutāni bhavantyādiyugagame /
yasmimsca praḷayam yānti punareva yugakṣaye //

yataḥ: yasmāt: from Which (or Whom) all beings arise when the first yuga dawns. *Yasmin:* in Which (or in Whom) *pralayam:* dissolution. *yānti:* attain. *punaḥ*: again. *eva* is to indicate certainty, means not in anything else. *yuga kṣaye:* in mahāpralaya; in the final deluge. *ca* after *yasmin* is to show that in the middle too they subsist in Whom. *vide* the śruti: *yato vā imāni bhūtāni jāyante;* etc.: 'That from Which all these beings are born etc.,' (Taitt. up.3.1).

तस्य लोकप्रधानस्य जगन्नाथस्य भूपते ।
विष्णोर्नामसहस्रं मे श्रृणु पापभयापहम् ॥ १२ ॥

tasya lokapradhānasya jagannathasya bhūpate /
viṣnornāmasahasram me ṣṛṇu pāpabhayapaham //

Of Him who is celebrated in the subjects of knowledge which are the instruments of (inner) sight and who is the Lord of the Universe, O! King! hear from me the thousand Names which ward off sin or fear.

tasya: of Him Who has these characteristics and Who is the one God. *lokapradhānasya* Who is celebrated by the subjects of study which are the cause of inner sight.[10] *Jagannāthasya*: the Lord or the owner (*svāmi*) of the Universe, the Paramātma in association with māyā, yet unattached to it. Of Him. *bhūpate*: O! King. *Viṣṇoḥ*: of Him who is pervasive. *nāmasahasram*: of the thousand Names. *pāpabhayāpaham*: which wards off sin and fear, *me*: from me. *śṛṇu*: listen carefully with concentration of mind.

'O! best of dvijas! Of Him who is the One and the All, listen to the Names which will be helpful to the people. Their effects vary according to the objects in view of the reciter. By repeating the Names, the corresponding results accrue. Whatever power belongs to a Name is effective whether for good or for evil in that sphere alone.' (Viṣṇudharma).

Though in respect of the Supreme (nirguṇa) Brahman, the use of the possessive indicating quality, action, class is not proper, yet, they are in place in regard to saguṇa Brahman which is a modification of the nirguṇa Brahman as It is of the nature of all things (in the

10. aneka samśayo' cchedi parokṣārthasya darśakam
sarvasya locanam śastram yasya nāsti andha eva saḥ.

universe) and as it warrants the application of all Names. So all Names can be applied to the Supreme Person.

यानि नामानि गौणानि विख्यातानि महात्मनः ।
ऋषिभिः परिगीतानी तानि वक्ष्यामि भूतये ।। १३ ।।

yāni nāmāni gauṇani vikhyātāni mahātmanaḥ /
ṛṣibhiḥ parigītāni tāni vakṣyāmi bhūtaye // 13

For securing prosperity, I shall enumerate those Names indicative of qualities which have been explained by the mahātmās and uttered by the ṛsis (in mantras).

Those Names which are *gauṇani,* which are connected with qualities and which have gained currency by such connection. Those that are *vikhyātāni,* celebrated. *ṛṣibhiḥ*: by (in) mantras and by those who have had a soul-sight of them. *parigītāni*: expressed fully in different contexts in stories of Parameśwara. *mahātma*: *mahānsca asau ātmā ca. yaccapnoti yadādatte yaccātti viṣayāniha / yaccāsya santato bhāvaḥ tasmad ātmeti kīrtyate //* : 'What gets, what eats (enjoys) the sense pleasures, what is of such constant nature is said to be the ātman'. This ātmā which is great is spoken of as mahātmā. *vakṣyāmi bhūtaye*: I shall utter the Names of Him of unimaginable glory for achieving the puruṣārthas (of dharma, artha, kāma and mokṣa) for those who are intent on their respective pursuits.

In the sahasranāma, Names like āditya are used. Though they apply to objects like the sun, such objects are non-different from the Supreme Being; they are praises of that Supreme. Hence their narration. *Vide,* Viṣṇu Purāṇa:

bhūtātmā cendriyātmā ca pradhānątmą tathą bhavān /

ātmā ca paramātmā ca tvamekaḥ pancadhā sthitaḥ //

'You are the same Ātman who appears in five-fold form as the physical objects, as the sense organs, as the Pradhāna (the stuff of the world) as the jīva and the Paramātmā.

jyotimṣi viṣṇurbhuvanāni visnurgirayo diśasca /
nadyah samudrāsca sa eva sarvam yadasti yannāsti ca vipravarya //

'The lights are Viṣṇu; the worlds are Viṣṇu, the mountains, directions the rivers and oceans, whatever is (visible) or is not (visible), He only is the All'.

Also because it is said in the Gita (10.21 to 42) beginning with *ādityānamaham viṣṇuḥ*: 'I am Viṣṇu among the Ādityas' and ending with *ekāmśena sthito jagat*: 'the universe stands (is sustained) by a particle of Me'. and also in the śruti: *puruṣa evedam viśvam karma tapo brahma parāmṛtam*: (Muṇd. Up. 3.10) 'all this universe, action, austerity, brahma and supreme amṛtam is the Supreme Person'.

Though the Names like Viṣṇu are repeated (in different places) the meaning differs by the context. So there is no redundancy. Names like Śrīpatih, Mādhavaḥ and the like differ in nomanclature though they have the same meaning. So, here too there is no redundancy. Even if the meaning is the same, repetition is not a fault as by the question originally asked viz., *nāmnām sahasrasya kim ekam daivatam*, 'Who is the one God denoted by the thousand Names?' all Names refer to the same God.

Names in the masculine gender refer to Viṣṇu, those in the feminine gender are to be understood as qualifying Devatā and those in the neuter gender refer to Brahman.

VIṢṆU SAHASRANĀMA STOTRA

The śruti beginning with *yataḥ sarvāṇi bhūtāni* which refers to Brahman which is the cause of the origination, preservation and dissolution of the universe speaks of the identity of the Saguṇa and the Nirguṇa Brahman. So, both kinds are spoken of by the Name *Viṣvam* (which is the first name in the Sahasranāma).

ॐ विश्वं विष्णुर्वषट्कारो भूतभव्यभवत्प्रभुः ।
भूतकृद्भूद्भावो भूतात्मा भूतभावनः ॥ १४ ॥

Om, Viśvam Viṣṇuḥ Vaṣatkāraḥ Bhūtabhavya bhavatprabhuḥ /
Bhūtakṛt Bhūtabhṛt Bhāvaḥ Bhutātmā Bhutabhāvanaḥ // 14

विश्वम् VIŚVAM: 1. Brahman is so called as It is the cause of viśvam, the universe. It is mentioned as the first Name to show that the cause is to be inferred from the effect and it applies to the Kārya Brahman like Virinci (Brahma) (and Viṣṇu and Rudra).

Or. 2. to show that this viśvam is not separate from the Supreme Puruṣa, He is called *Viśvam. vide* the śrutis: *brahmaivedam viśvam* (Mund. Up. 3-10): 'This viśvam, universe, is Brahman only', *puruṣa evedam viśvam*—this viśvam is not separate from the Supreme Puruṣa. *Viśvamevedam* this (Brahman) is *viśvam* only. Other than that, there is really nothing which exists.

Or 3. Brahman enters (viśati); so *viśvam*: *vide* the śruti. *tatśṛṣṭvā tadevānuprāviśat* (Taitt. Up. 2.6): having created it (the universe), It entered into it itself.'

Further 4. All the worlds (viśvāni) on destruction enter into This. So Brahman is called viśvam. *vide* the śruti: *yat prayantyabhisamviśanti*: 'That into Which at the end they enter'. (Taitt. Up. 3.1). He enters into the entire universe which is the effect, or, in This, the whole universe enters; in both ways Brahman is *viśvam.*

Or 5. The syllable OM is signified by the Name *Viśvam. Vide* from *anyatra dharmādanyatrādharmāt*: 'other than dharma and other than adharma' to *sarve vedā yatpadāmananti tapāmsi sarvaṇī ca yadvadanti yadiccanto brahmacaryam caranti tatte padam sangraheṇa bravīmi / Om ityetat / etad dvayevākṣaram brahma etaddvayevākṣaram param / etaddvayevākṣaram jñātvā yo yadiccati tasya tat /* : 'that state which is declared by all the Vedas, that which is the goal of all austerities, desiring which Brahman knowledge is pursued, I shall convey that state to you in brief. It is OM. These two only are the indestructible Brahman; these two only are the indestructible Supreme. Knowing these two indestructibles, whatever he desires, that is his.' (Kaṭh. Up. 1.2.15.16). Beginning with *etadvai satyakāma param cāparam brahma yadomkāraḥ*: 'This Omkāra, Satyakama! is the param (highest) and the aparam (lower) Brahma', to *yah punaretam trimātreṇa om ityetenaivākṣareṇa param puruṣam abhidhyāyati*: 'he (again) who by this word of three māntras, Om, mediates on the Supreme Puruṣa' in Praśnopaniṣad (5.2.5). *Om iti brahma*: 'Brahma is designated by the word Om.' *Om iti sarvam*: 'Everything is Om' is declared by Yajur Veda āraṇyakam. The Chāndogya says: *tadyathā sankunā sarvam parṇāni santrnnāni evam omkāreṇa sarvā vāk santṛnnā omkāra evedam sarvam*; 'as all fibres of a leaf are connected with the central stalk, so also all these forms of speech are connected with Omkāra. All this is Omkāra' (2.23.3). In the Māndukya beginning with *omityedakṣaram* 'this imperishable is Om,' we have

praṇavo hyaparam brahma pranavasca parā smṛtaḥ /
apūrvo 'nantarobāhyo na paraḥ praṇavo'-vyayaḥ //
sarvasyapraṇavo hyādiḥ madhyamantastathaiva ca /
evam hi praṇavam jñātvā vyaśnute
tadanantaram //
praṇavam hīśvaram vindyāt sarvasya hṛdaye
sthitam /
sarvavyāpinam Omkāram jñātvā dhīro na socati //
amātro' nantamātrasca dvaitasyopasamaḥ śivaḥ /
Omkāro vidito ena sa munirnetero janaḥ //

'Praṇava is the apara (lower) Brahma, praṇava is said to be the para (higher) Brahma. Without beginning and without end, without anything outside or higher, praṇava is undecaying. Of everything praṇava is the beginning, middle and the end. Understanding the praṇava thus, one attains it then. One should understand praṇava as God resident in the hearts of all. Understanding Omkāra as all pervasiva, the wise man never grieves. If Omkāra which is both *amātra* and *anantamātra* and which is end of duality making for auspiciousness is known, one becomes a muni, none else.' (Gaudapādakārika 1.26.29).

And there are also the srutis: *Om tadbrahma*, *Om tadātmā and Om tat sarvam*: 'that Brahman is Om, that Atmā is Om; that Satya is Om'.

Also:

'He who departs leaving the body uttering the one-syllabled Om and thinking of Me, attains the Supreme goal' (B.G.8.3).

That which the knowers of Veda call the Imperishable, and into which enter the samnyāsins, and desiring which they lead a life of continence (or engage themselves in inquiry into Brahman) that I shall declare to you briefly.'

'I am sapidity in water, O! son of Kunti! (BG. 8-11) I am the radiance in the Moon and in the Sun; I am the syllable Om in all the Vedas, sound in ether and manliness in man.' (B.G.7.8).

'Of utterances, I am the mono-syllable Om (B.G. 10.25). The first, compacted of three letters is Brahma, the Vedas which are established in it, that monosyllable is the transcendent Brahma; breath control is the supreme tapas (Apas Dhar. 1.4.13.6).

Omkārāḥ svargadvāram tasmat brahmādhyeṣyamānaḥ etadādi pratipadyeta, / vikatthām canyām krtvā evam laukikyā vācā vyāvartate brahma // : 'Omkara is the door to Heaven. So to those who study about Brahman, this is explained first. Giving up all useless secular talk Brahman is explained by words.' *praṇavādyās-tathā vedāḥ praṇave paryavasthitāḥ / vāngmayam praṇavaḥ sarvam tasmāt praṇavamabhyaset //* 'All Vedas have praṇava for their beginning; they are established in praṇava, the entire praṇava is of speech: therefore, every one should learn praṇava.' By these smṛtis too, by the word *Viśvam,* Omkara is indicated. As the word and what it signifies are absolutely non-different, *Viśvam,* which is referred to by Omkāra, is Brahman Itself. The Chāndogya (8.14.1): *sarvam khalu idam brahma tajjalāniti śānta upāsita:* 'all this is Brahma being the source, the sustenance and the sanctuary of all that. That from which all this manifold has sprung, into which it disappears and by which it lives. When all that is realised as the ātman, there is no room for desire and aversion. So the śruti says: let one worship It with equanimity.'

The following also should be noted in this connection:

'Let the essence of dharma be heard; after having heard, let one declare with determination. Let not one practise on others whatever is unfavourable to one-self' (Viṣṇu Dharma) (3.255.44).

That Yogi, O! Arjuna! is regarded as the Supreme who judges pleasure or pain everywhere, by the same standard as he applies to himself' (B.G.6.22).

'The nirguṇa Paramātmā rests in this body completely enveloping it. Him who is to be known by jñāna, I do not disregard nor transgress.'

'If I do not know that cause of all beings from the Vedas, I shall cross you and this mountain and as Hanuman did the Ocean.' (M.Bh.Vana.149.8.9).[11]

'If men on account of hatred are inimically inclined, being deluded, they are to be pitied by the wise as being under the sway of delusion. That is why those of a different vision are said by me to be distinct in nature.'

'Hear what I say briefly about those who have seen the truth. This whole world (constituted of all beings) is an expansion of Viṣṇu. Giving up the āsura nature, therefore, all things must be looked at as oneself by learned people attaining perfect one-ness.'

'We shall so endeavour as we shall attain bliss, O! daityas, acquiring equality of outlook. Such equality is worship of Acyuta. (Viṣṇu Purāṇa 1.17.82-85.90).

'This magnanimity, father, is not the result of any incantation nor is it wrought by nature. This is common

11. meaning as the latter will not happen, so, the former not knowing the cause will not happen. That is, it can be known from the Vedas.

to those in whose heart resides Acyuta.[12]

'He who meditates not wrong to others, but considers them as himself is free from the effects of sin as the cause does not exist.'

'Whoever inflicts injury on others by action, mind or speech gets a birth consequent on it and undergoes intense misery accordingly.'

'So realising that Keśava is resident in all creatures, I do not think of inflicting injury on others, nor do it or utter it.'

'In me who thinks of everything everywhere equally, how can sins bodily, mental or of by speech or wrought by gods or physical agencies ever happen?'

'Thus, knowing that Hari is resident in all beings, men of wisdom must practise constant devotion to all creatures.' (Viṣṇu Purāna 1.19.4-9).

'In acquiring friends the means are said to be sāma, dāna, bedha and danda (conciliation, gifts, differentiation, and punishment). But, I do not see the need of them, father; do not get angry. O! thou, long-armed! In the absence of anything to be accomplished, what is the use of the means.[12]

'When Govinda who is the Paramātman, who is the Lord of the Universe is pervaive of it, where, father is talk of friend are foe?' (Viṣṇu Purāṇa. 1.19, 35-37)[12]

'It is only in fools, the undiscriminating, the ignorant and the unrighteous that there is thought of what is to be enjoyed as mine and what is to be discarded as not mine.'

---

12. The idea is: when all objects are one's friends, where is the need to *acquire* a friend? When none is an enemy, why talk of the means to make a man as friend? Told by Prahlāda to his father.

'One who desires great prosperity must strive for virtues. He who desires mokṣa also must strive with a sense of equality. Celestial Beings, men, animals, birds, trees and crawling creatures are forms of Viṣṇu, the Ananta who appears as if differentiated. By one who know this, the whole creation comprising the unmoving and the moving should be looked as one self; for Viṣṇu takes the form of the entire universe.'

'Known thus, the Lord who is beginningless, the Parameśvara is pleased. When He is pleased there is liquidation of all grief.' (Viṣṇu Purāṇa 1.19.45.49).

'At the end of many lives the jñāni attains Me, That Mahātmā who realises that Vāsudeva is the All is rare.' (B.G.7.19).

In accordance with these and other texts to show that adoration, prostration etc., devoid of injury should be done, by the word *Viśvam* Brahman is indicated. For, the Lord has declared:

"He who does work for Me, he who looks on Me as the Supreme who is devoted to Me, who is free from attachment, who is without hatred for any being, he comes to Me, O! Paṇdava.' (B.G. 11.55).

"Know him to be a devotee of Viṣṇu who does not swerve from the dharmas of his varṇa (caste), who is of equanimous mind in respect of his friends and others, does not clamorously acquire or discard anything and who is of a pure unblemished mind.'

(Viśṇu Purāṇa 3.7.20)

'Vāsudeva resides in the heart of him who is not of impure mind, who is without jealousy, who is peaceful, of good conduct, who is the friend of all creatures, whose speech is pleasing and good and from whom all delusion has vanished.'

'If the Eternal (Supreme Being) resides in the heart of one, that person lives in the world with a comely form as the young sāla tree declares by its beauty the excellence of the juice that it has imbibed from earth' (Viṣṇu Purāṇa 3.7.23-24).

"Gor far away from those who rest their mind unsweringly on Ananta with the feeling 'all this and I are Vāsudeva,' 'Parameśvara is the Supreme Person and is One alone.' " (Viṣṇu Purāṇa 3.7.32).[12a]

'Servant, go very far from men whose impurities have been removed by disciplines of *yama* and *niyama* and whose minds are ever attached to Acyuta and who are free of passion, pride and jealousy.' (Viṣṇu Purāṇa 3.7.26).[12a]

Since by these and other texts, such are also the marks of a Vaiṣṇava (Viṣṇubhakta), praise and prostration to Him should be made without causing harm to others. Also by the śrutis: *sraddhayā deyam asraddhayā deyam sraddhayāgniḥ smidhyate:* 'It must be given with fervour, it must not be given without fervour, fire glows with ferver.'

'Best of Daityas! you shall have as your portion these six, a srāddha performed without one versed in the Vedas, the study of the Vedas without discipline, a sacrifice without dakṣiṇa (gift of money) an oblation without a ṛtvik (priest), a gift without fervour and an impure offering' (Hari Vamśa 3.72-2).[13]

'The merit (previously) acquired by those who hate Me, and similarly by those who hate My devotees and that acquired by those given to the daily worship of fire

12a. Told by Yama to his servants.
13. Told to Asuras by Viṣṇu when they asked for their portion of puṇya.

and yet engaging in buying and selling (trade) and by those who make gifts and sacrifices without earnestness- all that, O! chief of Daityas! shall be yours by My favour.' (Hari Vamśa 3-72.47-9)[13]

'Whatever is sacrificed, given or performed, and whatever austerity (tapas) is performed without fervour is called *asat* O! Partha! It is of no account in this world or in the next.' (B.G.17.287).

From these and other smṛti texts, it is evident that praise and prostrations etc., should be done with fervour and not from indifference. By the Lord's declaration (in B. G. 17.23) *Om tat sat iti nirdeśe bramaṇastrividhah smṛtaḥ:* 'Om Tat Sat,' this has been declared to be the triple designation of Brahman.' Though praise, prostrations etc., are not sāttvic and improperly done, they acquire proper form and become sāttvic if they are done with the use of these designations of Brahman. Thinking of one-self as Viṣṇu, praise, prostrations etc., must be made.

The Karma Kāṇda of the Mahā Bhārata says:-

'An aviṣṇu (one who does not think of one-self as Viṣṇu) should not sing the praises of Viṣṇu; an aviṣṇu should not offer flowers to Viṣṇu; an aviṣṇu should not meditate on Viṣṇu; an aviṣṇu will not attain Viṣṇu.'

In the Viṣṇu Dharma it is said:-

'O! sinless one! All these are the Names of the Supreme Brahman, one should utter these Names of the God of gods.' 'By properly worshipping the Guru of all the worlds, one attains undoubtedly whatever desires one longs for. Such worship enables one to get all one's wishes fulfilled.'

'Identifying himself with Govinda, not otherwise,

being one with Him, O! Dālbhya! man obtains all that he desires and also reaches the supreme state.'

In the Bhagavad Gīta (6.31) the Lord said:

'He who, established in oneness, worships Me abiding in all beings, that yogī lives in Me, whatever may be his mode of living.'

In the Viṣṇu Purāṇa (1.22.87) it is said:-

'To him who is firmly established in the thought: I am Hari, all this is Janārdhana, there is nothing other than Him as effect or cause, there does not arise another birth and he is not afflicted by the disease of dualities.'

Manu (2.2000)-

'Where the Guru is defamed or maligned, one should close one's ears or quit that place going somewhere else.'

Vyāsa Smṛti:

'Therefore Brahman Itself appears in the form of the Ācārya:-

Kātyāyana Smrti:-

'Than the mental torture of association with those who are against the contemplation of Sauri, it is better to be in the midst of a roaring fire.'

By this, it is clear that where there is abuse of Vāsudeva, one should not live there. Hence, it is said:-

'To him who has intense devotion to God, and as to God, so to the Guru, all that has been taught (and what has not been taught) becomes crystal clear' (Svet Up. 6.23).

By this mantra of the Sveteśvatara Upaniṣad, supreme devotion should be entertained to Hari and to the guru.

'Even if one utters His Name in spite of oneself, he

is freed from all sins even as stags which are terrified by a lion run away:' (Viṣṇu Purāṇa 6.8.19).

"By uttering Vāsudeva's Name knowingly or unknowingly, all (that sin) disappears like salt in water."

"The evil of Kali is very severe; it lands men in hell; but it disappears at once if Hari's Name is remembered once."(Viṣṇu Purāṇa 6.8.21).

"Even if remembered but once, Govinda burns away the multitude of sins like fire a bale of cotton."

"That which does not utter Govinda, Govinda, Govinda is the tongue of a serpent that lives in the anthill of the mouth."

"The creeper of sin lies in the form of a tongue of a man who does not keep on saying day and night the qualities of Govinda."

Even if the two letters of the Name of Hari हरि are pronounced once, then that man has girded up his loins to go on his journey to mokṣa."

"Even one prostration properly done to Kṛṣṇa is equal to the final baths after ten horse-sacrifices. The person who has performed ten horse sacrifices is born again (after the stock of his puṇya is exhausted). But a devotee of Kṛṣṇa is not born again' (M.Bh.Śānti. 46.123).

By these texts, it is declared that even in the absence of fervour and devotion, uttering the Lord's Name destroys all evil. What then needs to be said about the efficacy of uttering the Sahasrānāma with earnestness and devotion?

Manasā va agre samkalpyatyatha vācā vyāharati / yad hi manasā dhyāyati tadvāca vadati / : 'One first determines by the mind, then one utters by speech; what one thinks by the mind, that one expresses by speech' (Taitt Sam.6.1.7). By these two śrutis, it is clear that remembering and meditation are included in the utterance of Names.

Sage Parāsara concludes the Viṣṇu Purāṇa with—

"Resting the mind in Whom one does not go to hell, thinking of Whom, heaven too becomes a hindrance, when the mind is concentrated in Whom, the world of Brahma too becomes insignificant, when Who dwells in the mind of the pure, the Imperishable One confers liberation, what wonder that, if that Acyuta is praised, all sins vanish away? (6.8.56).

The Mahābhārata concludes with the following by Veda Vyāsa.

"After an exhaustive examination of all saśtras and inquiring again and again, this one conclusion is clearly established, namely Nārāyaṇa should be meditated on always." (M.Bh.Anu.186.11).

In the Kailāsa Yātra Parva of Harivamśa it is said also by Maheśvara that Hari only should be meditated on:

"By you governed by sattvic qualities, Hari alone should be meditated on; ye *vipras*, think of Keśava always by the syllable Om." (3.88.9).

It is keeping all this in mind, that the superiority of this dharma was expressed in the words: *eṣa me sarva-dharmāṇam dharmodhikatamomataḥ*. That Brahman which was declared in reply to the six questions beginning with *kimekam daivatam* etc., and ending with *kim japan mucyate jantuḥ etc.*, by the words *yataḥ sarvāṇi bhūtani* etc., that Brahman is indicated as explanation of *Viśvam*.

विष्णुः VIṢṆUḤ: 1. If the question is raised what is that? the answer is *Viṣṇuḥ*. In the Ṛgveda it is said *āsya jānanto nāma cidvivaktana mahaste viṣṇo sumatim bhajāmahe:* 'Conscious of this Thy glory, O! Viṣṇu! may we enjoy Thy grace!' (2.2.26). By this and other sentences, the attainment of true knowledge is ordained by the utterance of the Names of Viṣṇu. 1. *Viṣṇu:* derived from the expression *veveṣti,* 3rd person singular of *viś* meaning *vyāpnoti,* envelopes. It is the result of the combination of the suffix *nu* with *viś.* It means devoid of the limitations of space, time and object. *vide* the śruti *antarbahisca tat sarvam vyāpya nārāyaṇaḥ sthitaḥ:* 'pervading that (world) inside and outside stands Nārāyaṇa' (Nārā Up. 1.13.27).

Or, 2 the addition of the suffix *nu* to the root *viś* to enter gives the word *Viṣṇu.* In the Viṣṇu Purāṇa it is said: (3.1.45).

"Because all this is pervaded by that Supreme Being's power, therefore He is called Viṣṇuḥ. For the root *vis* signifies *entry into.'*

In the Mahā Bhārata it is said (Śānti Parva 350.42-43): "I am called Viṣṇu as I measured the sky and the earth and as I have pervaded the universe and beyond.

वषट्कारः VAṢATKĀRAḤ: 1. He for whom *vaṣat,* the oblation in yajñā is done is *Vaṣatkāra.*

Or 2. The sacrifice in which Vaṣatkāra is done, *vide*: the śruti: *yajño vai Viṣṇuḥ*: 'The sacrifice itself is Viṣṇuḥ' (Taitt.Sam.1.7.4).

Or 3. That Vaṣatkāra mantra by which one pleases the Gods is *Vaṣatkāra.*

Or 4. *Vaṣatkāra* is the name of a deity *vide: prajāpatisca vaṣatkārasca:* 'Prajāpati and Vaṣatkāra.' Also the smṛti: *caturbhisca caturbhisca dvābhyām pancabhireva ca / hūyate ca punardvābhyām sa me Viṣṇuḥ prasī-*

datu // "He who is invoked in sacrifices by four syllables[14] and four syllables,[15] by two [16] and five syllables,[17] and again by two,[18] let that Viṣṇu be pleased with me."

भूतभव्यभवत् प्रभुः BHŪTABHAVYABHAVAT PRABHUḤ: *Bhūtam* is past, *bhavyam* is future; *bhavat* is present. Their Lord *Prabutvam*: Lordship because He exists unconditionally regardless of differences of time.

भूतकृत् BHŪTAKṚT: 1. Because He creates beings assuming the rajoguṇa in the form of *Virinci* or Brahma.

Or, 2. Assuming the tamoguṇa, as Rudra He cuts or destroys or injures beings.

भूतभृत् BHŪTABHṚT: Assuming the sattvaguṇa, He sustains or protects or nourishes. So, *Bhūtabhṛt.*

भावः BHĀVAḤ: 1. He is in the form of the universe. 2. Or He merely exists. So, *Bhāvaḥ.* 3. Or Being as Sat is Bhāvaḥ.

भूतात्मा BHUTĀTMĀ: 1. Ātmā of the Bhūtas, their antaryāmī: the indwelling controller. *vide* the śruti: *eṣa ta ātmā antaryāmyamṛtaḥ*: He is your Ātmā, the indwelling controller and immortal.' (Bṛḥ. Up. 3.7.22).

भूतभावनः BHŪTABHĀVANAḤ: He originates or nourishes the bhūtas. So *Bhūtabhāvānaḥ.*

The doubt that subjection to the guṇas are predicated of the Lord by the Name *Bhūtakṛt* etc., (as explained above) is removed by the Names that follow.

पूतात्मा परमात्मा च मुक्तानां परमा गतिः ।
अव्ययः पुरुषः साक्षी क्षेत्रज्ञोऽक्षर एव च ।। १५ ।।

Pūtātmā Paramātmā ca Muktānānām paramā gatiḥ /

---

14. *a-srā-va-ya.* 15. *a-stu-sran-ṣat.* 16. *ya-ja.*
17. *ye-ya-jā-ma-he.* 18. *van-ṣat.*

Avyayaḥ Puruṣaḥ Sākṣī Kṣetrajñaḥ Aksaraḥ
evaca // 15

पूतात्मा PŪTĀTMĀ: He whose Ātmā is pure is Pūtātma. *vide* the śruti: *kevalonirguṇasca*: 'One only and qualitiless' (Śvet Up.11). The connection with the qualities for the Lord is stated to be of His own free will.

परमात्मा PARAMĀTMĀ: Parama Ātma: the Supreme Ātmā. Supreme because He is beyond material things which are results or causes and He is eternally pure, intelligent and free.

मुक्तानांपरमागतिः MUKTĀNĀM PARAMĀ GATIḤ: The ultimate goal attained by the liberated, the devatā to be reached. For, those who have reached Him do not come back (to samsāra). vide the Lord's assertion: *māmupetya kaunteya punarjanma na vidyate*: "Attaining Me, O' son of Kunti! there is no rebirth." (B.G. 8.16)

अव्ययः AVYAYAḤ: There is no *vyaya,* that is, destruction or change for Him. *vide* the śruti *ajaro'-maro'vyayaḥ*: 'not ageing, nor dying nor decaying'. (Bṛḥ. Up. 4.25)

पुरुषः PURUṢAH: 1. Exists in the *puram* or body. In the Mahā-Bhārata, it is said (Śānti Parva 212-52): *navadvāram puram puṇyam etairbhāvaiḥ samanvitam / vyāpya sete mahātmā yaḥ tasmāt puruṣa ucyate //* : This city (body) of nine openings has been acquired by meritorious deeds. As He exists pervading it entirely, He is called *Puruṣa*'.

Or 2. To express the idea that He was (āsīt) already before anything else, *pūrvam eva* by contraction and transposition of letters in āsīt, we get *puruṣah. vide* the *Taitt-śruti* (1.2.3). *pūrvameva'ḥamāsam iti, tat-*

purusaṣyapuruṣatvam: "I was even before." Hence the puruṣatva of Puruṣa'.

Or 3. He lives among the eminent persons, *puru* standing for eminence *puruṣ* utkarṣasāliṣu; *sīdati* lives.

Or 4. He gives many fruits (boons) *purūṇi phalāni sanoti* (*sanoti* means gives).

Or 5. At the time of destruction (samhāra), He brings about the end of the worlds: *purūṇi bhuvanāni syati* (*syati* means brings to end).

Or 6. Being full (*pūrṇaḥ*).

Or 7. Being permanent *sadanaḥ* so *puruṣaḥ vide*: M.Bh. Udyoga Parva 6.9.11): *purṇāt sadanaccaiva tato'sau puruṣottamaḥ*.

साक्षी SĀKṢĪ: Sees everything directly without obstruction by anything else, by natural intelligence; *sākṣāt ikṣate*, so *Sākṣi*. By virtue of the Pāṇini Sūtra (5.2.91): *saksadraṣṭari īkṣāyām* the suffix *in* is added (Sākṣin).

क्षेत्रज्ञ: KṢETRAJÑAḤ: *Kṣetram* is śarīram: body; He knows it, so *kṣetrajñah*. The *ka* prefix to *jñā* is by virtue of the Pāṇini Sūtra (3.2.3); *āto'nupasarge kaḥ*. *vide* the Lord's assertion: *kshetrajñam cāpi mām viddhi*: "Know Me to be the Knower of the kṣetra, field, body" (B.G. 13-2). Also the *Brahma Purāṇa* (found also in the M.Bh. Śanti Parva 361.6). *kṣetrākhyāni śarīrāṇi teṣām caiva yathā sukham / tāni vetti sa yogātmā tatah kṣetrajña ucyate //* 'the bodies are called kṣetras. Being a Yogi, He knows them at His pleasure'." So He is said to be the *Ksetrajña*.

अक्षर: AKṢARAḤ: He that is kṣetrajña Himself does not decay.

By *eva* in *akṣara eva* from the pāramārthic (transcendental) point of view, non-difference between the kṣetrajña (the jīvātman) and akṣara, the Paramātman is indicated. *vide* the śruti *tattvamasi*, 'That art thou'. By the rule *prasiddheḥ apramāṇatvat*, the difference between the jīvātman and Paramātman which is generally apparent from the vyāvahāric point of view is not valid.

योगो योगविदां नेता प्रधानपुरुषेश्वरः ।
नारसिंहवपुः श्रीमान् केशवः पुरुषोत्तमः ॥ १६ ॥

Yogaḥ Yogavidāmnetā Pradhānapuruseśvaraḥ /
Nārasimhavapuḥ Śrīmān Keśavaḥ Puruṣottamaḥ
// 16

योगः YOGAḤ: Controlling all the jñānendriyas along with the mind, realisation of oneness between the kṣetrajña and the Paramātman is yoga. As the Lord is attainable by it, He himself is called *Yoga*.

योगविदां नेता YOGAVIDĀM NETA: Those who inquire into, know or obtain yoga are *yogavidaḥ*. The chief of them, *neta*, by fulfilling the yoga, *aprāptasya prāptih* getting what has not been got, and *kṣema, prāptasya parirakṣaṇam*: safeguarding what has been got, the Lord is *Yogavidām neta; vide* the Lord's assertion: *teṣam nityābhiyuktānām yogakṣemam vahāmyaham*: "Of those who are stead-fastly devoted to Me (united with Me), I carry out their yogakṣema"

प्रधानपुरुषेश्वरः PRADHĀNAPURUṢEŚVARAḤ: *Pradhana* is prakrti or māyā, puruṣa is jīva; their Lord is *Pradhānapuruṣeśvaraḥ*.

नारसिंहवपुः NĀRASIMHAVAPUḤ: He Whose body in which the limbs of man and of a lion are seen is *Nārasimhavapuḥ*.

श्रीमान् ŚRĪMĀN: He in Whose chest Śrī (Lakṣmī) lives permanently is *Śrīmān*.

केशव: KEŚAVAḤ: 1. He who has handsome hairs is *Keśavaḥ*. The suffix *va* is added to extol: *keśādvo'-nyatarāsyām.*

Or 2. *ka, a* and *ī* signify the Trimūrtis (Brahma, Viṣṇu and Śiva). He in whose control they are is *Keśavaḥ*.

Or 3. Because He killed the demon Keśi, so *Keśavaḥ, vide* Nārada's words to Śrī Kriṣṇa in the Viṣṇu Purāṇa (5.6-23). 'O! Janārdana! Because the evil-natured Keśi was killed, therefore, You shall be renowned in the world by the Name of Keśava.'

पुरुषोत्तम: PURUṢOTTAMAḤ: 1. The best among Puruṣas. The objection that the use of the possessive (sixth) case is not to be used in determination does not apply here. Because, there is no reference to class etc. (quality and karma). The objection holds only where class, quality or action are specified as in *manuṣyāṇām kṣatriyaḥ sūratamaḥ, gavām kṛṣṇā, sampanna kṣīratamā,* and *adhvagānām dhāvan sīghratamaḥ.*

Or 2. It may be used in the dative (fifth) case, *vide* the Lord's words: '*yasmāt kṣaramatīto'hamakṣaradapi cottamaḥ.* 'As I am superior to the kṣara, the destructible and also to akṣara, the indestrictible, I am celebrated in the world and the Veda as Puruṣottama.'

सर्वः शर्वः शिवः स्थाणुर्भूतादिर्निधिरव्ययः ।
सम्भवो भावनो भर्ता प्रभवः प्रभुरीश्वरः ।। १७ ।।

Sarvaḥ Śarvaḥ Śivaḥ Sthāṇuḥ Bhūtadiḥ Nidhiḥ Avyayaḥ /
Sambhavaḥ Bhāvanaḥ Bhartā Prabhavaḥ Prabhuḥ Īśvaraḥ // 17

सर्व: SARVAḤ: Bhagavān Vyāsa in the Mahā

Bharata Udyoga Parva says: "As He is the origin and end of all that exists and does not, and as He has knowledge of all at all times, He is called Sarva". Therefore *Sarvaḥ.*

asatasca satascaiva sarvasya prabhavapyayāt /
sarvasya sarvadājñānāt sarvamenam pracakṣate //

शर्व: ŚARVAḤ: *Śṛṇāti* meaning *samharati* or *samhārayati*: destroys all that is born or causes them to be destroyed at the time of deluge (praḷaya). So, *Śarvaḥ.*

शिव: ŚIVAḤ: Being devoid of the three guṇas, pure, He is *Śivah. Śruti* says *sa brahma sa sivaḥ* (Nārā Up. 13). By the precept of non-difference between Śiva and Viṣṇu, by the name *Śiva* etc., Hari alone is praised.

स्थाणु: STHĀṆUḤ: So called as He is permanent, fixed (for there is no place where He is not to which He can be moved).

भूतादि: BHUTĀDIḤ The original cause of beings.

निधि: NIDHIḤ: At the time of praḷaya all beings are deposited in Him.

अव्यय: AVYAYAḤ: That Nidhi is qualified as *avyayaḥ.* It means the Nidhi that is undying.

संभव: SAMBHAVAḤ: His manifestations are by His own free will: *vide* the Lord's saying *dharmasamsthāpanārthāya sambhāvami yuge yuge.* 'For the establishment of dharma, I manifest Myself in each yuga' (Bh. G. 4.8). Also *atha duṣtavināśāya sadhūnām rakṣaṇāya ca / svecchayā sambhavāmyevam garbhadukhavivarjitaḥ //* : 'For the destruction of the wicked and protection of the good, I appear (as if born) devoid of the misery of passing through the womb'.

भावन BHĀVANAḤ: He dispenses fruits (of actions) to all who enjoy them. The being giver of all fruits is explained in the Brahma Sūtra (3.2.38) *phala-*

mata upaptteḥ, etc., 'The fruit of action is from Him, this being the logical position'.

भर्ता BHARTĀ: The support of the world as its foundation.

प्रभव: PRABHAVAḤ: 1. The great bhūtas (the great elements) eminently arise from Him.

Or 2. He whose origin, birth is eminent.

प्रभु: PRABHUḤ: So called as He has skill in all actions.

ईश्वर: ĪŚVARAḤ: His aiśvarya, lordship is not subject to any limitation. *vide* the *śruti: esa sarveśvaraḥ*: 'He is the Lord of all' (Mund Up. 9).

स्वयम्भूः शम्भुरादित्यः पुष्कराक्षो महास्वनः ।
अनादिनिधनो धाता विधाता धातुरुत्तमः ॥ १८ ॥

Svayambhūḥ Sambhuḥ Ādityaḥ Puṣkarākṣaḥ, Mahāsvanaḥ /
Anādinidhanaḥ Dhāta Vidhātā Dhāturuttmaḥ // 18

स्वयंभू: SVAYAMBHŪḤ: 1. For, He is born (manifests Himself) by Himself. *vide*: *Manu Smṛti* 1, 7) *sa eva svayam udbabhau*: 'He himself arose of His own accord.'

Or 2. He is above all.

Or 3. He Himself is all.

Or 4. He who is above all that which is eminent Or He who is eminent Himself, in both these ways *svayambhūḥ*. *vide*: *the śruti* (Īśa. Up. 8) *paribhūḥ svayambhūḥ*. He is everywhere and self-existent.

Or 5. Parameśvara who is of Himself, independent. *vide* (Kaṭha Up. 4.1). *Parāncikhāni vyatṛṇat svayambhūh*. "The self-existent turned the senses outwards'.

शंभु: SAMBHUḤ: He who dowers his devotees with *śam-sukham* beneficence.

आदित्य: ĀDITYAḤ: 1. The golden Puruṣa in the solar orb.

Or 2. Viṣṇu among the twelve Ādityas.

Or 3. He is the consort of Mother Earth unfragmented. *vide* the śrutis *iyam vā aditiḥ* (Taitt Sam. 5.1.7) and *mahīm devīm viṣṇupatnīm* (Taitt Brah. 3.1.2).

Or 4. Even as the one Sun shines as many on several receptacles of water, so the Ātmā shines as many in a number of bodies. Thus of a similar nature to āditya, He is called *Ādityaḥ*.

पुष्कराक्ष: PUṢKARAKṢAḤ: His eyes *akṣinī* are like lotuses *puṣkaras*.

महाश्वन: MAHĀŚVANAḤ: 1. He whose *svana* or sound is *mahān*, big, powerful.

Or 2. Whose sound is revered being of the nature of śruti. The *ā* in *mahāsvanaḥ* is justified by *san mahat* and the similarity in the use of *ā* and *mahat*. *vide* the *śruti asya mahato bhūtasya niśvasitametadṛgvedo yajurvedaḥ*, etc. (Bṛh. Up. 2.4.1). "Ṛgveda Yajurveda etc., took shape in the breathing of this mighty Bhūta.

अनादिनिधन: ANĀDINIDHANAḤ: *Ādi* is birth; *nidhanam* is destruction. He Who does not have these two.

धाता DHĀTĀ: So called because He supports the universe in the form of *Ananta*: Ādiśeṣa, etc.

विधाता VIDHĀTĀ: He who induces to action and dispenses their fruits.

Or 2. As the sustainer of Ananta and others, He bears eminently. *viseṣena dadhāti.*

धातुरुत्तम: DHĀTURUTTAMAḤ: is one word. He is superior to *Dhātu:* Virinci and others. Or two words: superior to all dhātus, the earth etc., the superior cit being the *Cit dhatu;* consciousness or intelligence as the sustainer of the world of effect and cause. As so sustaining He is called *Dhātuḥ.*

उत्तम: UTTAMAḤ: The most superior of all superior persons.

अप्रमेयो हृषीकेशः पद्मनाभोऽमरप्रभुः ।
विश्वकर्मा मनुस्त्वष्टा स्थविष्ठः स्थविरो ध्रुवः ॥१९॥

Aprameyaḥ Hṛṣikeśaḥ Padmanābhaḥ Amaraḥ Prabhuḥ /
Viśvakarmā Manuh Tvaṣṭā Sthaviṣṭaḥ Sthaviraḥ Dhruvaḥ // 19

अप्रमेय: APRAMEYAḤ: As He is devoid of sound etc. (form, taste, smell and touch), He cannot be known by pratyakṣa pramāṇa (which is based on the activity of the sense organs). Nor can He be known by inference as He has no mark which can be the basis of inference. He cannot be known by analogy as He has no parts, and, as analogy functions by comparing one part of a thing with a corresponding part of another thing. Implication too cannot be used to know Him as it is impossible to attain anything without Him. He is not known by the criterion of negation as He is always existent and He is the witness of all negation. Nor can He be known by śāstrapramāṇa being devoid of any peculiar features that can be deduced from the śāstras. Then, it may be asked, how is it said of Him (in the Brahma Sūtra 1.1.3). *sastrayonitvāt*: 'as the scriptures are the valid source of knowledge of Him'? It is replied: He is the witness of all pramāṇas (proofs) being the Supreme Light and He is not the object of proof; yet nescience superimposes on Him whatever is not He. That superimposition is removed with the help of śāstra. So *śastra-yonitvāt* is justified. As He cannot be known by any of the logical canons, He is *Aprameya* being the witness of all proof.

हृषीकेश: HṚṢĪKEŚAḤ: 1. Hṛṣīkas are indriyas or sense organs. Their *īśa* (lord) one who is of the nature of kṣetrajña who controls the senses.

Or 2. That Paramātmā in whose control are the senses is called *Hṛṣikeśa.*

Or 3. The *keśas* or rays of Him in the form of the sun and the moon delight (from *harṣ*) the world. So, He is *Hṛṣīkeśa. vide* the *śruti*: *suryarasmirharikeśaḥ purastāt.* Also in the Mokṣa Dharma it is said (M.Bh. Śānti Parva 352.1.2):

> "The Sun and Moon by their rays called keśas respectively awaken and send the world to sleep and uphold it. By such awakening and causing to sleep, the world is made happy. Thus by the action of Agni (the Sun) and Soma (Moon) (by the *agniṣoma*) ritual, I am called Hṛṣīkeśa, O! son of Pāṇḍu. I am the lawgiver and beneficent ruler of the Universe".

पद्मनाभ: PADMANĀBHAḤ: He in whose navel (*nābhi*) is the cause of the entire universe. *vide* the *śruti*: *ajasya nābhāvādhyekamarpitaṃ*: 'in the navel of the unborn (Brahma) all this is established.' (Taitt. Sam. 4.6.2).

अमरप्रभु: AMARAPRABHUḤ: The Lord of the Immortals.

विश्वकर्मा: VIŚVAKARMĀ: 1. He whose creation is the universe.

Or 2. The Universe whose action (creation) it is.

Or 3. He has the power of creating the wonderful manifold.

Or 4. By His similarity to Tvaṣta, the celestial architect known as Viśvakarmā.

मनु: MANUḤ: 1. So-called as He thinks. *vide* the śruti: *nānyatosti mantā*: there is no thinker apart from Him. (Bṛḥ. 3.7.23)

Or 2. Who is of the form mantra.

Or 3. Prajāpati.

त्वष्टा TVAṢṬĀ: As He reduces the size of all beings at the time of samhāra in praḷaya (to their subtle form), He is called *Tvaṣṭā*.

स्थविष्ठ: STAVISṬHAḤ: Very stout, the ancient and firm. *vide* the Ṛg Veda—*tveṣam hyasya sthavirasya nāma*: 'for celebrated is the name of this ancient One' (7.100.3).

Or 2. As indicating old age.

ध्रुव: DHRUVAḤ: As He is permanent. *Sthaviro Dhruvaḥ* is one name made up of an adjective and a noun.

अग्राह्यः शाश्वतः कृष्णो लोहिताक्षः प्रतर्दनः ।
प्रभूतस्त्रिककुब्धाम पवित्रं मङ्गलं परम् ॥ २० ॥

Agrāhyaḥ Śāśvataḥ Kṛṣṇah Lohitākṣah
Pratardanaḥ // 20
Prabhūtaḥ Trikakubdhāma Pavitram Mangalam
Param

अग्राह्य: AGRĀHYAḤ: He cannot be grasped by karmandriyas (organs of action) *vide*: *yato vāco nivartante aprāpya manasā saha*: 'That from speech returns without grasping It, along with the mind' (Taitt. up.2.4).

शास्वत: ŚĀŚVATAḤ: He is *śaśvat* at all times. So *Śāśvataḥ*, *vide* the śruti. *śāśvatam śivam acyutam*:

'ever existing Śivam and Acyuta' (Nāra up. 13).

कृष्णः KṚṢṆAḤ: Of the nature of Sat Cit and Ānanda. Intelligence, Knowledge and Bliss. *vide* Vyasa's words (in Mahā Bh. Udyoga Parva 70-5). *kṛṣirbhūvācakaḥ sabdo ṇasca nirvṛti vācakaḥ / viṣṇustad bhāvayogācca kṛṣṇobhavati śāśvataḥ. Kṛṣ* stands for existence *ṇa* stands for bliss, the union of these two is *Kṛṣṇa*.

Or 2. Because He is dark complexioned *vide* Mahā Bhārata (Śānti 343). *Kṛṣṇo varṇasca me yasmāt tasmāt Kṛṣṇohamarjuna:* O! Arjuna! because My colour is dark, so I am called Kṛṣṇa.'

लोहिताक्षः LOHITĀKṢAḤ: He whose eyes (akṣinī) are red (lohita) *sa mā vṛṣabho lohitākṣaḥ* (May the Supreme Lord who is lohitākṣa (protect me). (Taitt. Āraṇyaka 4.42).

प्रतर्दन: PRATARDANAḤ: Because in praḷaya (universal deluge) He afflicts (pratardyati) beings, He is *Pratardanaḥ*.

प्रभूतः PRABHŪTAḤ: Abundantly endowed with the qualities of wisdom, eminence etc.

त्रिकुकब्धाम TRIKAKUBDHĀMA: His abode is above, below and the middle regions. *Trikakubdhāma* is one word.

पवित्रम् PAVITRAM: That by which one is purified or 2. He who purifies the ṛṣi or the devata. That is *pavitram*.

मङ्गलं परम् MANGAḶAM PARAṂ: The Viṣṇu Purāṇa says *aśubhāni nirācaṣte tanoti subha santatim/ smṛtimātreṇa yat pumsām brahma tanmangaḷam viduḥ //* 'Brahman is known as mangaḷam (beneficent) which wards off evils and dowers with series of good by being merely remembered.

Or 2. He is *mangaḷam* due to His auspicious form, *param* Of all beings the highest, Brahma. *mangaḷam* and *param* make one word as adjective and noun.

ईशानः प्रणदः प्राणो ज्येष्ठः श्रेष्ठः प्रजापतिः ।
हिरण्यगर्भो भूगर्भो माधवो मधुसूदनः ॥ २१ ॥

Īśānaḥ Prāṇadaḥ Prāṇaḥ Jyeṣṭhaḥ Sreṣṭhaḥ Prajāpatiḥ /
Hiraṇyagarbhaḥ Bhūgarbhaḥ Mādhavaḥ Madhusūdanaḥ // 21

ईशान : ĪŚANAḤ: By reason of His controlling all things, He is called Īśānaḥ ('īś' means to control).

प्राणद : PRĀṆADAḤ: 1. He gives (dadāti- the vital breaths (prāṇas) and directs (ceṣtayati) their movements. *vide* the śruti *ko hevanyāt kaḥ prāṇayāt*: Who can live, who can breathe (without Him)? (Taitt. Up. 2-7).

Or 2. Takes away (*dyati, khaṇdayati*) the prāṇas in the form of Kāla (Death).

Or 3. He purifies the prāṇas (from *dāpayati* which means purifies).

Or. 4. Destroys the prāṇas (from *dāti*, lunati meaning destroys).

प्राण : PRĀṆAḤ: 1. From *praṇiti* i.e., breathes. The Name may refer to the kṣetrajñaḥ, the jīva, or the Paramātmā, *vide* the śruti *prānasya prānam* breath of breath etc., (Bṛḥ. up. 53.62).

Or 2. It means mukhyaprāṇa, the life principle.

ज्येष्ठ : JYEṢṬHAH: The oldest, *vide* the śruti: *prāṇovavā jyeṣṭhasca śreṣṭhasca*: prāṇa is the eldest and the most excellent (Br.up.8.1.1).

Or 2. The chief prāṇa *vide* Br. Sutra 2.4.8: *Sresṭhasca*. He is most excellent.

Or 3. Because He is the cause of all.

श्रेष्ठः SREṢṬHAḤ: 1. He is most praiseworthy. Or 2. He is above everything.

प्रजापतिः PRAJĀPATIḤ: Being Īśvara, He is the Lord of all beings.

हिरण्यगर्भः HIRAṆYAGARBHAḤ: He is the indweller in the golden egg, i.e., Brahma or Virinci, or His ātmā *vide* the śruti *hiraṇmaya garbhaḥ samavartatāgre:* Hiraṇyagarbha came into existence at the beginning (Taitt. Sam.4.1.87).

भूगर्भः BHŪGARBHAḤ: He in Whose womb is the earth (*bhū* meaning the earth, and *garbhaḥ,* the womb).

माधवः MĀDHAVAḤ: 1. The *dhava* or husband of *mā* or Śrī.

Or 2. He is made known by the Madhu Vidyā (in the Chāndogya Upaniṣad).

Or 3. In the Mahā Bhārata (Udyoga Parva 70-4) Vyāsa says: O! Bharata, know Mādhava by *mauna* silence, *dhyāna,* meditation and *yoga.* He who is known by these is *Mādhava. vide* Mahā Bhārata Udyoga Parva 69-4). *mā* signifies *mauna.* dhā signifies *dhyāna* and *vā yoga*).

मधुसूधनः MADHUSŪDHANAḤ: He killed (sūdhitavān), the demon called Madhu. *vide:* (The Mahā Bhārata Bhiṣma Parva 67-13-15). At the request of Brahmā, Puruṣottama slew the great asura of the name of Madhu born of Karṇamiśra. It is by his destruction, Janardhana was called *Madhusūdana* by gods, asuras, men and ṛṣis.

ईश्वरो विक्रमी धन्वी मेधावी विक्रमः क्रमः ।
अनुत्तमो दुराधर्षः कृतज्ञः कृतिरात्मवान् ।। २२ ।।

Īśvaraḥ Vikramī Dhanvī Medhāvī Vikramaḥ
Kramaḥ
Anuttamaḥ Durādharṣaḥ Kṛtajñaḥ
Kritiḥ Ātmavān / / 22

ईश्वरः ĪŚVARAḤ: So called as He possesses infinite power.

विक्रमी: VIKRAMĪ: *Vikrama* means prowess. Being associated with it, He is *Vikramī.*

धन्वी DHANVĪ: He has the bow, so *Dhanvī. vide* the Lord's assertion in the Gītā 10.31 *Rāmaḥ sastrabhṛtāmaham* 'I am Rama among the wielders of the bow.'

मेधावी MEDHĀVĪ: He who has *medhā,* the capacity to understand many treatises.

विक्रमः VIKRAMAḤ: 1. He measured (*vicakrame*) the entire universe. So *Vikramaḥ.*

Or 2. As He rides (*kramaṇāt*) the bird Garuda, otherwise called *vi.*

क्रमः KRAMAḤ: As He walks (*krama* to walk) or is the cause of walking. *vide* Manu Smṛti (12-121) *krante viṣṇum:* 'In the matter of walking, Viṣṇu.'

अनुत्तमः ANUTTAMAḤ: He who has no superior (*uttama*) to Him is *anuttama. vide* the śruti: *yasmāt param nāparamasti kincit*: 'Than Whom there is not anything above or below.' (Nārāyaṇa Up. 12). Also the Gīta: *na tvatsamostyabhyadhikaḥ kuto' nyaḥ*: 'There is none equal to Thee: How then could be one higher than Thee?'

धुराधर्षः DURĀDHARṢAḤ: He cannot be assailed by asuras and others.

कृतज्ञः KṚTAJÑAḤ: 1. He knows the actions of creatures, meritorious and otherwise.

Or 2. Even to those who make a small offering of

leaf, flower etc., He gives mokṣa (liberation).

कृतिः KṚTIḤ. 1. Human effort. 2. Or the act itself. 3. Or being the soul of all, He is considered as the basis of every act.

आत्मवान ĀTMAVĀN: As He is established in His own glory, He is *Atmavān. vide* the śruti: *sa bhagavaḥ kasmin pratiṣṭhitaḥ sve mahmni*: 'In what, my lord, does that Infinite abide? In Its own glory.' (Ch. Up. 7.24.1).

सुरेशः शरणं शर्म विश्वरेताः प्रजाभवः ।
अहः संवत्सरो व्यालः प्रत्ययः सर्वदर्शनः ॥ २३ ॥

Sureśaḥ Śaraṇam Śarma Viśvaretāḥ
Prajābhavaḥ
Ahaḥ Samvatsaraḥ Vyāḷaḥ
Pratyayaḥ Sarvadarśanaḥ / / 23

सुरेशः SUREŚAḤ: 1. The Lord of devas (surāḥ). 2. *su* is the prefix of the root *ra*. *su* stands for *sobhana* or auspicious, good and *ra* for giving. He is the Lord (Īśa) of suras who dower men with good.

शरणम् ŚARAṆAM: So called as He removes the pains of the afflicted.

शर्म ŚARMA: As He is of the form of supreme bliss.

विश्वरेताः VIŚVARETĀḤ. As He is the cause (from *retas*) of the Universe.

प्रजाभवः PRAJĀBHAVAḤ: He from whom all beings arise (*prajāh* and *bhavaḥ*).

अहः AHAḤ: So called as He is luminous (like the day).

संवत्सरः SAMVATSARAḤ: Viṣṇu who stands (is) in the form of Time (samvatsara or year being a part of time).

व्याल: VYĀLAḤ:. So called as He cannot be grasped (by the mind) as a serpent (vyāla) which cannot be grasped (by the hand).

प्रत्यर्थ: PRATAYAḤ: *Pratyaya* or prajña: consciousness. So called as He is the embodiment of consciousness (as He is citsvarūpa). *vide* the śruti *prajñānambrahma* (Ait. Up. 3.3).

सर्वदर्शन: SARVADARŚANAḤ: Whose eyes are of the nature of all darśanas, views of Reality (or one who is omniscient). As He is the ātman of everything, *vide* the śruti *viśvatascukṣuḥ* having eyes everywhere (Svet Up.3.3) and *viśvākṣam* (Nara Up.13.1).

अजः सर्वेश्वरः सिद्धः सिद्धिः सर्वादिरच्युतः ।
वृषाकपिरमेयात्मा सर्वयोगविनिःसृतः ।। २४ ।।

Ajaḥ Sarveśvaraḥ Siddhaḥ Siddhiḥ
Sarvādiḥ Acyutaḥ /
Vṛṣākapiḥ Ameyātma Sarvayogavinisṛtaḥ / / 24

अज: AJAḤ: He is not born (*jan* to be born) So *Ajaḥ. vide* the śruti *najāto najaniṣyate* 'is not born nor will be born' (Ṛgveda 1.81.5) (So birthless: ever existent) Also Mahā Bharata (Sānti 352.9) *nahi na jāto na jāyeya na janiṣye kadācana / kṣetrajñassarvabhūtānām tasmāt aham ajaḥ smṛtaḥ / /* : 'I was not born; I am not to be born nor will I be born at any time. I am the kṣetrajña of all beings. Therefore I am known as *ajaḥ* unborn.'

सर्वेश्वर: SARVEŚVARAḤ: The Lord of all Lords, *vide* the śruti: *eṣa sarveśvaraḥ*. 'He is the Lord of all' (Māṇd Up. 6.4.2).

सिद्ध: SIDDHAḤ: Being eternal and full always, He is Siddhaḥ.

सिद्धि: SIDDHIḤ: 1. As He is of the form of samvit or wisdom in all objects.

Or 2. As He is of wonderful form, He is *Siddhiḥ*. As svarga etc. are perishable, they are fruitless.

सर्वादि: SARVADIḤ: As He is the primal cause of all beings, the beginning (ādi) of all, sarva.

अच्युत: ACYUTAḤ: By reason of His inherent power, He is not one who fell, He does not fall and will not fall in the future. So He is *Acyutaḥ*. *vide* the śruti *sāsvatamśivamacyutam*: 'Permanent, auspicious and not falling.' (Nārā Up.13.1). So also did Bhagavān say in M.Bh. Śānti.352.16) *yasmārna cyutapūrvo'ham acyutastena karmaṇa*: 'By that karma by reason of which I did not fall before, I am Acyuta.'

Thus the first hundred Names have been explained.

वृषाकपि: VṚṢAKAPIḤ: Dharma is called Vṛṣaḥ as it rains all desires. *ka* stands for water. He protected, lifted the earth as Varāha. So He is called *Kapiḥ*. He is called *Vṛṣākapiḥ* as He is of the form of *vṛṣa* and *kapi* - *vide* Maha Bhārata (Śānti 352-24). ***Kapirvarāhaḥ sreṣtasca dharmasca vṛṣa ucyate / tasmāt vṛśakapim prāha kāśyapo mām prajāpatiḥ***: 'Kāsyapa Prajāpati called Me Vṛṣākapi as kapi means the big boar and dharma is said to be vṛṣā.'

अमेयात्मा AMEYĀTMĀ: He whose ātmā (nature) cannot be measured (determined) as of what extent by division.

सर्वयोगाविनि:सृत: SARVAYOGAVINISSṚTAḤ: 1. He who is devoid of all attachments. *vide* the śruti *asango hyayam puruṣaḥ*; 'This Puruṣa is unattached'. (Br.up. 4-3-15). Or 2. as He is apart from the paths of yogas detailed in all śāstras (He is the goal to be experienced, not merely the paths).

वसुर्वसुमनाः सत्यः समात्माऽसंमितः समः ।
अमोघः पुण्डरीकाक्षो वृषकर्मा वृषाकृतिः ॥ २५ ॥

Vasuḥ Vasumanāḥ Satyaḥ Samātmā
Asammitaḥ Śamaḥ /
Amoghaḥ Puṇḍarīkākṣaḥ Vṛṣakarmā
Vrsākrtiḥ / / 25

वसुः VASUḤ: 1 . All beings abide in Him (vasanti); therefore *Vasuḥ.*

Or 2. He too abides in them. So *Vasuḥ.*

Or 3. As the Lord described Himself, *vasūnām pāvakascāsmi*: 'I am Pāvaka among the Vasus, one of the eight Vasus.' (B. G. 10.23)

वसुमनाः VASUMANĀḤ: By *Vasu* which means wealth, excellence is indicated. He whose mind is excellent is *Vasumanāḥ.* That mind is said to be praiseworthy which is not polluted by kleśas (which include avidyā, asmitā, rāgā, dveṣa and abniveśa, nescience, egoism, passion, aversion and attachment) and upakleśas like intoxication, etc.

सत्यः SATYAḤ: 1. As He is of the form which is not untrue. *vide* the śruti *satyam jñānam anantam brahma.* 'Brahman is existence truth, knowledge and bliss.' (Taitt.Up.2.1).

Or 2. Because He is with and without form (visible and invisible) *vide* the śruti: *sacca tyaccha abhavat.* 'He was both *sat* and *tyat*' (making *satya*).

Or 3. *Sat* stands for prāṇa (breath), *ti* for annam (food) and *yam* for the sun. As He is of the form of prāṇa, anna, heat and light (which are the essentials for life) He is *Satyaḥ vide* the śruti *saditi prāṇāstītyannam yamityasavādityaḥ.* (Ait Āraṇ 2.1.5.6).

Or 4. Because He is good to the good people, He is called *Satyaḥ.*

समात्मा SAMĀTMĀ: 1. He whose ātmā (here mind), is *sama,* equanimous, unspoiled by attachment, aversion etc., is *Samātmā.*

Or 2. One who is the *sama ātmā,* the single (pervasive) ātmā in all beings is *Samātmā. vide* the sruti: *sama ātmeti vidyāt*: 'It should be understood that the ātmā is the same in all.' (Kausītaki Up. 3.9).

असम्मित: ASAMMITAḤ: He who is measured, determined by things is *mitaḥ* (*mā* meaning to measure). He who is unlimited or imm easurable is *Asammitaḥ.*

सम: SAMAḤ: 1. Unchanging at all times is *Samah.*

Or 2. He is ever with *mā* or Lakshmi *mayā* (3rd case singular of *ma*) *saha vartate.* So *Samaḥ.*

अमोघ: AMOGHAḤ: 1. When worshipped, praised or remembered, dowers one with the fruition of every desire, does not make it (such worship etc.) vain. Hence *Amoghaḥ.*

Or 2. His will is always unobstructed in His actions. *vide* the śruti: *satyakāmaḥ satyasamkalpaḥ*: 'His desire and samkalpa are ever realised.' (Ch. Up. 8.7.1)

पुण्डरीकाक्ष: PUṆDARĪKĀKṢAḤ: 1. He pervades the *puṇdarīkam,* the lotus of the heart. He is cognised in it, hence *Puṇdarīkākṣaḥ. vide* the sruti: *yatpundarīkam puramadhyasamstham*: 'the lotus is in the centre of the pura or *body.*' (Nārā Up. 10).

Or 2. He whose eyes are of the form of a lotus.

वृषकर्मा VṚṢAKARMĀ: His action is of the nature of dharma (*vṛṣa* means dharma).

वृषाकृति: VṚṢĀKṚTIḤ: He whose body is for dharma, i.e., who has taken a body for dharma. *vide* the Lord's assertion: *dharma samsthāpanārthāya sambhavāmi yuge yuge*: 'for the establishment of dharma, I take a body in age after age'. (B.G. 4.8)

रुद्रो बहुशिरा बभ्रुर्विश्वयोनिः शुचिश्रवाः ।

अमृतः शाश्वतः स्थाणुर्वरारोहो महातपाः ॥ २६ ॥

Rudraḥ Bahuśirāḥ Babhrūh Viśvayoniḥ Śuciśravāḥ
Amṛtaḥ Śaśvataḥ Sthāṇuḥ Varārohaḥ
Mahātapāḥ / / 26

रुद्रः RUDRAḤ: 1. At the time of destruction (involution) destroying the beings, He makes them cry. Hence *Rudraḥ*.

Or 2. *rudam rāti* (*ra* to give) He gives good and evil according to men's deserts. So *Rudraḥ*.

Or 3. *ruḥ* means sorrow or the cause of sorrow. So *Rudraḥ*.

Or 4. *dravayati* means melts (dissolves, makes to disappear); melts away sorrows. So *Rudraḥ*. He is so called by reason of *rodana* crying and *drāvaṇa* melting. *vide* Lingapurāṇa: *'rurduhkham duhkahetum vā vidrāvayati sa prabhuḥ / rudra ityucyate tasmāt śivah paramakāraṇam* / /

बहुशिराः BAHUŚIRĀḤ: He who has many heads, *vide*: (Puruṣa Sūkta) *sahasraṣirṣāpuruṣaḥ*.

बभ्रुः BABHRUḤ: He supports the world: *bibharti*. So *Babhruḥ*.

विश्वयोनिः VIŚVAYONIḤ: As He is the cause of the universe (*yoni* of *viśvam*). He is *Viśvayoniḥ*.

शुचिश्रवाः SUCIŚRAVĀḤ: His Names are pure (*suci*) or pleasing to hear. So *Sucisravāḥ*.

अमृतः AMṚTAḤ: He who has no *maraṇam* or death, immortal *vide* the śruti: *ajaro'maraḥ*, 'unageing, undying.' (Bṛh. Up. 4.4.25).

शाश्वतस्थाणुः ŚĀŚVATASTHĀṆUḤ: He is *śaśvata* and *sthānu* imperishable (eternal) and firm.

वरारोहः VARĀROHAḤ: 1. He Whose lap is superior (*vara-ārohaḥ yasya*).

Or 2. Ascending to (attaining) Whom is superior. For, to those who have ascended to (attained) Him, there is no possibility of coming back *na punaravartate* (Chānd. Up. 8.15.1) and the B. G. 10.11: *yam prāpya na nivartante*: after attaining Whom men do not come back'.

महातपाः MAHĀTAPĀḤ: 1. His *tapas* about creation is great. That tapas is jñāna, knowledge. *vide* the śruti. *yasya jñānamayam tapaḥ*: whose tapas is all jñāna. (Mund. Up. 1.1.9)

Or 2. His glory and prowess are tapas. He has them in an infinite measure. So, *Mahātapāḥ*.

सर्वगः सर्वविद्भानुर्विष्वक्सेनो जनार्दनः ।
वेदो वेदविदव्यङ्गो वेदाङ्गो वेदवित्कविः ॥ २७ ॥

Sarvagaḥ Sarvavidbhānuḥ Viśvaksenaḥ Janārdanaḥ /
Vẹdaḥ Vedavit Avyangaḥ Vedāngaḥ Vedavit Kaviḥ / / 27

सर्वगः SARVAGAḤ: He who goes (is) everywhere, is all-pervading as the cause of everything.

सर्वविद्भानुः SARVAVIDBHĀNUḤ: He who knows all (*vetti*) or attains all (*vindati*). So, Sarvavit. He also shines *bhāti*. So, *bhānuḥ*. *vide* the śruti *tamevabhāntamanubhātisarvam*: 'Everything shines by His luminosity'. Kaṭha Up. 2.2.7 and the B.G. 12). *yadādityagataṃ tejo jagadbhāsayate' khilam yaccandramasi yaccāgnau tattejo viddhi māmakam*: 'The light which residing in the sun illumines the whole world, that which is in the moon and in the fire-know that light to be

Mine' He is *sarvavit* and *bhānuḥ*. So He is *Sarvavid-bhānuh.*

विष्वक्सेन: VIṢVAKSENAḤ: Merely by whose preparation to give battle, the army of the demons runs away in all directions. He is *Viṣvaksenaḥ.* (*viṣvak.* in all directions and *sena*, army)

जनार्दन: JANĀRDANAḤ: 1. He who oppresses (*ardayati*) the (evil) men.

Or 2. Sends them to hell etc.

Or 3. He is be saught by men for salvation or worldly happiness. So, *Janardanaḥ.*

वेद: VEDAḤ: He makes one to know (*vedayati*) *vide* the Lord's assertion (B.G. 10.11) *teṣāmevānukampārtham ajñānajamtamaḥ / nāsayamyātmabhavasthaḥ jñānadipenabhāsvata*: 'Out of compassion for them, dwelling in their hearts, I destroy the ignorance-born darkness by the luminous lamp of wisdom.'

वेदवित् VEDAVIT: He knows the meaning of Veda truly, *vide* the Lord's assertion. *vedāntakṛt vedavidevacāham*: 'I am the author of the Vedānta (in the form of Vyāsa and others) and the Knower of Veda' (B.G.15.15). The Mahā Bhārata says: 'All the Vedas, Vidyās, Śāstras, yajñas and homas are Kṛṣṇa. Those Brāhmaṇas that know Kṛṣṇa in reality have performed all yajñās.'

अव्यङ्ग: AVYANGAḤ: 1. He who is full of jñāna etc., (from *vyanga* incomplete; *a-vyanga*-not incomplete, full).

Or 2. *vyanga* means manifest: *avyanga* is unmanifest. *vide* B.G. (2.25) *avyaktoyam*: 'He is unmanifest'

वेदाङ्ग: VEDĀNGAḤ: He of whom Vedas are parts is called *Vedāngaḥ.*

वेदवित् VEDAVIT: *vinte, vicārayati* He inquires into the Vedas.

कविः KAVIḤ: Seeing beyond *krantadarśī kavih,* all-seeing *vide* the śruti: *nānyo' tosti dṛṣṭā* etc. 'Other than Him there is no Seer'. (Bṛh. Up. 3.7); also the mantra beginning with *kavirmanīsī*: The Seer, Intelligent (Īśa. Up.8).

लोकाध्यक्षः सुराध्यक्षो धर्माध्यक्षः कृताकृतः ।
चतुरात्मा चतुर्व्यूहश्चतुर्दंष्ट्रश्चतुर्भुजः ॥ २८ ॥

Lokādhyakṣaḥ Surādhyakṣaḥ Dharmādhyakṣaḥ
Kṛtākṛtaḥ /
Caturātmā Caturvyūhaḥ Caturdamṣtraḥ
Caturbhujaḥ // 28

लोकाध्यक्षः LOKĀDHYAKṢAḤ: He presides over the worlds. He is the chief supervisory witness of all the worlds.

सुराध्यक्षः SURĀDHYAKṢAḤ: He is the presiding Lord of the gods (like Indra, Agni, Vāyu, Varuṇa, etc.) who hold sway over the worlds.

धर्माध्यक्षः DHARMĀDHYAKṢAḤ: He cognises dharma and adharma directly to give their appropriate rewards. So He is *Dharmādhyakṣaḥ* (*adyakṣaḥ* means one who presides or is the witness).

कृताकृतः KṚTAKṚTAḤ: He is as the effect, and as the cause. (He is both the cause and the effect).

चतुरात्मा CATURĀTMĀ: He whose glory is fourfold in creation etc., the Viṣṇu Purāṇa (1.22) says: 'Brahmā, Dakṣa and others and all beings are all the splendours of Hari as the instruments of creation. Viṣṇu, Manu and others, Time and all beings, O! Dvija, are the glories of Viṣṇu making for sustenance. Rudra, Kāla, Antaka (the God of Death) all creatures are the excellences of Janārdana for the purpose of paraḷaya (in which all creatures are destroyed.'

चतुर्व्यूहः CATURVYŪHAḤ: According to the statement of Vyāsa, "Janārdana who is in the vyūha form of great renown manifests Himself in a fourfold manner as Vāsudeva etc. and performed creation etc." So *Caturvyūhah.*[19]

चतुर्दंष्ट्रः CATURDAMṢTRAḤ: 1. He who has four protruding teeth in the incarnation of Nṛsimha.

Or 2. Due to the similarity of His four horns to teeth, He is called *Caturdamṣtraḥ. vide* the śruti: *catvārisṛngaḥ* 'possessing four horns'. (Rg. Veda 4.58.3)

चतुर्भुजः CATURBHUJAḤ: He has four arms. So *Caturbhujaḥ.*

भ्राजिष्णुर्भोजनं भोक्ता सहिष्णुर्जगदादिजः ।

अनघो विजयो जेता विश्वयोनिः पुनर्वसुः ।। २९ ।।

Bhrājiṣṇuḥ Bhojanam Bhoktā Sahiṣṇuḥ
Jagadādijaḥ /
Anaghaḥ Vijayayaḥ Jetā Viśvayoniḥ
Punarvasuḥ // 29

भ्राजिष्णुः BRĀJIṢNUḤ: Being wholly compacted of radiance only. He is *Brājisṇuḥ.*

भोजनम् BHOJANAM: Prakṛti or māyā (all things of the material world) is object of enjoyment. In the aspect of Prakṛti, He is *Bhojanam,* what is enjoyed.

भोक्ता BHOKTĀ: In the aspect of Puruṣa, He is the enjoyer. So, *Bhokta.*

सहिष्णुः SAHIṢNUḤ: He destroys Hiraṇyākṣa and

19. The four Vyūhas are Vāsudeva, Sankarṣana, Pradyumna and Anirudda.

others. So, *Sahiṣṇuḥ* (*Sahanam* is used in the sense of *abhibhavana* or killing).

जगदादिजः JAGADĀDIJAḤ: He Himself originates the universe in the beginning in the form of Hiraṇyagarbha.

अनघः ANAGHAḤ: (*gha* means sin) *anagha* means sinless. śruti (Ch. Up. 8.1.5) says *apahatapāpma.* "He is free from sin".

विजयः VIJAYAḤ: He excels the world by reason of His qualities of jñāna, aiśvarya, and vairāgya, knowledge, excellence and dispassion.

जेता JETĀ: As He excels by His nature all beings, so *Jetā.*

विश्वयोनिः VISVAYONIḤ: 1. The universe is His womb (*viśvam yaniḥ asya*).

Or 2. The cause of the whole universe (*visvascāsau yonisca*).

पुनर्वसुः PUNARVASUḤ: Resides in the bodies again and again in the form of the Kṣetrajña. So, called Punarvasuḥ. (*punaḥ* again, *vasati* dwells).

उपेन्द्रो वामनः प्रांशुरमोघः शुचिरूर्जितः ।
अतीन्द्रः संग्रहः सर्गो धृतात्मा नियमो यमः ॥ ३० ॥

Upendraḥ Vāmanaḥ Prāmsuḥ Amoghaḥ
Suciḥ Ūrjitaḥ /
Atīndraḥ Sangrahaḥ Sargaḥ Dhrtātmā Niyṁāḥ
Yamaḥ / / 30

उपेन्द्रः UPENDRAḤ: 1. Junior to Indra as his younger brother.

Or 2. Above Indra. *vide* Harivamśa (Indra says) *mamopari yathendrastvam sthāpito gobirīśvaraḥ /*

upendra iti kṛṣṇa tvām gāyanti bhuvi devatāḥ / / : 'You are placed above me by the Vedas. Therefore the gods speak of you as Upendra.'

वामन: VĀMANAḤ: 1. Because in the form of vāmana (a dwarf), He begged of Bali, so *Vāmanaḥ*.

Or 2. Worshipful (Khaṭha mantra 2.2.3) says: *madhye vāmanamāsīnam visve devā upāsate*: 'All devas worship Vāmana, the ātmā seated in the heart.'

प्रांशु: PRĀMŚUḤ: Tall. He Himself measuring the three worlds became tall. When the water symbolic of making a gift fell into His hands, Vāmana became avāmana, i.e., tall. The earth was His feet, the sky was the head, the moon and the sun were the eyes. Then as He showed His cosmic form, the moon and the sun rested on His chest. When he rose further and measured the sky, they rested on His naval. When he rose to the world of gods, they (the moon and the sun) came up to His knees. Thus His tallness is explained in Harivamśa.

अमोघ: AMOGHAḤ: He whose actions are never in vain.

शुचि: SUCIḤ: As purifying those who think of Him, praise Him and worship Him. The sruti says: *asparśasca mahān sucih.* 'He is untouched, great and pure'.

ऊर्जित: ŪRJITAḤ: He is extremely mighty.

अतीन्द्र: ATĪNDRAḤ: He is far superior to Indra in wisdom and greatness (*jñāna* and *aiśvarya*) which are native to Him.

सङ्ग्रह: SANGRAHAḤ: As He destroys all beings, He is *Sangrahah*.

सर्गः SARGAḤ: Either as what is be created or as the cause of creation He is *Sargaḥ*.

धृतात्मा DHṚTĀTMĀ: Whose ātmā is controlled (kept) in one state, not having birth and other change of states.

नियमः NIYAMAḤ: He establishes men in their respective places of authority. So *Niyamaḥ*.

यमः YAMAḤ: He is the inner controller.

वेद्यो वैद्यः सदायोगी वीरहा माधवो मधुः ।
अतीन्द्रियो महामायो महोत्साहो महाबलः ॥ ३१ ॥

Vedyaḥ Vaidyaḥ Sadāyogī Vīrahā Mādhavaḥ Madhuḥ /
Atīndriyaḥ Mahāmayaḥ Mahotsāhaḥ Mahābalaḥ / / 31

वेद्यः VEDYAḤ: Because He deserves to be known by those who seek liberation (*nisśreyasa*).

वैद्यः VAIDYAḤ: Because He is the knower of all vidyas, He is *Vaidyaḥ*.

सदायोगी SADĀYOGĪ: The eternal yogin as He is of manifested form.

वीरहा VĪRAHĀ: He kills asuras for safeguarding Dharma.

माधवः MĀDHAVAḤ: The Lord of *mā* or vidyā. So *Mādhavaḥ, vide* the Harivamśa. *mā vidyā ca hareḥ proktā tasya īśo yato bhavān / tasmān mādhava nāmạsi dhavaḥ svāmītiśabditaḥ*: 'mā is spoken of knowledge of Hari. As You are her Lord, therefore, You are of the name of *Mādhava* the master of *mā*.'

मधुः MADHUḤ: He generates supreme happiness like honey. So He is called *Madhuḥ*.

अतीन्द्रियः ATĪNDRIYAḤ: As He is without sound etc., He is not knowable by the sense-organs (*indriyas*) *vide* the śruti: *aśabdam asparśam*: (He is) 'soundless and touchless.' (Kaṭh. Up. 3.15)

महामायः MAHĀMĀYAḤ: He who subjects the illusionists themselves (*māyāvīs*) to illusion (*māyā*). *vide*: the Lord's statement, *mama māyā duratyayā*: 'My māyā is difficult to transcend'. (B.G. 7.14)

महोत्साहः MAHOTSĀHAḤ: He who takes great delight in the creation, preservation and subsumption of the universe.

महाबलः MAHĀBALAḤ: Being stronger than the strong, He is *Mahābalaḥ*.

महाबुद्धिर्महावीर्यो महाशक्तिर्महाद्युतिः ।
अनिर्देश्यवपुः श्रीमानमेयात्मा महाद्रिधृक् ॥ ३२ ॥

Mahābuddhiḥ Mahāvīryaḥ Mahāśaktiḥ
Mahādyutiḥ /
Anirdeśyavapuḥ Śrīmān Ameyātmā
Māhādridṛk // 32

महाबुद्धिः MAHĀBUDDIḤ: As He is more intelligent than the intelligent, He is *Mahābuddhiḥ*.

महावीर्यः MAHAVĪRYAḤ: His energy (*vīrya*) is the cause of the origination of *Mahat* (an evolute of Prakṛti) of the nature of avidyā. So, He is *Mahāvīryaḥ*.

महाशक्तिः MAHAŚAKTIḤ: He has immense *sakti* power or capacity. So *Mahāśaktiḥ*.

महाद्युतिः MAHĀDYUTIḤ: Splendorous inside and out. So, *Mahādyutiḥ*. *vide* the śruti. *svayam jyotiḥ*: 'radiant by Himself: (Bṛh. Up. 4.3.9) and *jyotiṣām jyotiḥ*: 'The Light of lights'. (Bṛh. Up. 4.4.16).

अनिर्देश्यवपुः ANIRDEŚYAVAPUḤ: As He can not

be indicated to others by saying "This is that". Because He is to be known by oneself. He has a body (nature) which cannot be so indicated. So, He is *Anirdeśyavapuḥ.*

श्रीमान् ŚRĪMĀN: He has all characteristics of Śrī which connotes aiśvarya. So, is *Śrīmān.*

अमेयात्मा AMEYĀTMĀ: He who has intelligence (here, ātmā) which cannot be measured by any creature is *Ameyātmā.*

महाद्रिधृक् MAHĀDRIDHṚK: He supported the big hills Mandara and Govardhana at the time of churning of the ocean and to protect the cows. So, He is *Mahādridhṛk.* (*mahā*-big; *adri*-hill; *dhṛ*-to support).

महेष्वासो महीभर्ता श्रीनिवासः सतां गतिः ।
अनिरुद्धः सुरानन्दो गोविन्दो गोविदां पतिः ।। ३३ ।।

Maheṣvāsaḥ Mahībhartā Śrīnivasaḥ Satāmgatiḥ /
Aniruddaḥ Surānandaḥ Govindaḥ Govindāmpatiḥ / /
33

महेष्वासः MAHEṢVĀSAḤ: (From *iṣu* arrow and *as* to throw) whose throwing the arrow is *mahān,* formidable. He is *Maheṣvasaḥ.*

महीभर्ता MAHĪBHARTĀ: So called as He supported the earth *mahī* submerged in the water (*mahīm babhāra*).

श्रीनिवासः ŚRĪNIVASAḤ: He on whose chest Śrī (Lakshmī) resides without separation.

सतांगतिः SATĀMGATIḤ: He who causes the realisation of the puruṣarthas by those who are *sat* i.e., vaidikas, who have learnt and practised the Vedas, the sādhus.

अनिरुद्धः ANIRUDDAḤ: Not obstructed by any one

in His manifestations (avatāras).

सुरानन्दः SURĀNANDAḤ: He who gives joy (*ānanda*) to the devas (Suras).

गोविन्दः GOVINDAḤ: *naṣṭām vai dharaṇīm purvamavindam vai guhāgatām / govinda iti tenāham devairvāghbir abhiṣṭutaḥ / /*: 'Previously I knew (avindam) the earth (go) concealed in a cave. So, I was praised by the devas as Govinda.' By this statement in Mokṣa Dharma He is *Govindaḥ. aham kilendro devānām tvam gavāmindratām gataḥ / govinda iti lokāstvām stoṣyanti bhuvi śāśvatam / /* : 'I attained Indratva (I am Indra) of the devas. You are the lord, Indra, of the cows. So, they will ever praise You on earth as *Govinda*.'

In the Harivamśa it is said: *gaureṣa tu tathā vāṇī tam ca vindayate bhavān / govindastu tato deva munibhiḥ kathyate bhavān / /* : 'Speech is called go. You confer it (vindayate). So munis proclaim You as *Govinda*.'

गोविदांपतिः GOVIDĀMPATIḤ: Gauḥ is vāṇī or speech or language. Those who know it are *govidaḥ*. Their supreme lord is *Govidāmpatiḥ*.

मरीचिर्दमनो हंसः सुपर्णो भुजगोत्तमः ।
हिरण्यनाभः सुतपाः पद्मनाभः प्रजापतिः ।। ३४ ।।

Marīciḥ Damanaḥ Hamsaḥ Suparṇaḥ Bhuja-
gottamaḥ /
Hiraṇyanābaḥ Sutapāḥ Padmanābhaḥ
Prajāpatiḥ / / 34

मरीचिः MARĪCIḤ: The effulgent among the effulgents. *vide* the Lord's statement: *tejastejasvinā-maham*'. 'I am the brightness of those who are bright' (B. G. 10-36).

दमन: DAMANAḤ: He who has the capacity in the form of Vaivasta and others to punish those who swerve from the duties of their offices.

हंस: HAMSAḤ: 1. He destroys the fear of (entanglement in) samsāra of those who realise "I am He" *(aham saha) (so' ham becomes Hamsaḥ).*

Or 2. By *hanti* which means *gacchati*: goes, He goes into or pervades all bodies. So, *Hamsaḥ. vide* the śruti-mantra (Kaṭh. Up. 3.2.2) *hamsa sucisat.*

सुपर्ण: SUPARṆAḤ: Of handsome wings. *vide* the śruti mantra (Svet. Up. 4.6). *dvā suparṇā*: 'two birds of beautiful plumage.'

भुजगोत्तम: BHUJAGOTTAMAḤ: The best of those who move on their chest (serpents).

हिरण्यनाभ: HIRAṆYANĀBHAḤ: 1. He whose naval (*nābhi*) is auspicious like gold. So, *Hiraṇyanābhaḥ.*

Or 2. Having a *hita,* beautiful navel.

सुतपा: SUTAPĀḤ: He performs auspicious tapas in Badarikāśrama in the form of Nara and Nārāyaṇa. *vide the smṛti: manasasca indriyaṇām ca hi ekāgryam paramam tapaḥ*: 'The one-pointedness of the mind and the senses is supreme tapas.'

पद्मनाभ: PADMANĀBHAḤ: 1. His naval (*nābhi*) is round like a lotus (padma). So, *Pamanābhaḥ.*

Or 2. As He shines in the centre of the lotus of the heart.

प्रजापति: PRAJĀPATIḤ: The *pati* or *pitā* (father) of all creatures.

अमृत्युः सर्वदृक् सिंहः सन्धाता सन्धिमान्स्थिरः ।
अजो दुर्मर्षणः शास्ता विश्रुतात्मा सुरारिहा ।। ३५ ।।

Amṛtyuḥ Sarvadṛk Simhaḥ Saṁdhātā Sandhimān
Sthiraḥ /
Ajaḥ Durmarṣaṇaḥ Śāstā Viśrutātmā
Surārihā // 35

अमृत्यु: AMṚTYUḤ: *Mṛtyuḥ* means dying or its cause. That He does not have either makes Him *Amṛtyuḥ*.

सर्वदृक् SARVADṚK: He sees by His native intelligence what all is done and omitted to be done by creatures. So *Sarvadṛk*.

सिंह: SIMHAḤ: Because He kills *hinasti*, therefore, *Simhaḥ*.

Thus the second hundred of Names has been explained.

संधाता SAMDĀTĀ: He associates (*samdhatte*) men with the fruits of their actions.

संधिमान् SANDHIMĀN: The enjoyer (of the fruits if actions) is He Himself. So, *Saṁdhimān*.

स्थिर: STHIRAḤ: Being always of the same form, He is *Sthiraḥ* or constant.

अज: AJAḤ: He goes (everywhere) or throws away His enemies *ajati gaccati kṣipati iti vā*.

दुर्मर्षण: DURMARṢANAḤ: He is unbearable by the asuras and others.

शास्ता ŚĀSTĀ: He disciplines every one by śrutis and smrtis.

विश्रुतात्मा VIŚRUTĀTMĀ: His nature which is marked by satyam, jñānam and ānandam (or anantam) is well-known. *viṣeṣena śrutaḥ*. So *Viśrutāṭmā*.

सुरारिहा SURĀRIHĀ: Because He kills the enemies of *suras,* devas.

गुरुर्गुरुतमो धाम सत्यः सत्यपराक्रमः ।
निमिषोऽनिमिषः स्रग्वी वाचस्पतिरुदारधीः ॥ ३६ ॥

Guruḥ Gurutamaḥ Dhāma Satyaḥ
Satyaparākramaḥ /
Nimiṣah Animṣaḥ Sragvī Vācaspat'irudhāra-
dhīḥ / / 36

गुरुः GURUḤ: 1. As He is the instructor of all vidyās (arts and sciences), He is *Guruḥ*.

Or 2. As He is the originator of a'' beings, He is *Guruḥ*.

गुरुतमः GURUTAMAḤ: As He originated the traditional teaching of Brahmavidyā to Virinci (Brahmā) and others, He is *Gurutamaḥ*. *vide* the mantra *yobrahmāṇam vidadhāti pūrvam*: 'He who first created Brahmā and instructed Him in all Vedas'. (Svet. Up. 6.18).

धाम DHĀMA: 1. Lustre, *vide* the mantra *nārāyaṇa parojyotiḥ*. Nārāyaṇa is the supreme radiance (Nārā. Up. 13).

Or 2. As He is the source of all desires. He is Dhāma. *vide* the śruti: *paramam brahma param dhāma*: 'Brahman is the supreme abode' (Muṇd. Up. 6.1).

सत्यः SATYAḤ: 1. Because He is *satyavacana* as His words always come true. *vide* the śruti *tasmāt satyam paramam vadanti*: 'therefore they say truth is paramount'. (Nārā. Up. 79).

Or 2. Because He is the Truth of truth. *vide* the śruti *prānāvai satyam teṣameṣa satyam*: the prānas are the truth and He is their truth. (Br. Up. 4.1.20).

सत्यपराक्रमः SATYAPARĀKRAMAḤ: He whose valour is never belied.

निमिषः NIMIṢAḤ: He whose eyelids are closed in His Yoganidrā.

अनिमिष: ANIMIṢAḤ: He whose eyes are never closed in His avatāra as the fish (Matsyāvatāra) or who is ever awake as the ātman (in everybody).

श्रग्वी SRAGVĪ: As of the form of tanmātras, the essence of the elements (the five bhūtas), He wears always the garland called Vaijayanti. (*Sragvī* one who wears the *srak* or garland).

वाचस्पतिरुदारधी: VACASPATIRUDĀRADHĪḤ: *Vācaspatiḥ* is *vācaḥ vidyāyāh patih*: the master of all vidyās. *Udāradhīḥ*: Whose *dhīh* or intellect is able to comprehend all knowledge. *Vācaspatirudāradhīḥ* is one Name.

अग्रणीर्ग्रामणीः श्रीमान्न्यायो नेता समीरणः ।
सहस्रमूर्धा विश्वात्मा सहस्राक्षः सहश्रपात् ।। ३७ ।।

Agraṇīḥ Grāmiṇīḥ Śrīmān Nyāyaḥ Netā
Samīriṇaḥ /
Sahasramūrdhā Viśvātmā Sahasrākṣaḥ
Sahasrapāt // 37

अग्रणी: AGRAṆIḤ: He leads the seekers of salvation to the first and foremost abode.

ग्रामणी: GRAMAṆIḤ: As He leads (controls) the collection of the bhūtas or elements.

श्रीमान् ŚRĪMĀN: He has splendour greater than everything. (śrī means kānti).

न्याय: NYĀYAḤ: Logic that establishes non-difference between the jīva and Brahman which is consistent with the canons of reasoning.

नेता NETĀ: The Director of the machine that is the world.

समीरण: SAMĪRAṆAḤ: In the form of breath He makes the elements act.

सहस्रमूर्धा SAHASRAMŪRDHĀ: He is thousand-headed. So, *Sahasramūrdhā*.

विश्वात्मा VIŚVĀTMĀ: The Ātmā of the Universe.

सहस्राक्षः SAHASRĀKṢAḤ: He who has thousand eyes.

सहस्रपात् SAHASRAPĀT: He who has thousand feet, *vide* the śruti *sahsraśirṣāpuruṣaḥ sahasrākṣhā sahasrapāt*: 'The Supreme Puruṣa has a thousand heads, a thousand eyes and a thousand feet.' (Puruṣa Sūkta).

आवर्तनो निवृत्तात्मा संवृतः सम्प्रमर्दनः ।
अहः संवर्तको वन्हिरनिलो धरणीधरः ॥ ३८ ॥

Āvartanaḥ Nivṛttātmā Samvṛtaḥ Sampramardanaḥ /
Ahaḥ Samvartakaḥ Vahniḥ Anilaḥ
Dharaṇidharaḥ / / 38

आवर्तनः ĀVARTANAḤ: He is possessed of the nature (or capacity) to turn the wheel of samsāra (*āvartana* is turning).

निवृत्तात्मा NIVṚTTĀMĀ: He whose nature is free (turned back) from the bonds of *śamsāra.*

संवृतः SAMVṚTAḤ: As He is covered (hidden) by avidyā (making the unenlightened unable to know Him).

संप्रमर्दनः SAMPRAMARDANAḤ: By His powers as Rudra, Kāla etc., He completely torments (evil doers) (*mardanaḥ, pramardanaḥ, samprardanah*).

अहस्संवर्तकः AHASSAMVARTAKAḤ: He causes the daytime, the sun, (*ahas*. day; *samvartakah* originator, one who causes the day).

वह्निः VAHNIḤ: By virtue of carrying (the *ahūtis* or oblations). He is *Vahniḥ.* (*vah* means to carry).

अनिलः ANILAH: 1. *anilayaḥ*, therefore *Anilaḥ*. He is not stationery, always moves.

Or. 2. *Anāditvāt anilaḥ.* He is beginningless, therefore *Anilaḥ.*

Or 3. By reason of lifting the hand (which affects the movement of the air.)

Or 4. By reason of breaking, He is Anilaḥ.[20]

धरणीधरः DHARANĪDHARAḤ: He bears the earth in the form of Ādiśeṣa or Varāha (*dharaṇīm datte so Dharaṇīdharaḥ*).

सुप्रसादः प्रसन्नात्मा विश्वधृग्विश्वभुग्विभुः ।
सत्कर्ता सत्कृतः साधुर्जह्नुर्नारायणो नरः ॥ ३९ ॥

Suprasādaḥ Prasannātmā Viśvadṛk Viśvabhuk Vibhuḥ
Satkartā Satkṛtaḥ Sādhuḥ Jahnuḥ Nārayaṇaḥ Naraḥ / / 39

सुप्रसादः SUPRASĀDAḤ: He whose grace makes for good, for it bestows salvation even on those like Śiśupāla and others who did Him wrong.

प्रसन्नात्मा PRASANNĀTMĀ: 1. He whose antaḥkarana (inner organ) is unaffected by rajas and tamas.

Or 2. Whose nature is *prasanna*, being merciful.

Or 3. As He has realised all His desires, He is ever satisfied.

विश्वधृक् VISVADṚK: He withstands the universe with confidence and power *viśvam dhṛṣṇoti. dhṛṣā* indicates confidence.

विश्वभुक् VIŚVABHUK: He enjoys the universe or protects it. *bhuj, bhuk,* to eat or to protect. So *Viśvabhuk.*

विभुः VIBHUḤ: He takes various forms as Hiraṇ-

20. The idea is that every one of our actions is instinct with God and He is called by the names of those actions.

yagarbha and others. *vide* the mantra *nityam vibhum*: is eternal and of various forms. (Muṇḍ 1.6)

सत्कर्ता: SATKARTĀ: He does good, so *Satkartā*.

सत्कृत: SATKṚTAḤ: Worshipped even by those who are worshipped.

साधु: SĀDUḤ: 1. As His actions are just, He is *Sādhuḥ*.

Or 2. He accomplishes everything.

Or 3. Realises things without extraneous aids.

जह्नु: JANHUḤ: 1. At the time of destruction, He makes men disappear (*apahnute*). So He is *Jahnuḥ*.

Or 2 & 3 He leads away from Himself, the Supreme, those who are devoid of intelligence or devotion.

नारायण: NĀRĀYAṆAḤ: 1. *Nara* is ātmā, from it arose ākāśa, etc., *nārāṇi*, the effects: He pervades them as their cause; so they are His abode. Therefore He is *Nārāyaṇa*. *vide* the mantra *yaccha kincit jagat sarvam drsyate srūyatepivā / antarbahisca tat sarvam vyāpya nārāyaṇah sthitaḥ / /*: 'Whatever is seen or heard, pervading all that in and out stands Nārāyaṇa.' (Nārā. Up. 13. 1-2).

Or 2. The categories were born from nara; they are called *nārāṇi*. He who has them as His abode is known as *Nārāyaṇa*. (M.Bh. Udyoga Parva 1.1.3.

Or 3. During praḷaya, involution, He is the abode of Jīvas or naras. *vide* the śruti: *yatprayantyabhisamviśanti*, That into which they enter.

Or 4. The Brahma Vaivarta Purāṇa says *nārānāmayanam yasmāt tasmānnārāyanaḥ smṛtaḥ* 'He is the abode of the *nāras*.'

Or 5. According to Manu Smṛti (1.10), the waters are said to be nāras, they are the children of Nara. They were His abode originally. So, He is called Nārāyaṇa.

Or 6. Narasimha Purāna says:

"Nārayaṇāya namaḥ (obesiance to Nārāyaṇa) is the eternal truth. It is the mantra which is the medicine to cure the deadly poison of samsāra. With uplifted hands I proclaim it. May ascetics of humble mind, and freed of all passions hear it."

नरः NARAḤ: *nayatiti naraḥ proktaḥ paramātmā sanātanaḥ* (*Vyāsa*). 'The eternal Paramātma is said to lead men to salvation. So, He is *Naraḥ*.'

असंख्येयोऽप्रमेयात्मा विशिष्टः शिष्टकृच्छुचिः ।
सिद्धार्थः सिद्धसंकल्पः सिद्धिदः सिद्धिसाधनः ॥ ४० ॥

Asaṃkhyehaḥ Aprameyātmā Visiṣtaḥ Śiṣtakṛt
Suciḥ /
Siddhārtaḥ Siddhasaṁkalpaḥ
Siddhidaḥ Siddhisādanaḥ // 40

असंख्येयः ASAMKHYEYAH: He in whom the difference of *sankhyā*, number, name and form do not obtain.

अप्रमेयात्मा APRAMEYĀTMĀ: His nature is not the subject of being determined by the canons of reasoning.

विशिष्टः VISIṢTAḤ: He excels all; therefore He is superior, *Viśiṣtah.*

शिष्टकृत् ŚIṢTAKṚT: 1. He ordains the law (law maker of the universe). *śiṣtam* means *śasanam; karoti:* makes: therefore, *Śiṣtakṛt.*

Or 2. He protects the good, the *śiṣtas,* so *Śiṣtakṛt* (*kṛt* is used in the sense of prōtection) Some roots which have general meaning are used in a special sense. Eg., In *kuru kaṣṭhāni* make firewood, *kuru* is used in the sense of fetch. Similarly, in *Śiṣtakṛt krt* has the meaning of protects.

सुचिः SUCIḤ: Without blemish: *niranjanaḥ* without anjana or spot.

सिद्धार्तः SIDDHĀRTAḤ: Whatever purposes He had, have been accomplished (sidda-arthaḥ) *vide* the śruti: *satyakāmaḥ* (Ch. Up. 8.1.5).

सिद्धसंकल्पः SIDDHASAMKALPAḤ: His *samkalpa* or resolution is *siddha* fulfilled. *vide* the śruti: *satyasaṁkalpaḥ*: His resolutions become true. (*ibid.*)

सिद्धिदः SIDDHIDAḤ: To those who perform actions He gives *dadāti* the fruit *siddham* according to their deserts. So, *Siddidaḥ*.

सिद्धिसाधनः SIDDHISĀDANAḤ: He is the means *sādana* to siddhi: fulfilment.

वृषाही वृषभो विष्णुर्वृषपर्वा वृषोदरः।
वर्धनो वर्धमानश्च विविक्तः श्रुतिसागरः॥ ४१॥

Vṛṣāhī Vṛṣabhaḥ Viṣnuḥ Vṛsaparvā Vrsodaraḥ /
Vardhanaḥ Vardhamānaḥ ca Viviktaḥ
Śrutisāgaraḥ / / 41

वृषाहीः VṚṢĀHĪ: *Vṛṣā* means dharma or merit, *puṇyam* that is *ahah:* a sacrifice done for twelve days etc. That accrues to Him. So *Vṛṣāhī*.

वृषभः VṚṢABHAḤ: He pours (varṣati) whatever they desire on His devotees.

विष्णुः VIṢNUḤ: By Vyasa's words *viṣṇurvikramaṇāt;* because He encompasses by (three) steps, He is Viṣṇuḥ (M.Bh.Udy.69-18).

वृषपर्वा VṚṢAPARVĀ: For those who wish to ascend to the highest state, they say dharmas are formed as the steps. Therefore He is *Vṛṣaparvā* (*vṛṣa:* dharma and *parva*: steps or staircase).

वृषोदरः VṚṢODARAḤ: He rains as it were

(varṣayati) the creatures from His womb *(udara)* So, *Vṛṣodaraḥ.*

वर्धन: VARDHANAḤ: He who makes things to increase (*vardhāyati*).

वर्धमान: VARDHAMĀNAḤ: He increases in the form of the universe. So *Vardhamānaḥ.*

विविक्त: VIVIKTAḤ: Though increasing like this, remains separate. So, *Viviktaḥ.*

श्रुतिसागर: ŚRUTISĀGARAḤ: The śruti (the Vedas) are laid in Him as in the ocean. So, *Srutisāgaraḥ.*

सुभुजो दुर्धरो वाग्मी महेन्द्रो वसुदो वसुः ।
नैकरूपो बृहद्रूपः शिपिविष्टः प्रकाशनः ॥ ४२ ॥

Subhujaḥ Durdharaḥ Vāgmī Mhendraḥ Vasudaḥ
Vasuḥ 42
Naikarūpaḥ Bṛhadrūpaḥ Sipiviṣṭaḥ Prakaśānaḥ

सुभुज: SUBHUJAḤ: He whose arms are beautiful and auspicious, which protect the world. So *Subhujaḥ.*

धुर्धर: DURDHARAḤ: 1. Supporting the earth which supports the worlds which cannot be supported by any other thing and who Himself cannot be supported by any one. So *dur dharah* (*dhar* to bear, *dur* difficult).

Or 2. He who is borne by the seekers of salvation with difficulty in their hearts at the time of contemplation (*durkhena dharyate*).

वाग्मी VĀGMĪ: From whom speech pertaining to Brahman has proceeded.

महेन्द्र: MAHENDRAḤ: The great Indra; The Lord of lords.

वसुद: VASUDAḤ: *Vasu* wealth. He gives it *(dadāti)* So, *Vasudaḥ vide* the śruti *annādo vasudānaḥ*: 'He is the consumer of food and the giver of wealth.' (Bṛh. U.6.4.24).

वसु: VASUḤ: 1. He Himself is that wealth which is given. So *Vasuḥ*.

Or 2. He veils His nature by māyā. (*vāsaḥ* which means a cloth worn round the limbs to cover them).

Or 3. He lives (is) only in ether (antarikṣa) nowhere else by His especial abode or *vāyu*. So, *Vasuḥ vide vasurantirakṣam*: vasu dwelling in the ether (Kaṭha Up.5.2).

नैकरूप: NAIKARŪPAḤ: He has no definite form. So, *Naikarūpaḥ vide* the śruti: *indromāyābhiḥ bahu rūpam īyate*: "Brahman assumes many forms by His māyā'. (Bṛh. Up. 4.5.19) and the smṛti: Viṣ. Pu. 2.12). *jyotīmṣi viṣṇuḥ*: 'The luminaries are Viṣṇu.'

बृहद्रूप BṚHDRŪPAḤ: His form (rūpam) is big (*bṛhat*) like the Boar (in the Varāhāvatāra).

सिपिविष्ट: SIPIVIṢṬAḤ: 1. Sipis are the sacrificial animals. He enters (*viśati*) into them in the form of the sacrifice. So *Sipiviṣṭaḥ vide* the śruti: *yajño vai viṣṇuḥ paśavaḥ sipiḥ yajna eva pasuṣu pratitiṣtati*: 'Verily the sacrifice is Viṣṇu: the sacrificial animals are the *sipiḥ* and Viṣṇu alone indwells in them.' (Taitt. Sam. 2.5.5).

Or 2. *sipis* are rays; one who has entered into them is *Sipiviṣṭaḥ*.

> By the combination of coolness and fitness to be rested in, the water is seen to be refreshing. By drinking and keeping them (in themselves) sipis are considered to be rays. As the Lord of the universe has entered into them, He is said to be *sipiviṣṭaḥ*.

प्रकाशन: PRAKĀŚANAḤ: As He possesses the capacity to illumine, He is called *Prakāśanaḥ*.

ओजस्तेजोद्युतिधरः प्रकाशात्मा प्रतापनः ।
ऋद्धः स्पष्टाक्षरो मन्त्रश्चन्द्रांशुर्भास्करद्युतिः ॥ ४३ ॥

Ojastejodyutidharaḥ Prakāsātmā Pratāpanaḥ
Ṛddhaḥ Spaṣṭākṣaraḥ Mantraḥ Candramśuḥ
Bhāskaradyutiḥ 43

ओजस्तजोव्युतिधरः OJASTEJODYUTIDHARAḤ: 1. *Ojah* means vital energy (prāṇabalam), *tejas* indicates qualities like valour etc., *dyutih* is brightness. He possesses them *(dhārayati)* So, *Ojasetejodyutidharaḥ.*

Or 2. *Ojas* and *tejas* are two Names, vide the Bhagavān's statement: *balam balavatāmaham; tejas tejasvināmaham:* 'I am the strength of the strong, I am the valour of the valorous'. He possesses *dyuti* the effulgence which is jñāna. So *dyutidharaḥ* (B.G. 7.11 and 7-10).

प्रकाशात्मा PRAKĀŚĀTMĀ: He whose ātmā is radiant.

प्रतापनः PRATĀPANAḤ: He makes the universe hot (*pratapayati*) by His glories like the sun etc.

ऋद्धः ṚDDHAḤ: Richly endowed with dharma, jñāna, vairāgya (righteousness, wisdom, dispassion) and other qualities.

स्पष्टाक्षरः SPAṢTAKṢARAḤ: He is marked by clear utterances of the syllable Om in an accented form *(udāttam).*

मन्त्रः MANTRAḤ: 1. He is of the form of Ṛk, Yajus and Sāman which are mantras.

Or 2. as He is taught (to men) by mantras, He is called *mantra.*

चन्द्रांशुः CHANDRĀMŚUḤ: So called as He gives joy like the rays of the moon to minds afflicted by the heat of samsāra.

भास्करद्युतिः BHASKARADYUTIḤ: Because of similarity with the brightness of the sun, He is *Bhāskaradyutiḥ.*

अमृतांशूद्भवो भानुः शशबिन्दुः सुरेश्वरः ।
औषधं जगतः सेतुः सत्यधर्मपराक्रमः ॥ ४४ ॥

Amṛtāmsūdbhavaḥ Bhānuḥ Śaśabinduḥ Sureśvaraḥ
Auṣadhaṃ Jagataheṭuḥ
Satyadharmaparākramaḥ // 44

अमृतांशूद्भवः AMRTAMŚŪDBHAVAḤ: He from whom arose the moon of the nectareous rays when the ocean was churned is known as *Amṛtāmśūdbhavaḥ.*

भानुः BHANUḤ: He shines, therefore He is *Bhānuḥ. vide* the śruti: *tamevabhāntam anubhāti sarvam:* 'Everything shines after only Him who is shining.' (Kaṭh.Up.4.15).

शशबिन्दुः ŚAŚABINDUḤ: 1. 'As He has a mark like a hare, He is *Saśabinduh,* or Moon.

Or 2. He nourishes the creatures like a moon. So He is *Śaśabinduḥ. vide* the Lord's statement *puṣṇāmi ca auṣadīḥ sarvāḥ somobhūtvā rasātmakaḥ*: 'Becoming the moon of the form of *rasas,* I nourish all the herbs.' (B.G. 15.13).

सुरेश्वरः SUREŚVARAḤ: The Lord of the devas and those who bestow good (auspiciousness).

औषधम् AUṢADHAM: As He is the medicine for the disease of samsāra, He is *Auṣadham.*

जगतस्सेतुः JAGATASSETUḤ: By reason of His emancipation of the world and by His non-destruction of differences of varṇas and āśramas and being like a bund preserving them, He is *Jagatassetuḥ. vide* the śruti: *eṣa seturvidharaṇa eṣam lokānām asaṃbhedāya*: 'He is the bund of all these preserving the worlds from confusion.' (Br. Up. 6.4.22).

सत्यधर्मपराक्रमः SATYADHARMA PARĀKRAMAḤ: He whose dharmas, jñāna and other qualities and valour (parākrama) are true, unfalsified is *Satyadharma parākramaḥ*.

भूतभव्यभवन्नाथः पवनः पावनोऽनलः ।
कामहा कामकृत्कान्तः कामः कामप्रदः प्रभुः ॥ ४५ ॥

Bhūtabhavyabhavannāthaḥ Pavanaḥ Pāvanaḥ Analaḥ //
Kāmahā Kāmakṛt Kāntaḥ Kāmaḥ Kāmapradaḥ Prabhuḥ // 45

भूतभव्यभवन्नाथः BHŪTABHAVYABHAVANNĀTHAḤ: 1. The Lord of the collection of bhūtas (elements or beings) in the past, future and present.

Or 2. He is implored by them.

Or 3. He teases them.

Or 4. He rules over them.

Or 5. Orders them. So *Bhūtabhavyabhavannāthaḥ*.

पवनः PAVANAḤ: Makes blow as the wind: *pavate*. So He is *Pavanaḥ*. *vide* the śruti *bhiṣāsmāt vātaḥ pavate*: 'The wind blows by fear of Him'. (Taitt. Up. 2.8).

पावनः PĀVANAḤ: He purifies. So He is *Pavanaḥ*. *vide* the Lord's statement: *pavanaḥ pavatām asmi*: 'I am the purifier among those who purify'. (B.G. 10.31).

अनलः ANALAḤ: 1. He receives the prāṇas into Himself being the self (jīva): *aṇān prāṇān ātmatvena lāti*.

Or 2. *alam*, satiety dies not exist for Him (as the Fire), hence *Analaḥ*.

कामहा KĀMAHĀ: He destroys the lusts of seekers of salvation, devotees and evil-doers. So *Kāmahā* (*har* to kill).

कामकृत्: KĀMAKṚT: 1. He fulfils the desires of good people.

Or 2. He is the father of Kāma or Pradyumna.

कान्त: KĀNTAḤ: Extremely handsome, brilliant in appearance.

काम: KĀMAḤ: Much desired (sought after) by the seekers of the puruṣārthas.

कामप्रद: KĀMAPRADAḤ: He gives plentifully what they desire to His devotees. So, *Kāmapradaḥ*.

प्रभु: PRABHUḤ: He flourishes magnificently (*prakarṣeṇa bhavati*). Hence Prabhuḥ.

युगादिकृद्युगावर्तो नैकमायो महाशनः।
अदृश्योऽव्यक्तरूपश्च सहस्रजिदनन्तजित् ॥ ४६ ॥

Yugādikṛt Yugāvartaḥ Naikmāyaḥ Mahāśanaḥ /
Adṛśyaḥ Vyaktarūpaḥ ca Sahasrajit Anantajit / / 46

युगदिकृत् YUGĀDIKṚT: As being the institutor of the yugas, according to the difference of Time, He is *Yugādikṛt* or because He starts the *ādi*, the beginning, of Yuga.

Thus the third hundred of Names has been explained.

युगावर्त: YUGĀVARTAḤ: As Time, He rotates (*āvartayati*), the Kṛta and other yugas.

नैकमाय: NAIKAMĀYAḤ: His māyā is not one; but He wields many māyās.

महाशन: MAHĀŚANAḤ: At the end of a Kalpa, He swallows everything. As His eating (*aśana*) is big (*mahat*), He is *Mahāśanaḥ*.

अदृश्य: ADṚŚYAḤ: He cannot be known by any of the buddindriyas.

व्यक्तरूप: VYAKTARŪPAḤ: 1. His form is manifested when He assumes a concrete shape (*sthūla rūpa*).

Or 2. Being self-radiant, He is visible to the yōgis.

सहस्रजित् SAHASRAJIT: He conquers thousands of asuras in battle. So *Sahasrajit.*

अनन्तजित् ANANTAJIT: By His unimaginable power, He excelled all (*ananta* endless in number of) creatures in battle or sport.

इष्टो विशिष्टः शिष्टेष्टः शिखण्डी नहुषो वृषः ।
क्रोधहा क्रोधकृत्कर्ता विश्वबाहुर्महीधरः ॥ ४७ ॥

Iṣtaḥ Aviśiṣtaḥ Śiṣtestaḥ Sikhandī Nahusaḥ Vṛsaḥ /
Krodhahā Krodhakṛt Kartā Viśvabhāhuḥ
Mahīdharaḥ // 47

इष्टः IṢTAḤ: 1. Dear being of the form of the highest bliss.

Or 2. He is worshipped by sacrifice.

अविशिष्टः AVIŚIṢTAḤ: Being the *antaryāmī,* the inner pervasive Ruler of all, He is Aviśiṣtaḥ (*viś* to enter, to reside in).

शिष्टेष्टः ŚIṢTEṢTAḤ: 1. Dear to śiṣtas or learned persons or jñānis.

Or 2. Because learned persons or jñānis are dear to Him, He is *Śiṣtestaḥ. vide* the Lord's statement: *priyoḥi jnanino'tyanthạm aham sa ca mama priyaḥ*: 'I am very dear to the jñāni and he is also dear to Me'. (B.G. 7.17).

Or 3. He is *iṣtaḥ,* worshipped by the *śiṣtas*, learned men or jñānis, so *Śiṣteṣtaḥ.*

सिखण्डी SIKHANDĪ: Sikhanda or peacock-feather adorns His head when He puts on the garb of a cowboy. So *Sikhandī.*

नहुष: NAHUṢAḤ: As He binds (*nahyati*) all creatures by His power of māyā, He is *Nahuṣaḥ,* the great Binder.

वृषः VṚṢAḤ: 1. As He rains all desires, He is *Vṛṣaḥ* (*vṛṣaṇa* is to rain).

Or 2. Dharma. *vide* (M.Bh. Śānti 352-23). *vṛṣohi bhagavān dharmaḥ smṛto lokeṣu bhārata / naighantuka-padakhyānaiḥ viddhi mām vṛṣa ityuta* // : "The worshipful dharma is considered in the world as Vṛṣa. The lexicographers speak of *vṛṣa* as *dharma.* Know Me to be *Vṛṣa.*"

क्रोधहा KRODHAHĀ: He destroys the anger of good men.

क्रोधकृत् KRODHAKṚT: He creates anger among evil persons.

कर्ता KARTĀ: What is done or created is action, that is the world; the creator of the worlds is *Kartā. vide* the śruti. (Kauśītaki Up. 4.18) *eteṣām puruṣāṇam yah kartā yasya vai tat karma sa vai veditavyaḥ*: 'He Who is the maker of all these persons, Whose is that work, He verily is to be known.'

Or KRODHAKṚTKARTĀ may be taken as one Name meaning the slayer (kartā=slayer, cutter) of the *krodakṛts,* the asuras who are easily prone to anger.

विश्वबाहुः VIŚVABĀHUḤ: 1. With arms as the support of all, He is *Viśvabhāhuḥ.*

Or 2. He has arms on all sides. *vide* the śruti. *visvatobāhuḥ*: 'Has arms everywhere.' (Svet. Up. 3.3).

महीधरः MAHĪDHARAḤ: (*dhar* to hold, to accept). He holds the earth *mahī* or He accepts worship. *mahī* is earth or worship. So, *Mahīdharaḥ.*

अच्युतः प्रथितः प्राणः प्राणदो वासवानुजः ।
अपां निधिरधिष्ठानमप्रमत्तः प्रतिष्ठितः ॥ ४८ ॥

Acyutaḥ Prathitaḥ Prāṇaḥ Prāṇadaḥ Vāsavānujaḥ /
Apāmnidhiḥ Adhiṣṭhānam Apramattaḥ
Pratiṣṭhitaḥ // 48

अच्युत: ACYUTAḤ: Unchanging. He is devoid of the six changes (birth, existence, growth, transformation, decline and death). *vide* the śruti: *śaśvatam śivamacyutam*: 'eternal, auspicious and not changing.' (Nārāyaṇa Up. 13.1).

प्रथित: PRATHITAḤ: Famous by reason of the actions of creation etc. (preservation and destruction) of the world.

प्राण: PRĀṆAḤ: Makes creatures breathe (*prāṇayati*) by being the pervasive thread. *vide*: the Ṛk, *prāṇo va ahamasmi*: 'I am indeed the prāṇa (breath)'. (Ait. Aran. 2.2.3).

प्राणद: PRĀṆADAḤ: Gives the prāṇa (strength) to the devas (dadāti), Or destroys (dyati) the strength of the asuras.

वासवानुज: VĀSAVĀNUJAḤ: Born as the younger brother (*anuja*) of Vāsava to Aditi by Kaśyapa. Hence *Vāsavānujaḥ*.

अपांनिधि APĀMNIDHIḤ: The reservoir of waters. (*āpah*=waters; *nidhi*=store). vide: the Lord's statement: *sarasām asmī sāgaraḥ*: 'Of reservoirs, I am the ocean'. (B.G. 10.24).

अधिष्ठानम् ADHIṢṬHĀNAM: He is Brahman who pervades all things as their material cause. *vide* the Lord's declaration: *matsthāni sarvābhūtani*. 'All beings are in Me'. (B.G. 9.4).

अप्रमत्त: APRAMATTAḤ: Is not careless in apportioning fruits of their actions to respective persons. So *A-pramattaḥ*.

प्रतिष्ठित: PRATIṢṬHITAḤ: Established in His own eminence. *vide* the śruti. *sa bhagavan kasmin pratiṣṭhitaḥ* etc., *sve mahimni*: 'In what is He (the ātman) established? In His own eminence'. (Ch. Up. 7.2.4.1).

स्कन्दः स्कन्दधरो धुर्यो वरदो वायुवाहनः ।
वासुदेवो बृहद्भानुरादिदेवः पुरन्दरः ॥ ४९ ॥

Skandaḥ Skandadharaḥ Dhuryaḥ Varadaḥ Vāyuvāhanaḥ /
Vāsudevaḥ Bṛhadbhānuḥ Ādiđevaḥ Purandaraḥ // 49

स्कन्द: SKANDAḤ: 1. He flows (*skandati*) in the form of nectar.

Or 2. Dries up in the form of Vāyu (wind). (*skanda* has both meanings).

स्कन्दधर: SKANDADHARAḤ: He establishes the way of dharma or *skanda*. So, *Skandadharaḥ*.

धुर्य: DHURYAḤ: He bears the burden (*dhuram*) of creation etc., of all beings. So *Dhurayaḥ*.

वरद: VARADAḤ: 1. He bestows the boons (*varam*) that are desired.

Or 2. Gives the dakṣiṇa (*varam*) in sacrifices officiating as the yajamāna. *vide* the śruti: *gaur vai varaḥ*: the cow indeed is the vara i.e., dakṣiṇa. (Āpastamba Sūtra 5.11.4).

वायुवाहन: VĀYUVĀHANAḤ: Makes the seven winds or *āvahas*, etc., blow. (They are *avahan, pravahan, samvahan, udvahan, parivahan* and *paravahan*).

वासुदेव: VĀSUDEVAḤ: 1. *vas* to reside. He resides everywhere.

Or 2. He veils everything (*vas,* to cover) by his māyā. So, *vāsuh*.

divyat: Sports, desires to conquer, conducts, shines, produces, moves. Hence *devaḥ*. He who is both *vāsu* and *deva* is *Vāsudevaḥ*. In the Udyoga Parva of the Mahābhārata, it is said:

'Like the Sun with his rays, I envelop the Universe. Also as I reside in beings, I am said to be Vāsudeva.

As I am in (permeate) all beings and I am the source of all gods, I am to be known by yogis who have realised the truth as Vāsudevaḥ.'

(Śānti Parva 350.41).

The Viṣṇu Purāṇa says (6.5.80):

'He resides everywhere and in all here; so He is called by the learned as Vāsudeva.

'In the Paramātman reside all beings and He resides in all beings. Hence, He is known as Vāsudeva'.

भृहद्भानु: BṚHADBHĀNUḤ: His mighty (powerful) rays penetrate into the sun, moon (and stars) (and illumine them). He illumines the universe by them. So, He is said to be *Bṛahadbhānuḥ*.

आदिदेव: ĀDIDEVAḤ: 1. *ādi* is *kāraṇam* or cause. The deva or God who is the primal cause (of everything) is *Ādidevah*. He who possesses brilliance and other qualities is *deva*.

पुरंदर: PURANDARAḤ: He destroys (dara) the cities (puras) of the enemies of the gods. So, *Purandaraḥ* the compound should be *Puradara* and not *Purandara*. But Pāṇini has emphatically declared that *Vācamyama* and *Purandara* are exceptions.

अशोकस्तारणस्तारः शूरः शौरिर्जनेश्वरः ।
अनुकूलः शतावर्तः पद्मी पद्मनिभेक्षणः ॥ ५० ॥

Āśokaḥ Tāraṇaḥ Tāraḥ Śuraḥ Śauriḥ Janeśvaraḥ /
Anukūlaḥ Śatāvartaḥ Padmī
Padmanibhekṣaṇaḥ // 50

अशोक: AŚOKAḤ: Free from the six waves of samsāra like grief. (The six waves which keep on afflicting a person, subject to samsāra are birth and death pertaining to the body, hunger and thirst pertaining to the prāṇa and attachment and aversion pertaining to the mind). So, *Aśokaḥ.*

तारण: TĀRAṆAḤ: He helps one to cross the samsāra sāgara. So, *Tāraṇaḥ.*

तार: TĀRAḤ: He protects one from the fears characterised by conception, birth and death. So, *Tāraḥ.* (*Tāraṇam* is protection).

शूर: SŪRAḤ: Sūraḥ because of valour.

शौरि: ŚOURIḤ: The son of Sūraḥ, born of Vasudeva.

जनेश्वर: JANEŚVARAḤ: The Lord of men, of creatures.

अनुकूल: ANUKŪLAḤ: Being the Ātman of all, He is friend of all. For no one will do what is unfavourable to oneself.

शतावर्त: SATĀVARTAḤ: 1. His coming to be, incarnation, for upholding dharma is on hundreds of occasions (innumerable).

Or 2. He is in hundreds of nerves in the form of prāṇa.

पद्मी PADMĪ: There is a lotus in His hand; so *Padmī.*

पद्मनिभेक्षण: PADMANIBHEKṢAṆAḤ: His two eyes are like the lotus. So *Padmanibhekṣaṇah.*

पद्मनाभोऽरविन्दाक्षः पद्मगर्भः शरीरभृत् ।
महर्द्धिरृद्धो वृद्धात्मा महाक्षो गरुडध्वजः ।। ५१ ।।

Padmanābhaḥ Aravindākṣaḥ Padmagarbaḥ Śarīrabhṛt /
Mahaṛddhiḥ Ṛddhaḥ Vṛddhātmā Mahākṣaḥ Garudadvajaḥ // 51

पद्मनाभः PADMANĀBHAḤ: He is in the middle part of a lotus (nābhi) in its pericarp. So *Padmanābhaḥ.*

अरविन्दाक्षः ARAVINDĀKṢAḤ: His eyes are similar to the lotus. Hence *Aravindākṣaḥ.*

पद्मगर्भः PADMAGARBHAḤ: As He is to be worshipped in the middle of the lotus of the heart, He is *Padmagarbhaḥ.*

शरीरभृत् ŚARĪRABHṚT: In the form of food, He nourishes or in the form of prāṇa, He sustains the bodies of the embodied. So, *Śarīrabhṛt.*

Or 2. He assumes a body by His māyā.

महर्द्धिः MAHARḌDHIḤ: His prosperity (ṛddhiḥ) is enormous (mahatī).

ऋद्धः ṚDDHAḤ: As He grows (increases) in the form of the universe, He is *Ṛddhaḥ*, one who increases.

वृद्धात्मा VṚDDHĀTMĀ: *vṛddhaḥ*, ancient. He whose Ātmā is ancient is *Vṛddhātmā.*

महाक्षः MAHĀKṢAḤ: He whose two eyes are great, or He whose many eyes are great is *Mahākṣaḥ.*

गरुडध्वजः GARUDADHVAJAḤ: He whose flag bears the emblem of a garuda.

अतुलः शरभो भीमः समयज्ञो हविर्हरिः ।
सर्वलक्षणलक्षण्यो लक्ष्मीवान्समितिञ्जयः ।। ५२ ।।

Atulaḥ Śarabhaḥ Bhīmaḥ Samayajñāḥ Haviḥ /
Hariḥ /

Sarvalakṣaṇalakṣaṇyaḥ Lakṣmīvān

Samitiṁjayaḥ // 52

अतुल: ATULAḤ: There is no comparison, *tulā*, for Him. Hence *Atulaḥ*. *vide* the śruti: *na tasya pratimāsti yasya nāmā mahat yaśaḥ*: 'Of Him there is no likeness, Whose Name and fame are great'. (Swet. Up. 4.19) and the smṛti: *na tvat samo'styabhyadhikaḥ kutonyaḥ*. 'There is none equal to Thee and how can there be another who excels Thee?' (B.G. 11.43).

शरभ: ŚARABHAḤ: *Śarāḥ* means *sarīrāṇi*, bodies as they waste away. *śīryamānatvāt*. In them (the bodies), the pratygyātmā, the ātmā that is inside (who is non-different from the Paramātman) *bhāti* shines. So He is known as *Śarabhaḥ*.

भीम: BHĪMAḤ: Of Him everything is afraid; *bibheti*. So *Bhīmaḥ*. It may also be taken as ABHĪMAḤ in which case, it will mean He causes no fear to those who tread the right path.

समयज्ञ: SAMAYAJÑAḤ: 1. As He knows the time for creation, preservation and dissolution, He is *Samayajñaḥ*.

Or 2. He knows the six systems of philosophy, *ṣat* samyān. So, He is *Samayajñaḥ*.

Or 3. Looking at all beings with an equal eye is worship of Him. *saravabhuteṣu samatvam* being equal in all beings is His worship. Therefore also He is *Samayajñaḥ*. *vide* Prahlada's words: *samatvam āradhanam acyutasya*: 'Equal consideration of all is worship of Acyuta.' (Viṣ. Pu. 1.17.90).

हविर्हरि: HAVIRHARIḤ: 1. He takes the oblation (the *havirbhāgam*) in sacrifices. So *Havirhariḥ*. *vide* the Lord's utterance: *aham hi sarvayajñāmām bhoktā ca prabhureva ca*: 'In all sacrifices, I am the enjoyer (eater) and the Lord of the sacrifice.' (B.G. 9.2.4).

Or 2. He is worshipped (*hūyate*) through the *havis* oblation of cooked rice). So He is *Haviḥ*. *vide* the śruti: *abadhnan puruṣam paśum*: 'They bound the Puruṣa as the paśu' (sacrificial offering). (*Puruṣa Sūkta*). By it His being *havis* is spoken of.

Merely when remembered, He destroys samsāra or sins of men (harati). So. *Hariḥ*.

Because of His yellow coloured garb (*pītāmbara*) He is *Hariḥ*. (By the reflection of the *pītāmbara*, He is yellow-complexioned. *vide* Vyasa's words: *harāmyagham ca smartṛṇām havirbhāgam kratuṣvaham / varnasca me harirveti tasmāt haviraham smṛtaḥ / /* : 'I destroy the sins of those who remember Me. I also receive oblations in sacrifices. My complexion also is yellow. So I am named Hari'. (M. Bh. Santi. 352.3).

सर्वलक्षणलक्षण्य: SARVALAKṢANALAKṢAṆYAḤ: Jñāna obtained by all pramāṇas (canons of proofs) is *sarva lakṣanaḥ*. He who is indicated by it is *Sarvalakṣaṇalakṣaṇyaḥ*. He is the transcendental Truth.

लक्ष्मीवान् LAKṢMĪVAN: The Goddess Laksmī resides in His chest permanently. So *Lakṣmīvan*.

समितिंजय: SAMITIMJAYAḤ: He conquers war or *samiti* (i.e. victorious in war).

विक्षरो लोहितो मार्गो हेतुर्दामोदरः सहः ।
महीधरो महाभागो वेगवानमिताशनः ॥ ५३ ॥

Vikṣaraḥ Rohitaḥ Mārgaḥ Hetuḥ Damodaraḥ Sahaḥ
Mahīdharaḥ Mahābhāgaḥ Vegavāṇ Amitāśanaḥ 53

विक्षर: VIKṢARAḤ: *kṣara* or *nāśa*, destruction for Whom does not exist. Undying.

रोहितः: ROHITAḤ: He who by His own accord assumes the red hue or the form of the fish (whose fins are red).

मार्गः: MĀRGAḤ: The seekers of salvation seek that Divinity (*mārgayanti*). So Mārgah.

Or 2. He by (on account of) Whom the supreme bliss is obtained, He is *Mārgaḥ*.

हेतुः: HETUḤ: He is Himself the material cause and the instrumental cause (*hetu*) (of the world). So *Hetuḥ*.

दामोदरः: DĀMODARAḤ: He is attained by superior (udāra, utkrṣta) disciplines of *dama* etc., Hence, *Dāmodara, vide* the M. Bh. (Udy. Par. 69-8) *damāddāmodaram viduḥ:* He is known as Dāmodara as He is attained by dama (self-control) etc.

Or 2. Because He was bound with a rope by Yasoda in the waist. *vide* Brahma Purāṇa (18.42) *tayormadhyagatam baddham dāmna gāḍham tayodare / tatasca dāmodaratām sa yayau dāmabandhanāt:* 'She (Yasodā) bound Him with a rope betwixt them (the two trees). He became *Dāmodara* due to binding with a rope (*dāma*).

Or 3. He is *Dāmodara* by the words of Vyāsa, *dāma* means worlds; He in whose belly are the worlds is *Dāmodara. dāmānilokanāmāni tāniyasyodarāntare ena damodaro devaḥ.*

सहः: SAHAḤ: He excels or forgives all. So *Sahaḥ*.

महीधरः: MAHĪDHARAḤ: He supports the earth in the form of mountain (*mahī*: earth *dharati*: supports). *vide* the Viṣṇu Purāṇa (2-12.38) *vanāni viṣṇuh girayo diśasca* 'the forests are Viṣṇu, also the mountains and directions.'

महाभाग: MAHĀBHĀGAḤ: 1. Assuming a body of His own free will, He eats excellent food which is His portion as havirbhāgaḥ.

Or 2. Great fortune arises as a result of His incarnations.

वेगवान् : VEGAVĀN: *Vega* means speed. He who has it is Vegavān: Speedy. *vide anejadekam manaso javīyaḥ;* the unmoving, which is swifter than the mind (Īś.Up.4).

अमिताशन: AMTĀŚANAḤ: He eats the (entire) universe during samhāra (general destruction). So, *amita* (not within limits) *aśanaḥ*: eater.

उद्भवः क्षोभणो देवः श्रीगर्भः परमेश्वरः ।
करणं कारणं कर्ता विकर्ता गहनो गुहः ।। ५४ ।।

Udbhavaḥ Kṣobhaṇaḥ Devaḥ Śrīgarbhaḥ
Parameśvaraḥ /
Karaṇam Kāraṇam Kartā Vikartā Gahanaḥ
Guhaḥ // 54

उद्भव: UDBHAVAḤ: 1. As He is the material cause of the origination *(utpatti)* of the universe, He is *Udbhavaḥ.*

Or 2. Because He is free (udgataḥ) from *bhava* samsāra.

क्षोभण : KṢOBHAṆAḤ: At the time of creation, entering into Prakṛti and Puruṣa, He agitated them (to movement). So, He is *Kṣobhaṇaḥ* (*Kṣobhaṇa* is agitation, curdling). The Viṣṇu Purāṇa (1.2.29) says: *prakrtim puruṣam caiva praviśya ātmeccayā hariḥ / kṣobhayāmāsa bhagavān sargakāle vyayāvyayau / /* 'Bhagvān Hari, entering Prakrti and Purusa at the time of creation, agitated the perishable (Prakrti) and the imperishable (Purusa).

देवः DEVAḤ: Because He sports by creation, etc. or wishes to conquer the celestials and others, or functions in all beings, shines as their ātman, is praised by those given to praise, goes everywhere, so *Devaḥ. vide* the mantra: *eko devah*: there is only one Deva. (Sve. Up. 6.11).

श्रीगर्भः ŚRĪGARBHAḤ: *Śrī* or splendour exists in His womb, in the stomach as the world. So, He is *Śrīgarbhaḥ.*

परमेश्वरः PARMEŚVARAḤ: He is supreme and is able to control or rule (over everything). So, He is *Parameśvaraḥ. vide* the Lord's statement: *samam sarvabhūteṣu tiṣṭhantam parameśvaraṁ*: 'Parameśvara who is the same in all beings.' (B.G.13.17).

करणम् KARAṆAM: The most extraordinary cause for the origination of the world. (*asādhāraṇakāraṇam karaṇam*).

कारणम् KĀRAṆAM: He is both the material and the instrumental cause (of the universe).

कर्ता KARTĀ: The Independent (doer).

विकर्ता VIKARTĀ: The creator of the varied universe. He is the Lord Viṣṇu Himself.

गहनः GAHANAḤ: It is not possible to know His form, His capacity or actions. So, He is *Gahanaḥ:* inscrutable.

गुहः GUHAḤ: He conceals *(gūhate)* His real form by His māyā. So *Guhaḥ.*

व्यवसायो व्यवस्थानः संस्थानः स्थानदो ध्रुवः ।
परर्द्धिः परमः स्पष्टस्तुष्टः पुष्टः शुभेक्षणः ।। ५५ ।।

Vyavasāyaḥ Vyavasthānaḥ Samsthānaḥ
Sthāndaḥ Dhruvaḥ /
Pararddiḥ Paramaspaṣṭaḥ Tuṣṭaḥ Puṣṭaḥ
Subhekṣanaḥ / / 55

व्यवसाय: VYAVASĀYAḤ: As He is of the nature of jñāna (samvit) pure and simple, He is *Vyavasāyaḥ* (c. f. *vyavasāyātmikā buddiḥ* in the B. G.).

व्यवस्थानम: VYAVASTHĀNAḤ: 1. Everything is based on Him. So, *Vyavasthānaḥ.*

Or 2. The regulator of the guardians of the Worlds and their appropriate duties and those who are born of wombs, born from eggs, born cleaving the earth; of the Brāhmaṇa, Kṣatriya, Vaiśya and Sūdra castes and of the intermediate castes, of the Brahmacarya, Gṛhastha, Vānaprasta and Sanyāsa aśramas.

संस्थान: SAMSTHĀNAḤ: 1. Here is the resting place of creatures in the form of praḷaya (deluge).

Or 2. His abode is excellent. So, *Samasthānaḥ. samīcīnam sthānam.*

स्थानद: STHĀNADAḤ: He confers on Dhruva and others their place *(sthāna)* according to their karmas. So *Sthānadaḥ.*

ध्रुव: DHRUVAH: As He is imperishable, He is *Dhruvaḥ.*

परार्द्ध: PARARDHIḤ: He has supreme *ṛddhi* or magnificence.

परमस्पष्ट: PARAMASPAṢṬAḤ: 1. His is supreme splendour. So, Paramaḥ.

As supremely eminent being not dependent on another or as clear of the nature of *samvid* (intelligence), spaṣṭaḥ. So, *Paramaspaṣṭaḥ.*

तुष्टः TUṢTAḤ: Being solely of the nature of absolute bliss, *Tuṣṭaḥ.*

पुष्टः PUṢTAḤ: As He is full of everything, He is *Puṣṭaḥ.*

शुभेक्षणः SUBHEKṢANAḤ: He whose *īkṣaṇam,* look is *subham* auspicioūs, conferring salvation on those who seek it, enjoyment on those who aspire for it, dispelling all doubts, purifying sinners, breaking all knots of the heart, burning away all karmas and rooting out avidyā. Hence, He is *Subekṣanaḥ. vide* the śruti beginning with *bhidyate hṛdayagranthiḥ:* 'the knot of the heart is broken' (Mund.Up.2.8).

रामो विरामो विरजो मार्गो नेयो नयोऽनयः ।
वीरः शक्तिमतां श्रेष्ठो धर्मो धर्मविदुत्तमः ।। ५६ ।।

Rāmaḥ Virāmaḥ Virataḥ Mārgaḥ Neyaḥ
Nayaḥ Anayaḥ /
Vīraḥ Śaktimatām Śreṣṭhaḥ Dharmaḥ
Dharmaviduttamaḥ / / 56

रामः RĀMAḤ: 1. The yogis delight in beholding or contemplation of Him who is characterised by permanent bliss (*nityānanda*). So *Rāmaḥ.* The Pādma Purāṇa says: *ramante yoginoyasmin nityānande cidātmani / iti rāmapadanaitatparam brahma abhidhīyate / /* 'Brahman is indicated by the word Rāma to show that yogis revel in permanent bliss of *cidātman,* the ātman which is pure consciousness.'

Or 2. As Rāma, the son of Dasratha, of His own free will assumed a handsome figure.

विरामः VIRĀMAH: There is cessation (*virāma*)

of samsāra (characterised by repeated birth and death) for creatures in (when they attain) Him.

विरतः VIRATAḤ: The attachment (*rata*) to sense pleasures vanishes for Him. So, *Viratah*.

मार्गः MĀRGAḤ: He by knowing Whom yogis Who aspire for salvation are considered to have attained immortality is the Way (to immortality). So *Mārgaḥ*. *vide* the śruti: *nanyaḥ panthā vidyate'yanāya:* 'There is no other path to immortality.' (Svet.Up.6.15).

नेयः NEYAḤ: By right knowledge the jīva is led to being of the nature of identity with the Paramātman.

नयः NAYAḤ: He who leads is *Nayaḥ*.

The Lord is referred to in three ways as Mārgaḥ, Neyaḥ and Nayaḥ. He is the Way, the Goal and He who leads to it.

अनयः ANAYAḤ: There is no leader for Him. So *Anayaḥ*.

Thus has the fourth hundred of the Names has been explained.

वीरः VĪRAḤ: Being valorous, He is *Vīraḥ*.

शक्तिमतां श्रेष्टः SAKTIMATAM ŚREṢTHAḤ: More powerful than (powerful gods like) Brahma etc.

धर्मः DHARMAḤ: 1. He supports all beings. So, *Dharmaḥ*. *vide* the śruti: *aṇureṣa dharmaḥ:* 'this dharma is subtle' (Kaṭha. Up.1.21).

Or 2. He is worshipped by dharmas. So, *Dharmaḥ*.

धर्मविदुत्तमः DHARMAVIDUTTAMAḤ: He Whose commands are the śrutis and smṛtis is alone the greatest of those who know dharmas. Hence *Dharmaviduttamaḥ*.

वैकुण्ठः पुरुषः प्राणः प्राणदः प्रणवः पृथुः ।
हिरण्यगर्भः शत्रुघ्नो व्याप्तो वायुरधोक्षजः ॥ ५७ ॥

Vaikuṇṭhaḥ Puruṣaḥ Prāṇaḥ Prāṇadaḥ
Praṇavaḥ Pṛtuḥ /
Hiraṇyagarbhaḥ Satrughnaḥ Vyāptaḥ Vāyuḥ
Adhokṣajaḥ / / 57

वैकुंठः VAIKUṆTHAḤ: *Kuṇṭhaḥ* means path. The obstruction of paths (natural inclinations) is *Vikuṇṭha.* He who causes *Vikuṇṭha* is *Vaikuṇṭaḥ.* At the start of the universe, He united the elements (pancabhūtas) which, scattered, had a tendency to fly off at random) and obstructed their (independent) movement. So, He is called *Vaikuṇṭhaḥ.* The Sānti Parva of Mahā bhārata (343-351) says: *mayā samśleśitā bhūmiḥ adbhiḥ vyoma ca vāyuna / vāyusca tejasā sārdham vaikuṇṭhatvam tato mama //* : 'By Me was the earth united with the waters, the ether with air and air with fire. Hence being Vaikuṇṭha (the Name Vaikuṇṭha) pertained to me.'

पुरुष: PURUṢAḤ: 1. As He was before all.

Or 2. As He destroys all sins, He is *Puruṣah. vide* the śruti *sa yat purvo'smat sarvan pāpmana auṣat tasmāt puruṣaḥ*: 'because He is the first of all this and consumed all sins.' (Brh.Up.3.4.1).

Or 3. He resides in the city (of the body) *puri śayanāt. vide* the śruti: *sa vā ayam puruṣaḥ sarvāsu pūrṣu puri śayaḥ* 'He is called Puruṣa who resides in all bodies.' (Bṛh.Up.4.5.18).

प्राण: PRĀṆAḤ: 1. As kṣetrajña He breathes.

Or 2. assuming the form of prāṇa (breath) He makes the organs and limbs of the body function. In the Viṣṇu Purāṇa, it is said: *cestām karoti śvasanasvarūpī.* "In the form of breath, He acts".

प्राणद: PRĀṆADAḤ: At the time of praḷaya He

cuts off the prāṇas of living beings (*da* is used in the sense of cutting).

प्रणव: PRAṆAVAḤ: 1. Is praised, So *Praṇavah. vide* the śruti: *tasmāt omiti praṇauti.* "So He is praised by the sound Om'.

Or 2. He is made obeisance to (from *nam* to bow). Sanatkumāra said: *praṇamantīha yam vedāh tasmāt praṇava ucyate:* 'As the Vedas make obeisance to Him, He is said to be *Praṇava'.*

पृथु: PṚTHUḤ: As He is expanded as the universe, He is *Pṛthuḥ.*

हिरण्यगर्भ: HIRAṆYAGARBHAḤ: The golden egg *(hiraṇyamayam aṇdam)* which was the cause of the birth of Hiraṇyagarbha arose from His vital power, that was in His womb. So, *Hiraṇyagarbhaḥ.*

शत्रुघ्न: SATRUGHNAḤ: He kills the enemies of the devas, *tridaśas,* who have only three stages of life (childhood, boyhood and eternal youth, as they are not subject to old age and death).

व्याप्त: VYĀPTAḤ: One who permeates all effects as their cause.

वायु: VĀYUḤ: Blows, carries the smell. The Lord said: *puṇyogandhaḥ pṛthivyām ca* 'I am the agreeable (auspicious) odour on the earth.' (B.G.7.9).

अधोक्षज: ADHOKṢAJAḤ: 1. He who does not decline. *vide* the Udyoga Parva (69-10). *adho na kṣīyate jātu yasmāt tasmāt adhokṣajaḥ*: 'As He does not ever decline, He is Adokṣajaḥ.' *(adhaḥ na kṣīyate).*

Or 2. *adhaḥ* down, stands for the earth, *akṣam* is the sky. *ja* is to be born. He who incarnated as the Virāt Puruṣa extending from the earth to the sky is *Adhokṣajaḥ.*

Or 3. Knowledge of Him arises only when the sense organs which go down (outward) are turned inward. Hence, He is said to be *Adhokṣajaḥ*. *adhobhute hyakṣagaṇe pratygarūpapravāhite / jāyate tasya vai jñānam tena adokṣajaḥ ucyate / /*

ऋतुः सुदर्शनः कालः परमेष्ठी परिग्रहः ।
उग्रः संवत्सरो दक्षो विश्रामो विश्वदक्षिणः ॥ ५८ ॥

Ṛtuḥ Sudarśanaḥ Kālaḥ Parameṣṭhī Parigrahaḥ /
Ugraḥ Samvatsaraḥ Dakṣaḥ Viśrāmaḥ
Viśvadakṣiṇaḥ / / 58

ऋतु: ṚTUḤ: In His aspect of Time, He is signified by the word *ṛtu* (season) So *Ṛtuḥ*.

सुदर्शन: SUDARŚANAḤ: 1. *Darśaṇa*, knowledge of Him leads to the auspicious fruit of liberation. So, He is *Sudarśanaḥ*.

Or 2. His *darśana*, eyes are *sobhana*, auspicious and are like lotus petals.

Or 3. He is seen (realised) easily by devotees. So, *Sudarśanaḥ*.

काल: KĀLAḤ: He counts (*kalayati*) everything (to determine their duration of life). Hence *Kālaḥ*, *vide* the Lord's statement: *kālah kalayatām aham*: 'I am the Kāla (Time) of those who count.' (B.G. 10.30).

परमेष्ठी PARAMEṢṬHĪ: He resides in His own eminence in the hṛdayakāsa the supreme ether of the heart. So, *Parameṣṭhī* (*parama* is supreme; *is* from *sthā* to reside) *vide* the mantra: *parameṣṭhī vibhrājate.* 'The Parameṣthī shines'. (Āpastamba Dharma Sūtra 1.23.2).

परिग्रह: PARIGRAHAḤ: (*Paritaḥ gṛhyate*). 1. He is grasped on all sides by those who take refuge in Him.

Or 2. as He is omnipresent, He is grasped by the mind on all sides.

Or 3. He receives the leaf, flower, etc. (fruit and water) offered by His devotees (*parigrinhāti*). So, *Parigrahaḥ*.

उग्र: UGRAḤ: As He causes fear to the Sun and others. *vide* the śruti: *bhīṣodeti sūryaḥ;* by fear of Him the Sun rises (Tait. Up. 2.7).

संवत्सर: SAMVATSARAḤ: All beings reside in Him (*samvasanti*), therefore *Samvatsaraḥ*.

दक्ष: DAKṢAḤ: 1. As He grows in the form of the universe or because He does all actions quickly, He is *Dakṣaḥ*.

विश्राम: VIŚRĀMAḤ: For those who are entangled in the ocean of samsāra containing the six waves of hunger, thirst, etc., caught up by the great griefs of avidyā etc., and the small griefs like pride etc., and long for rest, He gives rest and release. So *Viśrāmaḥ*.

विश्वदक्षिण: VIŚVADAKṢIṆAḤ: 1. More powerful (dakṣiṇaḥ) than all or skilful in all actions. So, *Viśvadakṣiṇaḥ*.

विस्तारः स्थावरः स्थाणुः प्रमाणं बीजमव्ययम् ।
अर्थोऽनर्थो महाकोशो महाभोगो महाधनः ॥ ५९ ॥

Vistāraḥ Sthāvaraḥ Sthāṇuḥ Pramāṇam
Bhījamavyayam /
Arthaḥ Anarthaḥ Mahākośaḥ Mahābhogaḥ
Mahādhanaḥ / / 59

विस्तार: VISTĀRAḤ: He in whom all worlds are expanded (*vistīryante*). So *Vistāraḥ*.

स्थावरस्थाणु: STHĀVARASTHĀṆUḤ: Being firm, He is *Sthāvaraḥ*. Firm objects like the earth etc., rest in Him. So, *Sthāṇuḥ* (motionless). He is *sthāvara* and *sthāṇuḥ,* firm and motionless. So, He is *Sthavarasthāṇuḥ.*

प्रमाणम् PRAMĀṆAM: He is of the nature of knowledge acquired by proof. So, He is *Pramāṇam.*

बीजमव्ययम् BĪJAMAVYAYAM: Unchanging cause (*bījam*: cause, *avyayam*: not changing, immutable). So, *Bījamavyayam.* This is a Name with an adjective.

अर्थः ARTHAḤ: Being of the nature of bliss, He is yearned after (*arthyate*) by all. Hence *Arthaḥ.*

अनर्थः ANARTHAḤ: He has nothing to seek. Being of fulfilled desire, He has nothing to desire. So, *Anarthaḥ.*

महाकोशः MAHĀKOŚAḤ: His coverings of *annamaya* and the rest (material sheaths etc.) are big. So, *Mahākośaḥ.*

महाभोगः MAHĀBHOGAḤ: His blissful form is great. So, *Mahābhogaḥ.*

महाधनः MAHĀDHANAḤ: His wealth which is the means to enjoyment is immense. Hence *Mahādhanaḥ.*

अनिर्विण्णः स्थविष्ठोऽभूर्धर्मयूपो महामखः ।
नक्षत्रनेमिर्नक्षत्री क्षमः क्षामः समीहनः ॥ ६० ॥

Anirvinnaḥ Sthaviṣṭhaḥ Abūh Dharmayūpaḥ
Mahāmakhaḥ /
Nakṣatranemiḥ Nakṣatrī Kṣamaḥ Ksāmaḥ
Samīhanaḥ // 60

अनिर्वण्णः ANIRVĪṆṆAḤ: Being of fulfilled desires, He has no regrets. So, *Anirviṇṇaḥ* (*nirveda* is regret).

स्थविष्ठः STHAVIṢṬHAḤ: He stands in the form of Virāt. *vide* the śruti. *agnirmūrdha cakṣuṣī candra-*

sūryau: 'The fire is His head, sun, and moon His eyes'. (Muṇd. Up. 1.4).

अभूः ABHŪḤ: 1. Unborn.

Or 2. *Bhū* in the sense of firm existence, Who exists in the last resort; *vide* the Sūtra *bhū sattayām.*

Or 3. The earth.

धर्मयूपः DHARMYŪPAḤ: As the animal which is tied to the sacrificial post, the dharmas that will please Him are tied on Him. So, *Dharmayūpah.*

महामखः MAHĀMAKHAḤ: The sacrifices offered to whom lead to liberation and so, are great. So *Mahāmakhaḥ* (*makha* is sacrifice).

नक्षत्रनेमिः NAKSATRANEMIḤ: It is said, 'the planets, the sun, the moon etc. the stars fixed (*nakṣatras*) and moving (*tāras*) are bound to Druva by the bonds of Vāyu'. Druva governs the motions of the celestial bodies and resides at the tail of the Śimśumāra. At the heart of the wheel is Viṣṇu like a nave regulating them all. The Svādhyāya Brāhmaṇa describes the śimśumāra and says: *Viṣṇorhṛdayam* 'Viṣṇu is the heart'. (Taitt. Āraṇyaka 2.19). Viṣṇu is the *nemi* or nave of the nakṣatras. So, *Nakṣatranemi.*

नक्षत्री NAKṢATRĪ: In the form of the moon, He is *Nakṣatrī. vide* the Lord's statement: *nakṣatrāṇām aham śāsī*: Among the stars I am the moon. (B.G. 10.21).

क्षमः KṢAMAḤ: 1. Expert in all actions. So *Kṣamaḥ.*

Or 2. He forgives, So *Kṣamaḥ. vide* Vālmīki (on Rāma) *kṣamayā pṛthvī samaḥ*: in forgiveness like the earth'.

क्षामः KṢĀMAḤ: When all modifications subside, He remains as the true Self.

समीहनः SAMĪHANAḤ: He desires (purposes) well in acts like creation, etc.

यज्ञ इज्यो महेज्यश्च क्रतुः सत्रं सतां गतिः ।
सर्वदर्शी विमुक्तात्मा सर्वज्ञो ज्ञानमुत्तमम् ॥ ६२ ॥

Yajñaḥ Ijyaḥ Mahejyaḥ ca Kratuḥ Satram
Satāmgatiḥ /
Sarvadarśī Vimuktātmā Sarvajñaḥ
Jñānamuttamam // 61

यज्ञः YAJÑAḤ: 1. As He is in the form of all sacrifices (*yajñas*), so, *Yajñaḥ.*

Or 2. By His form as sacrifice, He is the producer of happiness to all devas. *vide* the śruti: *yajñovai viṣṇuḥ:* 'the yajñā indeed is Viṣṇu' (Taitt. Sam. 2.5.5).

इज्यः IJYAḤ: He himself is to be worshipped by the sacrifice. *vide* the Harivamśa: *ye yajanti makhaiḥ puṇyaiḥ devatādīn pitṛn api / ātmānam atmanā nityam viṣṇumeva yajanti te //* : Those who worship the gods and their ancestors by holy sacrifices, worship Viṣṇu as the Self through the self.

महेज्यः MAHEJYAḤ: Of all devas, He is to be specially worshipped as bestowing liberation. So, *Mahejyaḥ.*

क्रतुः KRATUḤ: The sacrifice associated with a post.

सत्रम् SATRAM: 1. The sacrifice in which the command for the coming together of the learned is given.

Or 2. He protects good people (*sat* good and *tra* to protect).

सतांगतिः SATĀMGATIḤ: There is no other refuge but He for seekers of liberation (*satām: mumuksūṇām:* for those who desire mokṣa).

सर्वदर्शी SARVADARŚĪ: By His native intelligence, He sees what is done and not done by all creatures.

विमुक्तात्मा VIMUKTĀTMĀ: 1. By nature He is *vimuktaḥ*, liberated.

Or 2. He is both liberated and ātmā. *vide* the śruti: *vimuktasca vimucyate* (Kaṭh. Up. 2.2.1).

सर्वज्ञः SARVAJÑAḤ: He is the all (*sarvam*) and the knower (jñāḥ). So. *Sarvajñaḥ*. *vide* the śruti: *idam sarvam yadayam ātmā*: All this is the ātmā (Bṛh. Up. 2.4.6).

ज्ञानमुत्तमम् JÑĀNAMUTTAMAM: This is a Name with an adjective. He is jñānam (knowledge), the most superior, unproduced (because ever existent), unlimited and which is most efficacious for all. That Jñānamuttamam is Brahma *vide* the śruti: *satyam jñānam anantam brahma*. Brahman is Truth, Knowledge and Infinite (Taitt. Up. 2.1).

सुव्रतः सुमुखः सूक्ष्मः सुघोषः सुखदः सुहृत् ।
मनोहरो जितक्रोधो वीरबाहुर्विदारणः ।। ६२ ।।

Suvrataḥ Sumukhaḥ Sūkṣmaḥ Sughoṣaḥ
Sukhadaḥ Suhṛt /
Manoharaḥ Jitakrodhaḥ Vīrabāhuḥ
Vidāraṇaḥ // 62

सुव्रतः SUVRATAḤ: His vrata (vow) is sobhanam (auspicious). In the Rāmāyaṇa, Rama said: *sakṛdeva prapannāya tavāsmīti ca yācate / abhayam sarvathā tasmai dadāmyetad vratam mama / /*: "To him who takes refuge in Me but once imploring 'I am Thine', I give freedom from fear in all ways. This is My vow". (Rāmāyaṇa 6.18.33).

सुमुखः SUMUKHAḤ: 1. His countenance is handsome. In the Viṣṇu Purāṇa it is said: *prasanna vadanam cāru padmapatrāyatekṣaṇam*: 'His face is pleasing and beautiful with large eyes resembling the lotus leaf'. (6.7).

In the Rāmāyaṇa, it is said:—

"The Śrīmān hearing His father's behest with a cheerful mind, agreed to it with the following words. 'I shall abide by your words sporting in the great forest for nine and five years'. There was no agitation in the mind of Rāma who was superior to all men when he was to be exiled to the forest relinquishing His kingdom."

Or 2. He is Sumukha as He was satisfied having taught all Vidyas (arts and sciences). *vide* the śruti: *yo'brahmānam vidhadāti pūrvam yo vai vedāmsca prahinoti tasmai*: 'Who created Brahma at first and instructed Him in the Vedas.' (Sve. Up. 6.18).

सूक्ष्मः SŪKṢMAḤ: Subtle being free from physical causes like sound. Sound etc., are the gross cause of ākāśa and the rest successively. *vide* the śruti: *sarvagatam sūkṣmam*: 'omnipresent and subtle'. (Muṇ. Up. 1.6).

सुघोषः SUGHOṢAḤ: 1. His loud voice constituting the Vedas is auspicious.

Or 2. Because His loud voice is thundering like the cloud, He is *Sughoṣaḥ*.

सुखदः SUKHADAḤ: 1. He endows righteous people with happiness (*sukham dadāti*).

Or 2. He destroys the happiness of unrighteous people (*dyati khaṇdayati*, cuts off, destroys). *sukham dyati*.

सुहृत् SUHṚT: As He benefits men without expecting a recompense, He is *Suhṛt*.

मनोहर: MANOHARAḤ: He attracts or sways the mind as He is compacted of extraordinary bliss. So *Manoharaḥ. vide* the sruti: *yo vai bhūmā tat sukham nālpe sukhamasti*: 'That which is big is bliss; there is no joy in the small'. (Chānd. Up. 7.23.1).

जितक्रोध: JITAKRODHAḤ: He by whom anger has been conquered. He kills the enemies of the devas to establish the Vedic way, but not swayed by anger.

वीरबाहु: VĪRABĀHUḤ: Killing the foes of the *tridaśas* (devas), establishing the Vedic way, His arm is powerful. So *Vīrabāhuḥ*.

विदारण: VIDĀRAṆAḤ: He destroys (*vidārayati*) unrighteous men. Hence *Vidāraṇaḥ*.

स्वापनः स्ववशो व्यापी नैकात्मा नैककर्मकृत् ।
वत्सरो वत्सलो वत्सी रत्नगर्भो धनेश्वरः ।। ६३ ।।

Svāpanaḥ Svavaśaḥ Vyāpī Naikātmā
Naikakarmakṛt /
Vatsaraḥ Vatsalaḥ Vatsī Ratnagarbhaḥ
Dhaneśvaraḥ // 63

स्वापन: SVĀPANAḤ: By His māyā, He renders men oblivious of their nature, of their Ātmajñana.

स्ववश: SVAVAŚAḤ: Independent as He originates, preserves and destroys the Universe Himself (without extraneous aid).

व्यापी VYAPĪ: 1. As He is omnipresent like the ether. *vide* the śruti. *ākāśavat sarvagatasca nityaḥ*: 'like ether being everywhere and eternal'.

Or 2. As He pervades all effects as their cause, so, He is *Vyāpī*.

नैकात्मा NAIKĀTMĀ: He is in various forms in the different manifestations of His instrumental powers. So *Naikātmā* (*na ekātmā:* not of one form).

नैककर्मकृत् NAIKAKARMAKṚT: He does many actions like *utpatti, sampatti* and *vipatti*, creation, preservation and dissolution of the worlds. (*na ekakarmakṛt*).

वत्सरः VATSARAḤ: Everything lives here, *vasati atra akhilam.* So *Vatsaraḥ.*

वत्सलः VATSALAḤ: As He is dear to His devotees, He is *Vatsalaḥ.*

वत्सी VATSĪ: 1. As He is the protector of the calves (*vatsas*). He is *Vatsalaḥ* (*vatsa*: calf).

Or 2. Because in His aspect as the father of the world, all are His children. (*vatsa*: child).

रत्नगर्भः RATNAGARBHAḤ: As gems are in its bottom (womb), the ocean is known as *ratnagarbhaḥ*. He is of the form of the ocean.

धनेश्वरः DHANEŚVARAḤ: He is the Lord of wealth (*danānām iśvaraḥ*).

धर्मगुब्धर्मकृद्धर्मी सदसत्क्षरमक्षरम् ।
अविज्ञाता सहस्रांशुर्विधाता कृतलक्षणः ॥ ६४ ॥

Dharmagup Dharmakṛt Dharmī Sat Asat Kṣaram Akṣaram /
Avijñātā Sahasramśuḥ Vidhātā Kṛtalakṣaṇaḥ / / 64

धर्मगुप् DHARMAGUP: He safeguards Dharma (*dharmam gopayati*). So *Dharmagup. vide* the Lord's statement: *Dharmasamsthāpanārthāya sambhavāmi yuge yuge*: 'To establish dharma I incarnate in age after age'. (B.G. 4.8).

धर्मकृत् DHARMAKṚT: Though He transcends the distinction of dharma and adharma, He does only righteous deeds for establishment of Dharma. So *Dharmakṛt.*

धर्मी DHARMĪ: Supports dharma. Hence *Dharmī.*

सत SAT: He is the true supreme Brahman (which truly exists), *vide* the śruti: *sadeva saumya idam agra āsīt:* 'Existence alone, dear one, was in the beginning.' (Chānd. Up.6.2).

असत् ASAT: The lower Brahman (conditioned, which is not true in the ultimate pāramārthic sense). So, *Asat. vide* the śruti: *vācārambhaṇam vikaro namadheyam:* 'All modifications of the Sat are only names, a way of speaking.' (Ch.Up.6.6.14).

क्षरम् KṢARAM: All beings.

अक्षरम् AKṢARAM: *Kūtasṭhaḥ* (the inner unchanging soul) *vide* the Lord's statement: *dvāvimau pururuṣau loke kṣarasca akṣara eva ca / kṣaraḥ sarvāṇi bhūtāni kūtasṭho' kṣara ucyate / /* 'There are two puruṣas in the world, the perishable and the imperishable. All beings are the perishables, the kūṭasṭha is called the imperishable' (B.G.15.16).

अविज्ञाता AVIJÑĀTĀ: The jīva is the knower *vijñātā* limited by the false idea like doership etc., which do not pertain to the ātman. He who is different from the jīva is *Avijñātā,* Viṣṇu.

सहस्रांशु: SAHASRĀMŚUḤ: The rays of the sun and other luminaries are truly His. So He is the chief Sahasrāmsuḥ *vide* the śruti: *yena sūryastapati tejaseddah:* 'Kindled by whom the sun scorches,' and the smṛti: *yadādityagatam tejah:* 'that brilliance which is in the sun' (B.G. 15.12). —

विधाता VIDHĀTĀ: He specially supports Ādiśeṣa, the diggajas the elephants in the cardinal directions, the mountains which support all other things. (*vi, viśeṣeṇa dhāta* is *vidhātā*).

कृतलक्षण: KṚTALAKṢAṆAḤ: 1. He is the eternal plenal consciousness, caitanya.

Or 2. By Him have been created the lakṣaṇas, namely the saśtras. Later in this work it will be said: *vedāh sāśtrāṇi vijñānam etat sarvam janārdanāt:* 'The Vedas sāśtras, wisdom all are from Janārdana.'

Or 3. The distinctions of like kind, of different kind of all things have been made by Him.

Or 4. The mark (lakṣaṇa) of śrīvatsa that is His has been made by Him. Therefore, *Kṛtalakṣaṇaḥ.*

गभस्तनेमिः मत्त्वस्थः सिहो भूतमहेश्वरः ।
आदिदेवो महादेवो देवेशो देवभृद्गुरुः ।। ६५ ।।

Gabhastinemiḥ Sattvasṭhaḥ
Simhaḥ Bhūtamaheśvaraḥ /
Ādidevaḥ Mahādevaḥ
Deveśaḥ Devabhṛtguruḥ / / 65

गभस्तिनेमि: GABHASTINEMIḤ: He is in the middle of the planetary constellation called *Gabhasticakra.*

सत्त्वस्थ: SATTVASTHAḤ: 1. He eminently abides in the effulgence of the sattvaguṇa.

Or 2. He abides in all creatures. So *Sattvasṭhaḥ.*

सिहः SIMHAḤ: 1. Being valorous, He is like a lion.

Or 2. By omission of the prefix *Nara* like Satyabhāma being called Bhāma, He (who is Narasimha). is *Simhaḥ.*

भूतमहेश्वर: BHŪTAMAHEŚVARAḤ: 1. The great Lord of all beings.

Or 2. *Bhūtena,* i.e., satyena, in truth, He is supreme Lord (*mahān īśvaraḥ*) So, *Bhūtamaheśvaraḥ.*

आदिदेव: ĀDIDEVAḤ: 1. All beings are drawn to

Himself (as their origin), *ādīyante.* So *ādiḥ*; *ādi* and *devaḥ* is *Ādidevaḥ*.

महादेव: MAHĀDEVAḤ: Abandoning all concepts, He glories in the great wealth of ātmajñāna, yoga and aiśvarya. Therefore, He is said to be *Mahādevaḥ*.

देवेश: DEVEŚAḤ: Especially the Lord of the devas.

देवभृत्गुरु: DEVABHṚTGURUḤ: 1. Sakra (Indra) is the protector of the devas. He who orders him too is *Devabhṛtguruḥ*.

Or 2. By protecting the devas or by swallowing (*nigaraṇa*) i.e., by mastery of all Vidyas, He is *Devabhṛtguruḥ*.

उत्तरो गोपतिर्गोप्ता ज्ञानगम्यः पुरातनः ।
शरीरभूतभृद्भोक्ता कपीन्द्रो भूरिदक्षिणः ॥ ६६ ॥

Uttaraḥ Gopatiḥ Goptā
Jñānagamyaḥ Purātanaḥ /
Śarīrabhūtabhṛt Bhoktā Kapīndraḥ
Bhūridakṣiṇaḥ / / 66

उत्तर: UTTARAḤ: 1. He uplifts or releases (men) from the bonds of birth and samsāra.

Or 2. Superior to all. *vide* the śruti. *viśvasmāt indra uttaraḥ*: 'He (Brahman or the Lord) is superior to the whole universe .' (Ṛg. Veda 10.86.1).

गोपति: GOPATIḤ: 1. From protecting cows, He is called Gopatiḥ who dons the garb of a *gopa* (cowherd).

Or 2. *go* means the earth. As He is its *pati* lord of the earth. He is *Gopatiḥ*.

गोप्ता GOPTĀ: Ruling over all creatures, He protects the world. So. *Goptā*.

ज्ञानगम्य: JÑĀNAGAMYAḤ: He is attained not by

karma, not by upāśana and karma, but only by jñāna. Hence *Jñānagamyaḥ*.

पुरातनः PURĀTANAḤ: As He is not limited by time, He exists even before. (There is no time when He is not, past, present or future) Hence *Purātanaḥ*.

शरीरभूतभृत ŚARĪRABHŪTABHṚT: He is in the form of prāṇa (vital breath) which sustains the elements which make up the body. So, *Śarīrabhutabhṛt*.

भोक्ता BHOKTĀ: 1. As He protects or 2. As He enjoys association with supreme bliss, He is *Bhoktā*.

Thus the fifth hundred of Names has been explained.

कपीन्द्रः KAPĪNDRAḤ: 1. *Kapi* means *Varāha; Indra* means superior; Kapīndra is the great Varāha (an incarnation of Viṣṇu).

Or 2. *Kapi* means monkey, lord of the monkeys, Śrī Rāghava.

भूरिदक्षिणः BHŪRIDAKṢIṆAḤ: *Bhūri* means much, abundant yajñadakṣiṇas obtain in Him who performs sacrifices to show (to the world) the proprieties of yagnās. So, He is *Bhūridakṣiṇaḥ*.

सोमपोऽमृतपः सोमः पुरुजित्पुरुसत्तमः ।
विनयो जयः सत्यसन्धो डशार्हः सात्वतां पतिः ।। ६७ ।।

Somapaḥ Amṛtapaḥ Somaḥ Purujit Purusattamaḥ /
Vinayaḥ Jayaḥ Satyasandaḥ Dāsārhaḥ
Sāttvatāmpatiḥ / / 67

सोमपः SOMAPAḤ: 1. He drinks Soma in all yajñās in the form of the god who is sacrificed to.

Or 2. In the form of the sacrificer (yajamāna) showing the proprieties of dharma. So, *Somapaḥ*.

अमृतपः AMṚTAPAḤ: 1. He drinks the nectar *(amṛtam)* of His own Self.

Or 2. rescuing the (pot of) amṛtam from the asuras

who attempted to carry it away, after making the devas drink it, He himself drank it. So, *Amṛtapaḥ*.

सोम: SOMAḤ: 1. He nourishes the plants in the form of the moon.

Or 2. Śiva in association with Uma (His consort) (Sa-Uma, Umayā saha is *Somaḥ*).

पुरुजित् PURUJIT: He conquers many (foes) *puru* means *bahu:* many, *jit* is conqueror. *Purujit* is the conqueror of many).

पुरुसत्तम: PURUSATTAMAḤ: Being of universal form *puru*; excellent, He is *sattamah*, superlatively good or existent. He is *puru* and *sattamaḥ* i.e., *Purusattamaḥ*.

विनय: VINAYAḤ: He punishes the evil-doers to humility (vinaya). So *Vinayaḥ*.

जय: JAYAH: He is victorious over all beings.

सत्यसन्ध: SATYASANDHAḤ: His resolves *sandhas* always come true. *vide* the śruti. *satyasamkalpah*: 'Of true resolve.' (Ch. Up. 8.1.5).

दासार्ह: DĀŚĀRAḤ: 1. *dāśa* is gift, *dānam*. He deserves gifts.

Or 2. Kṛṣṇa born in the Daśarha, yādava race.

सात्वतांपति: SĀTTVATĀMPATIḤ: The Lord and Protector of those who observe the Sāttvatantra, their yogakṣemakaraḥ: *yoga* is getting, *kṣema* is safeguarding).

जीवो विनयितासाक्षी मुकुन्दोऽमितविक्रमः ।
अम्भोनिधिरनन्तात्मा महोदधिशयोऽन्तकः ॥ ६८ ॥

Jīvaḥ Vinayitā Sākṣī Mukundaḥ
Amitavikramaḥ |
Ambhonidhiḥ Anantātmā Mahodadhiśayaḥ
Antakaḥ / / 68

जीवः JĪVAḤ: Supporting the Prāṇas in the form of Kṣetrajña, He is called *Jīva.*

विनयितासाक्षी VINAYITĀSAKṢĪ: 1. Humility (vinayitvam) is *Vinayitā.* He witnesses it directly in men. So, *Vinayitāsākṣī.*

Or 2. The form of the root *naya* expressing *gati*, going, is *Vinayitā;* He who leads (to Himself.)

Or *asākṣī*: *asākṣatdraṣṭā*: One who does not see anything different from the ātman.

मुकुन्दः MUKUNDAḤ: He gives mukti, confers salvation (*muktim dadāti*) So, Mukundaḥ. There is similarity of letters between *mukti* and *mukunda.* So according to Nirukta (lexicography) *Mukunda* means *muktim dadati;* confers mukti.

अमितविक्रमः AMITAVIKRAMAḤ: 1. Whose vikramas, three steps were *amitāḥ* unlimited (in Trivikrama incarnation).

Or, 2. Whose *vikrama* or valour is *amitam,* enormous.

अंभोनिधिः AMBHONIDHIḤ: 1. Ambhas, devas etc., are made to rest in Him. So, *Ambhonidhiḥ. vide* the Śruti: *tānivā etāni catvāri ambhāmsi.* They are the four ambhas, gods, men, fore-fathers (pitṛṣ) and assuras. (Taitt.Brah.2.2.8).

Or 2. The ocean. *vide* the Lord's declaration: *sarasām asmi sāgaraḥ*: Of reservoirs, I am the ocean. (B.G. 10.2.4).

अनन्तात्मा ANANTĀTMĀ: As He is unlimited by space, time or object, He is *Anantātmā.*

महोदधिशयः MAHODADHIŚAYAḤ: When having reduced all beings to their primal state and having converted the world to one expanse of water, He reclines in it, He is *Mahodadhiśayah.*

अन्तक: ANTAKAḤ: As He brings about the end of all beings (causes their death), He is Antakaḥ (*anta* is end).

अजो महार्हः स्वाभाव्यो जितामित्रः प्रमोदनः ।
आनन्दो नन्दनोनन्दः सत्यधर्मा त्रिविक्रमः ।। ६९ ।।

Ajaḥ Mahārhaḥ Svābhavyaḥ Jitāmitraḥ
Pramodanaḥ /
Ānandaḥ Nandanaḥ
Nandaḥ Satyadharmā Trivikramaḥ / / 69

अज: AJAH: Kamaḥ was born of *Ā,* आ that is Viṣṇu. So *a-jah,* born of *ā* आ that is Viṣṇu. Kāma was born of Viṣṇu i.e., He is of the form of Kāma (Manmaṭha).

महार्ह: MAHĀRHAḤ: *Mahaḥ* is puja, worship. He deserves it. So, *Mahārhaḥ.*

स्वाभव्य: SVĀBHĀVYAḤ: As He is eternal and self-existent, He is by nature such that He cannot be born (*svabhāvena abhāvyaḥ*). (*bhava* indicates birth).

जितामित्र: JITĀMITRAḤ: *Amitrāḥ:* Enemies; *jita:* overcome.. He has conquered the internal enemies of attachment, aversion etc., and the external enemies like Rāvaṇa, Kumbhakarṇa, Śiśupāla and others.

प्रमोदन: PRAMODANAḤ: 1. By drinking the nectar of His own Self (by contemplation of His own Ātmaṇ), He is *Prāmodanaḥ,* always pleased.

Or 2. He causes delight to contemplators merely as a result of their dyāna, thought of Him.

आनन्द: ĀNANDAḤ: Bliss. His form (nature) is *ānanda,* bliss. So *Anandaḥ. vide* the śruti *etasyaivānandasyānyāni bhūtāni mātrāmupajīvanti:* 'Of this ānanda, that of other beings is only a part.' (Bṛh.Up.4.3.32).

नन्दन: NANDANAḤ: He pleases (*nandayati*). So, *Nandanaḥ.*

नन्द: *NANDAḤ:* Rich with all things to be attained

Or अनन्द: ANANDAH. He is not subject to sense pleasure, *vide* the śruti: *yo vai bhūmā tatsukhaṁ nālpe sukhamasti:* 'What is great, that is felicity; there is no felicity in the small'. (Ch.Up.7.23).

सत्यधर्मा: SATYADHARMĀ: His dharma, jñāna etc., are true. So, *Satyadharmā.*

त्रिविक्रम: TRIVIKRAMAḤ: 1. He whose three steps encompassed the three worlds, *vide* the śruti: *trīṇi padā vicakrame:* 'He measured by three steps.'

Or 2. By whom the three worlds were measured. The Hari Vamśa says: *triritypeva trayo lokāh kīrtitā munisattamaiḥ / kramate tāṁstridhā sarvāṁstrivikram'osijanārdana //* : "The great munis said of You, O! Janārdana that You strode three steps. Therefore You are said to be Trivikrama."

महर्षिः कपिलाचार्यः कृतज्ञो मेदिनीपतिः ।
त्रिपदस्त्रिदशाध्यक्षो महाश्रृङ्गः कृतान्तकृत् ॥ ७० ॥

Maharṣiḥ Kapilācaryaḥ Kṛtajñāḥ Medinīpatiḥ /
Tripadaḥ Tridaśādyakṣaḥ
Mahāsṛṅgaḥ Kṛtāntakṛt / / 70

महर्षिकपिलाचार्य: MAHARṢIḤ KAPILĀCĀRYAH: This is one Name with an adjective. *mahān ṛṣiḥ* is *Maharṣiḥ*. He is great as he saw (with intuitive eye) the entire body of the Vedas. Others are only ordinary ṛṣis as they saw only a part of the Vedas. Kapila is also Ācārya as he is teacher of the knowledge of Sāmkhya which is also Truth. *vide* the Vyāsa Smṛti: *suddhātmā tattva vijñānanam sāmkhyam iti obhidhīyate*: 'the knowledge of the truth of the pure Ātman is called Sāmkhyam. ' Also the *śruti: ṛṣim prasūtam kapilam mahāntam*: 'He who endowed his son Ṛṣī Kapila' (Sve. Up. 5.2) and also B.G. (10.26): *siddhānām kapilomuniḥ*: 'Of perfect ones, I am the sage Kapila.'

कृतज्ञ: KṚTAJÑAḤ: *Kṛtam* is the effect, the world. *jñā* is the ātmā. He who is both the *kṛtam* and the *jñā* the world and its knower, the Ātman is *Kṛtajñaḥ*.

मेदिनीपति: MEDINĪPATIḤ: *Medinī*: earth, *patiḥ*: the Lord; the Lord of the earth.

त्रिपद: TRIPADAḤ: He has (placed) three steps. So, *Tripadaḥ. vide* the śruti. *trīṇi padā vicakrame*: 'He who measured by His three strides'. (Taitt Br.2.4.6).

त्रिदशाध्यक्ष: TRIDAŚĀDHYAKṢAḤ: By combination with guṇas (sattva, rajas and tamas) arise three states (of the mind, *jāgrat* (waking) and the rest (*svapna,* dream and *suṣupti,* dreamless sleep). Their witness is *Tridaśādhyakṣaḥ*.

महाश्रृङ्ग: MAHĀŚṚNGAḤ: In His *matsya* (fish) form (Matsyāvatāra) He sported in the waters of *praḷaya* (deluge) binding the boat (of life) to His great horn (*śrnga*).

कृतान्तकृत् KṚTĀNTAKṚT: 1. He brings the *anta*, the end of everything, that is *kṛta* created. So. *Kṛtāntakṛt.*

Or 2. He cuts off, destroys (*kṛntati*) Kṛtānta, the God or Death. Hence *Kṛtāntakṛt.*

महावराहो गोविन्दः सुषेणः कनकाङ्गदी :
गुह्यो गभीरो गहनो गुप्तश्चक्रगदाधरः ॥ ७१ ॥

Mahāvarāhaḥ Govindaḥ Suṣeṇaḥ Kanakāngadī /
Guhyaḥ Gabhīraḥ Gahanaḥ Guptaḥ
Cakragadhādharaḥ / / 71

महावराहः MAHĀVARĀHAḤ: *Mahān varāhaḥ*. The great Boar (in the Varāhāvatāra to lift the earth from the waters into which it was hidden by Hiranyākṣa).

गोविन्दः GOVINDAḤ: 1. He (the Lord) is attained by *go* which stands for *vāṇi* speech.

Or 2. He (the jīva who is non-different from Brahman knows (the Truth that is Brahman) by the texts of Vedānta. *vide* the Viṣṇutilika: *gobhireva yato vedyo govindaḥ samudāhṛtaḥ*: 'as You are known by *go*, Vedāntic texts alone You are said to be Govinda.'

सुषेणः SUṢEṆAḤ: He who possesses the auspicious groups of *senas*, armies of the form of gaṇas. So *Suṣenaḥ*.

कनकाङ्गदी KANAKĀNGADĪ: He has golden armlets.

गुह्यः GUHYAḤ: 1. He is to be known by the Upaniṣads which are imparted in secret *guhya*.

Or 2. He dwells in the cave, *guha*, in the ether of the heart in *hṛdayākāśa*. So *Guhyaḥ*.

गभीरः GABHĪRAḤ: The unfathomable or Supreme in wisdom, wealth, strength valour etc., (*jñāna, aiśvarya, bala, vīrya*).

गहनः GAHANAḤ: 1. Being impenetrable (to the unqualified).

Or 2. He is the witness to the appearance or disappearance of the three states of consciousness, being free from them.

गुप्तः GUPTAḤ: The concealed, as He cannot be attained by speech and the mind. *vide* the śruti. *eṣa sarveṣu bhūteṣu gūḍho'tmā na prākāśate*: 'concealed in all beings this Ātman does not shine.' (Katha Up.1.3.12).

चक्रगदाधरः CAKRAGADĀDHARAḤ: *Cakram*, the

discus is of the nature of the *manastattva; gadā* the club is of the nature of the *buddhi tattva*. He is the bearer of the *cakra* and the *gadā* for protecting the world. So He is *Cakragadādharaḥ*.

वेधाः स्वाङ्गोऽजितः कृष्णो दृढः सङ्कर्षणोऽच्युतः ।
वरुणो वारुणो वृक्षः पुष्कराक्षो महामनाः ।। ७२ ।।

Vedhāḥ Svāngaḥ Ajitaḥ Kṛṣṇaḥ
Dṛḍhaḥ Sankarṣaṇocyutaḥ /
Varuṇaḥ Vāruṇaḥ Vṛkṣaḥ
Puṣkarākṣaḥ Mahāmanaḥ / / 72

वेधाः VEDHAḤ: The creator, therefore, Vedhāḥ.

स्वाङ्गः SVĀNGAḤ: He Himself is the instrument in bringing about effects *sva-angaḥ*. Hence *Svāngaḥ*.

अजितः AJITAḤ: In no incarnation has He been conquered. So *Ajitaḥ*.

कृष्णः KṚṢṆAḤ: *Kṛṣṇadvaipāyanaḥ*. Dark and island-born. (Sage Vyāsa) *vide*: the Viṣṇu Purāṇa statement: *kṛṣṇa dvaipāyanam vyāsam viddhi nārāyaṇam prabhum / kohyanyaḥ puṇḍarīkākṣāt mahābhāratakṛt bhavet / /* 'Know Kṛṣṇadvaipāyana Vyāsa to be the Lord Nārāyaṇa. For, who other than the Puṇḍarīkākṣa (the lotus-eyed Nārāyaṇa) could have been the author of the Mahābhārata?' (3.4.5).

दृढः DṚḌAḤ: Firm because there is no sliding in His nature or capacity.

सङ्कर्षणोच्युतः SANKARṢAṆOCYUTAḤ: At the time of destruction, *samhāra*, He draws to Himself, *sankārṣati*, all beings together to Himself. So, *Sankarṣanaḥ*. Does not slide down from His nature. Therefore *Acyutaḥ*. Sankarṣanocyutaḥ is one Name with an adjective.

वरुणः VARUṆAḤ: As Sun that draws to itself all rays when it sets, He is *Varuṇa*. *vide* the mantra:

imam me varuṇa śrudhī havam: 'O! Varuna listen to my hymn.' (Taitt.Sam.2.10.11).

वारुण: VĀRUṆAḤ: Varuṇa's son, Vaśiṣta or Agastya.

वृक्ष: VṚKṢAḤ: He stands unshaking (firm) like a tree. So *Vṛkṣah. vide* the śruti: *vṛkṣa iva stabdho divitiṣtatyekaḥ*. 'Alone He stands in the sky firm like a tree.' (Sve. Up.3.9).

पुष्कराक्ष: PUṢKARĀKṢAḤ: 1. The root *akṣa* which has the meaning of pervading is added to the word *puṣkara*. So, we get *puṣkarakṣaḥ* (meaning all pervading).

Or 2. meditated in the lotus of the heart where He shines in His native effulgence.

महामना: MAHĀMANĀḤ: By mere thought He accomplishes the actions of creation, preservation and dissolution; therefore *Mahāmanāḥ. vide* the Viṣṇupurāṇa *manasaiva jagatsṛṣtim samhāram ca karoti yaḥ*: 'He who does the creation of the world and its destruction merely by His mind.' (5.22.15).

भगवान् भगहानन्दी वनमाली हलायुधः ।
आदित्यो ज्योतिरादित्यः सहिष्णुर्गतिसत्तमः ॥ ७३ ॥

Bhagavān Bhagahā Āṇandī Vanamālī Halāyudhaḥ /
Ādityaḥ Jyotirādityaḥ Sahiṣṇuḥ Gatisattamaḥ / / 73

भगवान् BHAGAVĀN: *Bhaga* means the six attributes, abundant aiśvarya (riches), dharma, yaśas (fame) śrī (prosperity) vairāgya (dispassion) and mokṣa (salvation) *aiśvaryasya samagrasya dharmasya yaśasaḥ śriyaḥ / vairāgyasyātha mokṣasya ṣaṇṇām bhaga itīraṇā //* He who has *bhaga* is *Bhagavān*. In the Viṣṇu Puraṇa it is said: *utpattim praḷayam caiva bhūtānām āgatim gatim / vetti vidyāmavidyām ca sa vācyo bhagavāniti //*

'He knows the origination and dissolution of beings, their coming and going, both vidyā and avidyā. So He is said to be Bhagavān'. (6.5.7.8)

भगदा BHAGAHĀ: At the time of samhāra, He destroys aiśvarya, etc.

आनन्दी ĀNANDĪ: He is called *Ānandī* as He is of the nature of happiness or has a plenitude of it.

वनमाली VANAMĀLĪ: He wears the garland called *Vaijayanti* made out of the *tanmātras,* subtle elements.

हलायुध: HALĀYUDHAḤ: In the form of Balabhadra, He has a plough for His weapon.

आदित्य: ĀDITYAḤ: He Who is born as Vāmana of Aditi and Kaśyapa.

ज्योतेरादित्य: JYOTIRĀDITYAḤ: He who resides as the splendorus effulgence in the orb of the sun

सहिष्णु: SAHIṢṆUḤ: He bears the dualities of cold, heat, etc., so He is *Sahiṣṇuḥ.*

गतिसत्तम: GATISATTAMAḤ: The refuge (*gati*) and the best (the most superior) Existent (*sattamaḥ*). So *Gatisattamaḥ.*

सुधन्वा खण्डपरशुर्दारुणो द्रविणप्रदः ।
दिविस्पृक्सर्वदृग्व्यासो वाचस्पतिरयोनिजः ॥ ७४ ॥

Sudhanvā Khaṇḍaparaśuḥ Dāruṇaḥ Draviṇapradaḥ /
Divaspṛk Sarvadṛk Vyāsaḥ Vācaspatiḥ
Ayonijaḥ / / 74

सुधन्वा SUDHANVĀ: He has the beautiful bow of (signifying) the sense organs (*dhanus* is bow).

खण्डपरशु: KHAṆḌAPARAŚUḤ: 1. By reason of punishing the enemies He is *Khaṇḍaḥ.* In the form of Parasurāma, son of Jamadagni, He has an axe (*paraśu*). So He is *Khandaparaśuḥ.*

Or 2. It may be taken as *akhaṇdaḥ paraśuḥ*, unbreakable axe; wielding it.

दारुण: DĀRUṆAḤ: As being hard on the enemies of the righteous path, He is *Dārunaḥ*.

द्रविणप्रद: DRAVIṆAPRADAḤ: He gives the desired wealth *draviṇa* to His devotees. So *Draviṇapradaḥ*.

दिवस्पृक् DIVASPṚK: As He touched the sky in His Trivikrama incarnation, He is *Divaspṛk*.

सर्वदृग्व्यास: SARVADṚGVYĀSAḤ: 1. As Vyāsa, He expounded at length all knowledge.

Or 2. *Sarvadṛk* means *jñānam,* knowledge of all forms.

Or 3. *Sarvadṛk* means He sees everything. *Vyāsa* the classifier. Vedas were classified fourfold in the forms of Rk., etc. The first the Ṛg Veda was made of twenty-one parts, the second Yajur Veda was made of one hundred and one parts, the Sāma Veda was made of a thousand parts, the Atharva Veda in nine branches Thus other purāṇas also were made by him, *vyastāni*. So he was called Vyāsa. In that aspect, the Lord too is called Vyasa, i.e., Brahmā.

वाचस्पतिरयोनिज: VĀCASPATIRAYONIJAḤ: *Vācaḥ vidyāyāḥ patih Vācaspatih*: 'The Lord of Knowledge.'

Ayonijaḥ means not born of a mother. *Vacaspatirayonijaḥ* is a name with an adjective.

त्रिसामा सामगः साम निर्वाणं भेषजं भिषक् ।
संन्यासकृच्छमः शान्तो निष्ठा शान्तिः परायणम् ॥ ७५ ॥

Trisāmā Sāmagaḥ Sāma Nirvāṇam Bheṣajam
Bhiṣak /
Sanyāsakṛt Śamaḥ Śāntaḥ Niṣtha Śantiḥ
Parāyaṇam // 75

त्रिसामा TRISĀMA: The singers of Sāma praised

Him by the three Sāmas named Devavrata. So *Trisāma*.

सामगः SĀMAGAḤ: He sings the Sama. So *Sāmagaḥ*.

साम SĀMA: By the Lord's statement: *vedānām sāma vedo'smi*: Of the Vedas, I am the Sāma Veda, (B.G. 10.22). He is the Sāma Veda.

निर्वाणम् NIRVĀṆAM: He is of the nature of supreme bliss characterised by the cessation of all sorrows.

भेषजम् BHEṢAJAM: He is the medicine for the disease of samsāra.

भिषक् BHIṢAK: He is the physicians as He taught in the Gita the knowledge that will relieve one of the disease of samsāra. *vide* the *śruti*: *bhiṣaktamam tva bhiṣajam śṛṇomi*: 'You are the best of all physicians'. (Ṛg. Veda. 2.33.4).

सन्यासकृत् SANYĀSAKṚT: He created the Samnyāsāśrama to aid in attaining liberation.

शमः ŚAMAḤ: 1. He declared that *śama* is chiefly the means to knowledge (of ātmajñāna). So, He Himself is *Samaḥ*. *vide* the śruti. *yatīnām praśamo dharmo niyamo vanavāsinām / dānameva gṛhasṭhānam śuśrūṣa brahmacārinam //* : 'For the *yatis* (samnyāsins) *sama* is the chief dharma, *niyama* (restraint) of the *vānaprastas*, *dana* (giving) of *gṛhasthas* and service (*śuśrūṣa*) of the *brahmacārins*'.

Or 2. He controls all creatures; therefore, He is *Śamāḥ*.

शान्तः ŚĀNTAḤ: As He is unattached to sense-pleasures, He is *Śāntaḥ*. *vide* the śruti: *niṣkaḷam niṣkriyam śāntam*: 'without parts, without action, tranquil'. (Sve. Up. 6.19).

निष्टा: NIṢṬHĀ: During pralaya all beings rest

in Him for long; so *Niṣṭhā* or the Abode.

शन्तिः ŚĀNTIḤ: The Peace arising from freedom from all avidyās.

परायणम् PARĀYAṆAM: That Śānti is Brahman itself, the Supreme leading to the highest state without doubt of coming back. So *Parāyaṇam.* It may also be taken in the masculine gender (as *param ayanam yasya saha*: He Whose is the supreme goal).

शुभाङ्गः शान्तिदः स्रष्टा कुमुदः कुवलेशयः ।
गोहितो गोपतिर्गोप्ता वृषभाक्षो वृषप्रियः ॥ ७६ ॥

Śubhangaḥ Śāntidaḥ Sraṣṭā Kumudaḥ
Kuvaleśayaḥ /
Gohitaḥ Gopatiḥ Goptā Vṛṣabhakṣaḥ
Vṛṣapriyaḥ / / 76

सुभाङ्गः SUBHĀNGAḤ: He bears (possesses) a handsome body, hence *Subhāngaḥ.*

शान्तिदः ŚĀNTIDAḤ: He confers sānti (peace) characterised by freedom from attachment and aversion (*rāga* and *dvēṣa*), etc., *Śānti-daḥ,* the Giver of peace.

श्रेष्टा SRAṢṬĀ: He created all beings in the beginning of creation. So *Sraṣṭā.*

कुमुदः KUMMUDAḤ: He delights in the earth. (*kau bhūmyām modate*).

कुवलेशयः KUVALEŚAYAḤ: 1. *kuvalam* is water as it is round (or in) the earth. He lies *śeṭe* (sleeps) on it. So *Kuvaleśayaḥ.*

Or 2. Takṣaka the serpent lies inside a *kuvala,* badari fruit; that Takṣaka too is a manifestation of the Lord. So *Kuvaleśayaḥ.*

Or 3. *kuvala* is the belly of serpents as they crawl on the ground. He lies on it, on the belly of the Seṣa. So *Kuvaleśayaḥ.*

गोहित: GOHITAḤ: 1. For the welfare of the cows He lifted the Govardhana hill. So *Gohitaḥ,* good to the cows.

Or 2. He assumed a body for decreasing the earth's burden. (*go* means *bhūmi*). So, *Gohitaḥ.*

गापति: GOPATIḤ: The Lord of the earth. (*go-patih*).

गोप्ता GOPTĀ: 1. The protector of the world.

Or 2. He conceals His self by His māyā. So *Goptā.*

वृषभाक्ष: VṚṢABHĀKṢAḤ: 1. His eyes akṣ̄ni rain all that is desired. Hence *Vṛsabhākṣaḥ.*

Or 2. *vṛṣabha* means *dharma.* That itself constitutes His eyes. So, *Vṛsabhākṣaḥ.*

वृषप्रिय: VṚṢAPRIYAḤ: 1. He to whom *vṛṣa* or *dharma* is dear, *priya.*

Or 2. He is dharma (vṛṣaḥ) and dear (priyaḥ). So *Vṛṣapriyaḥ.*

अनिवर्ती निवृत्तात्मा संक्षेप्ता क्षेमकृच्छिव:।
श्रीवत्सवक्षा: श्रीवास: श्रीपति: श्रीमतांवर: ।। ७७ ।।

Anivartī Nivṛttātmā Snkṣeptā Kṣemakṛt Śivaḥ /
Śrīvatsavakṣaḥ Śrīvāsaḥ Śrīpatiḥ
Śrīmatāmvaraḥ // 77

अनिवर्ती ANIVARTĪ: 1. He does not turn back from the devāśura war (without victory).

Or 2. He does not return (resile) from dharma, it being dear to Him. So *Anivartī.*

निवृत्तात्मा NIVṚTTĀTMĀ: By nature, His ātmā, i.e., mind has turned back from sense pleasures. He is *nivṛtta-ātmā.*

संक्षेप्ता SAMKṢEPTĀ: The expanded universe is contracted by Him into its subtle form at the time of samhāra (in praḷaya).

क्षेमकृत् KṢEMAKṚT: He safeguards what has been acquired.

शिव: ŚIVAḤ: Because He purifies by the mere remembrance of His name, He is *Śivaḥ*.

Thus the sixth hundred of the Names has been explained.

श्रीवत्सवक्षा: ŚRĪVATSAVAKṢAḤ: There is the mark called Śrīvatsa on His breast. So *Śrīvatsavakṣāḥ*.

श्रीवास: ŚRĪVĀSAḤ: Srīḥ (Lakshmī) resides in His chest without separation. Hence *Śrīvāsaḥ*.

श्रीपति: ŚRĪPATIḤ: 1. (The husband of Śrī). At the time of churning the ocean (for amṛta), rejecting the devas and asuras, Śrīḥ (Lakṣmī) chose Him for Her husband (*pati.*) So, *Śrīpatiḥ*.

Or 2. *Śrīḥ* may mean *parā saktiḥ*. Her husband is *Srīpatiḥ*. *vide* the sruti: *parāsya saktirvividhaiva śrūyate*: 'His supreme śakti is heard to be of varied forms.' (Sve. Up. 6.8).

श्रीमतांवर: SRĪMATĀMVARAḤ: Rg. Yajus and Sāma are the Srīḥ of those who possessed it, Brahma and others. He is the greatest of them. So *Śrīmatāmvaraḥ*. *vide* the sruti: *rg. sāmāni yajumṣi sā hi śrīramṛtā satām:* 'Ṛk. Sāma and Yajus are the Srı of the good making for immortality'. (Taitt. Brahmana. 1.1.1).

श्रीद: श्रीश: श्रीनिवास: श्रीनिधि: श्रिवभावन:

श्रीधर: श्रीकर: श्रेय: श्रीमांल्लोकत्राश्रय: ।। ७७ ।।

Śrīdaḥ Śrīśaḥ Sīnivāsaḥ Srīnidhiḥ Srivibhāvanaḥ /
Śrīdharaḥ Srīkaraḥ Śreyah Srīmān
Lokatrayaśrayaḥ / / 78

श्रीद: ŚRĪDAḤ: He confers Śrī, wealth, on His devotees. So *Srīḍaḥ*.

श्रीश: ŚRĪŚAḤ: The Lord of Śrī.

श्रीनिवासः ŚRĪNIVĀSAḤ: He resides always with the wealthy. By the word *Śrī,* wealthy persons *Śrīmantaḥ* are implied.

श्रीनिधिः ŚRĪNIDHIḤ: In Him who is all powerful, all treasures (śriyaḥ) are deposited. So He is *Śrīnidhiḥ.*

श्रीविभावनः ŚRIVIBHĀVANAḤ: He distributes various kinds of wealth to all people according to their karmas.

श्रीधरः ŚRĪDHARAḤ: He bears on His chest Śrī who is the mother of all creatures.

श्रीकरः ŚRĪKARAḤ: He dowers with Śrī those that remember Him, praise Him and worship Him. He is *Śrī-karaḥ.*

श्रेयः ŚREYAḤ: *Śreyaḥ* is characterised by attainment of non-separating (permanent) *sukha.* That pertains only to the Absolute. Hence He is *Śreyaḥ.*

श्रीमान् ŚRĪMĀN: He has Śrī. So *Śrīmān.*

लोकत्रयाश्रयः LOKATRAYĀŚRAYAḤ: As He is the refuge of the three worlds, He is *Lokatrayāśrayaḥ.*

स्वक्षः स्वङ्गः शतानन्दो नन्दिर्ज्योतिर्गणेश्वरः ।
विजितात्मा विधेयात्मा सत्कीर्तिश्छिन्नसंशयः ॥ ७९ ॥

Svakṣaḥ Svangaḥ Satānandaḥ Nandhiḥ
Jyotirgaṇeśvaraḥ /
Vijitātmā Avidheyātmā Satkīrtiḥ
Chinnaśamśayaḥ // 79

स्वक्षः SVAKṢAḤ His eyes are auspicious and resemble the lotus (*su-akṣaḥ*). So *Svakṣaḥ.*

स्वङ्गः SVANGAḤ: His limbs are auspicious. So Svangaḥ. (*Su-angaḥ*)

सतानन्दः SATĀNANDAḤ: *Paramānanda* supreme bliss is one only. Due to differences of limitations, it is broken into hundreds. So, *Satānandaḥ* (sataānandāḥ).

vide the śruti: *etasyaiva ānandasya anyāni bhūtāni mātrām upajīvanti:* 'Of this ānanda (bliss), other beings enjoy only a part.' (Brh. Up.6.3.32).

नन्दि: NANDIḤ: The concrete form of paramānanda, supreme bliss.

ज्योतिर्गणेश्वर: JYOTIRGAṆEŚVARAḤ: The Lord of all luminous bodies: *vide* the śruti: *tameva bhāntam anubhāti sarvam*: 'All that shines after Him when He shines' (Kaṭha Up.5.15) and smṛtis like *yadādityagatam tejaḥ*: 'That light which is in the sun'. (B.G. 15.12).

विजितात्मा VIJITĀTMĀ: He by whom the *ātmā,* i.e. the *manas* has been conquered (subdued).

अविधेयात्मा AVIDHEYĀTMĀ: His ātmā or nature (svarūpam) is not under the sway of anybody (*a-vidheya ātmā*).

सत्कीर्ति: SATKĪRTIḤ: His renown is ever true *(sat),* never belied.

छिन्नसंशय: CHINSAMŚAYAḤ: To Him for whom everything is directly discernible, there is no doubt whatever. So *Chinsamśayaḥ.*

उदीर्णः सर्वतश्चक्षुरनीशः शाश्वतस्थिरः ।
भूशयो भूषणो भूतिर्विशोकः शोकनाशनः ।। ८० ।।

Udīrṇaḥ Sarvatascakṣuḥ Anīśaḥ Śaśvatsthiraḥ /
Bhūṣayaḥ Bhuṣaṇaḥ Bhūtiḥ Viśokaḥ
Śokanaśanaḥ // 80

उदीर्णं: UDĪṚṆAḤ: As He is apart from and above all beings, transcendent, He is *Udīrṇaḥ.*

सर्वतस्चक्षु: SARVATTASCAKṢUḤ: He sees everywhere everything by His own intelligence, *vide* śruti *viśvatascakṣuḥ*: 'Having eyes everywhere' ((Nārāyaṇa Up. 1).

अनीश: ANĪŚAḤ: He has no lord (superior to Him). *vide* the śruti: *na tasyeśe kascar.a*: 'none rules over Him' (Mahā Nārāyaṇa Up. 1).

शाश्वतस्थिर: ŚAŚVATASTHIRAḤ: Through existing always, He never undergoes any change (eternal and unchanging. *Śāsvatasthiraḥ* is one Name.

भूशय: BHŪṢAYAḤ: When He searched for a path across the ocean when He wished to go to Lanka, He lay on the ground. So bhū-sayaḥ. (The reference is to Śrī Rāma).

भूषण: BHŪṢANAḤ: By the many incarnations which He took of His free will, He adorned the earth. So Bhūṣanaḥ, ornament.

भूति: BHŪTIḤ: 1. *Bhavanam* means existence or glory. The Existent or the Glorious.

Or 2. He is the cause of all the glories. So *Bhūtiḥ*.

विशोक: VIŚOKAḤ: As He is of the form of supreme bliss, no grief ever touches Him. *Vi-śokah.*

शोकनाशन: ŚOKANĀSANAḤ: He destroys the griefs of His devotees by their mere thought of Him.

अर्चिष्मानर्चितः कुम्भो विशुद्धात्मा विशोधनः ।
अनिरुद्धोऽप्रतिरथः प्रद्युम्नोऽमितविक्रमः ॥ ८१ ॥

Arciṣman Arcitaḥ Kumbhaḥ Visuddhātmā
Viśodhanaḥ /
Aniruddhaḥ Apratirathaḥ Pradyumnaḥ
Amitavikramaḥ // 81

अर्चिष्मान् ARCIṢMĀN: He by whom the luminaries, the sun, moon, etc., get their luminosity is alone pre-eminent *Arciṣmān.*

अर्चित: ARCITAḤ: Worshipped even by Brahmā and others who are worshipped by all the worlds.

कुम्भः KUMBHAḤ: Like the nave of a wheel, everything is made to rest in Him. So *Kumbhaḥ*.

विशुद्धात्मा VIŚUDDHĀTMĀ: Being beyond the three guṇas He is *viśuddha*, pure. He is also the (parama) Ātmā. So, He is *Visuddhātmā*.

विशोधनः VIŚODHANAḤ: As He erases sins by mere thought of Him, He is *Viśodhanaḥ*.

अनिरुद्धः ANIRUDDHAḤ: 1. Of the four vyūha forms (manifestations) of God, He is the fourth.

Or 2. He is never overcome by His enemies. So *Aniruddhaḥ*.

अप्रतिरथः APRATIRATHAḤ: There is no opponent (*pratiraṭha*)—rival—to Him. So, *Apratirathaḥ*.

प्रद्युम्नः PRADYUMNAḤ: 1. He has infinite wealth *prakṛṣtam dyumnam,* i.e., *dhanam*).

Or 2. One of the four vyūhas.

अमितविक्रमः AMITAVIKRAMAḤ: 1. Of unlimited, incomparable valour.

Or 2. He whose valour has not been impaired.

कालनेमिनिहा वीरः शौरिः शूरजनेश्वरः ।
त्रिलोकात्मा त्रिलोकेशः केशवः केशिहा हरिः ॥ ८२ ॥

Kālaneminihā Vīraḥ Śauriḥ Śurajaneśvaraḥ /
Trilokātmā Trilokeśaḥ Keśavaḥ Keśihā Hariḥ / / 82

कालनेमिनिहा KĀLANEMINIHĀ: He killed the asura, Kālanemi.

वीरः VĪRAḤ: Valiant.

शौरिः ŚAURIḤ: Born in the Śūra clan.

शूरजनेश्वरः ŚŪRAJANEŚVARAḤ: By His superior prowess, exceedingly greater than heroes like Indra, etc. (Śurajanāṇām-Iśvaraḥ).

त्रिलोकात्मा TRILOKĀTMĀ: 1. As He is the inner ruler (*antaryāmi*) of the three worlds, He is their ātmā.

Or 2. The three worlds are not really different from Him. So, *Trilokātmā*.

त्रिलोकेश: TRILOKEṢAḤ: Subject to His command, the three worlds perform their respective actions. Hence *Trilokeśaḥ*.

केशव: KEṢAVAḤ: 1. *keśa* is the name given to the rays of the sun, etc. As He has them, He is Keśava: *vide* the Mahābhārata: *amśavo ye prakāśante mama te keśasamjñitāḥ / sarvajñāḥ keśavam tasmāt mām āhurdvijasattamāḥ / /* : 'My rays which illumine are called keśas. Therefore, learned people, the best among the dvijas call me *Keśava*'.

Or 2. The śaktis or powers called Brahmā, Viṣṇu and Śiva are designated as *Keśas*. Having them, He is *Keśava*. The word keśa is used as synonym for śakti in the śruti: *trayaḥ keśinaḥ*: 'there are three keśins'. (Ṛg. Veda. 1.64.44) and in Viṣṇu Purāṇa: *mat keśau vasudhātale*: 'My keśas (are) in the earth' (5.1.61). Here too the word keśa is used as a synonym for śakti. The Harivamśa (279.47) says: *ko brahmeti samākhyāta īśo'ham sarvadehinām / āvām tavamśasambhūtau tasmāt keśavanamavan / /* : Śiva says to Viṣṇu: '*ka* means Brahma and I am Īśa, the Lord of all that are embodied. We (Brahma and I) are Your parts (amśas). So, you have the name *Keśava*'."

केशिहा KEŚIHĀ: He killed the asura named Keśi. So, *Keśihā*.

हरि: HARIḤ: He liquidates (harati) samsāra with its cause (avidyā).

कामदेवः कामपालः कामी कान्तः कृतागमः ।
अनिर्देश्यवपुर्विष्णुर्वीरोऽनन्तो धनञ्जयः ॥ ८३ ॥

Kāmadevaḥ Kāmapālaḥ Kāmī Kāntaḥ Kṛtāgamaḥ /
Anirdeśyavapuḥ Viṣṇuḥ Vīraḥ Anantaḥ Dhanamjayaḥ / / 83

कामदेवः KĀMADEVAḤ: He is desired (*kāmyate*) by those who wish to have the four puruṣārthas, dharma, etc. So, He is *Kāma.* He is *Kāma* and *deva.* So, He is *Kāmadeva.*

कामपालः KĀMAPĀLAḤ: He safeguards the desires of those who desire. Hence *Kāmapālaḥ* (*kāmān pālayati.*)

कामी KĀMĪ: As His desires are ever fulfilled, He is *Kāmī.*

कान्तः KĀNTAḤ: 1. He bears a very handsome body.

Or 2. At the close of the second parārdha, the end of Brahmā too arises from Him. (*ka* means Brahmā; *anta* is end). So *Kāntaḥ.*

कृतागमः KṚTĀGAMAḤ: The *āgamas* made up of śruti and smṛti were 'done' (produced) by Him. So *Kṛta-āgamaḥ vide* the Lord's statement: *śrutiḥ smṛtiḥ mamaiva ājñe:* 'Śruti and Smṛti are my commands' and also *infra* in this work: *Vedāśśāstrāṇi vijñānam etat sarvam janārdanāt:* 'the Vedas, śāstras, and wisdom, all these are from Janārdana'.

अनिर्देश्यवपुः ANIRDEŚYAVAPUḤ: Due to transcending the guṇas, it is impossible to indicate His form as 'this', 'that' or 'like this'. So, *Anirdeśyavapuḥ.*

विष्णुः VIṢṆUḤ: His splendour pervades the firmament and remains beyond. So, *Viṣṇuḥ. vide* the Mahābhārata: *vyāpya me rodasī pārtha kāntirabhyadhikā sṭhitā / kramaṇādvāpyaham pārtha viṣṇurityabhisamjñitaḥ / /* : 'As my splendour pervades and exceeds the firmament and as I have traversed the entire universe, I am designated Viṣṇu.' (Śānti Parva 342-43).

वीरः VĪRAḤ: By reason of His having *gati* (motion) etc., *vide* the Dhātupāṭha: *vī gati vyāpti prajana kānti- asana khādaneṣu*: the root *vī* is used for motion, pervasion, creation, effulgence, throwing and eating (samhāra). So, He is *Vī-raḥ*.

अनन्तः ANANTAḤ: 1. As He pervades, as He is eternal, and is of the nature of all ātmās, He is without limits of space, time and object. Hence *Anantaḥ*. *vide* the śruti: *satyam jñānam anantam brahma*: 'Brahman is existence, wisdom and unlimited'. (Taitt. Up. 2.1).

Or 2. By the Viṣṇu Purāna text: *gandharvāpsarasaḥ siddhāh kinnaroraga cāraṇāḥ / nāntam guṇānām gacchanti tenānato'yamavyayaḥ / /* : 'the gandharvas, apsaras, siddhas, kinnaras, uragas and cāraṇas cannot exhaust the recital of His (divine) qualities. For that reason He is *Ananta* and Avyaya, imperishable'.

धनंजयः DHANAMJAYAḤ: Arjuna acquired by conquest abundant wealth left over after a sacrifice. He is *Dhanamjayaḥ*. The Lord identifies Himself with Arjuna and calls Himself Dhanamjaya. For, the Lord said: *pāṇdavānām (aham) dhanamjayaḥ'*. 'Among the Pāṇdavas, I am Dhanamjaya'. (B.G. 10.37). Hence the name to Him.

ब्रह्मण्यः ब्रह्मकृत् ब्रह्मा ब्रह्म ब्रह्मविवर्धनः।
ब्रह्मवित् ब्राह्मणो ब्रह्मी ब्रह्मज्ञो ब्राह्मणप्रियः ॥ ८४ ॥

Brahmaṇyaḥ Brahmakṛt Brahmā Brahma
Brahmavivardhanaḥ /
Brahmavit Brāhmaṇaḥ Brahmī Brahmajñaḥ
Brāhmaṇapriyaḥ / / 84

ब्रह्मण्य: BRAHMAṆYAḤ: *Tapo vedāsca viprāśca jñānam ca brahmasamjñitam*: 'austerity, the Vedas, sages and wisdom are indicated by the word 'Brahma'. As He is beneficial to them, the Lord is called *Brahmaṇyaḥ*.

ब्रह्मकृत्: BRAHMAKṚT: As He created *tapas* (austerities) etc. He is *Brahmakṛt.*

ब्रह्मा BRAHMĀ: Being Brahmā, He created all things.

ब्रह्म BRAHMA: Being great and all-pervading, He is Brahma characterised by *Satyam,* etc.; *vide* the śruti: *satyam jñānam anantam Brahma:* Brahma is of the nature of 'existence, knowledge and infinitude'. (Taitt. Up. 2.1). The Viṣṇu Purāṇa says: (6.7.53) *pratyastamitabhedam yat sattāmātramagocaram / vacasāmātma samvedyam tat jñānam brahmasamjñitam / / :* 'That knowledge which negates difference, which refers to pure existence, which is beyond grasp of the senses and realised in the Self is indicated by Brahma".

ब्रह्मविवर्धन: BRAMAVIVARDHANAḤ: As He promotes *tapas,* etc. He is *Brahmavivardhanaḥ* (*tapas* is called *Brahma*).

ब्रह्मवित् BRAHMAVIT: He knows the Vedas and their meanings correctly. Hence *Brahmavit.*

ब्राह्मण: BRĀHMANAḤ: In the form of the Brāhmaṇas He expounds the Vedas to the whole world. So, He is *Brāhmaṇaḥ.*

ब्रह्मी: BRAHMĪ: All things indicated by the word

Brahman (*tapas*, Vedas, vipras and jñānam) are parts of Him. So He is *Brahmī*.

ब्रह्मज्ञः BRAHMAJÑAḤ: He knows the Vedas which are Himself.

ब्राह्मणप्रियः BRĀHMAṆAPRIYAḤ: Dear to the Brāhmaṇas or Brāhmanas are dear to Him. The Lord said: One who does not duly salute a Brahmaṇa as is proper, who kills, curses, or speaks harshly to him, is a sinner burnt up by the forest fire of Brahman and must be put to death or otherwise punished; he does not belong to Me.' In the Mahābhārata it is said: 'That God whom the holy Devaki begot of Vasudeva like the radiant fire from *araṇi* wood for the protection of Brāhmaṇas on earth'.

महाक्रमो कहाकर्मा महातेजा महोरगः ।
महाक्रतुर्महायज्वा महायज्ञो महाहविः ॥ ८५ ॥

Mahākramaḥ Mahākarmā Mahātejāḥ
Mahoragaḥ /
Makākratuḥ Mahāyajvā Mahāyajñaḥ
Mahāhaviḥ / / 85

महाक्रमः MAHĀKRAMAḤ: His are great strides. *vide* the śruti *śam no viṣṇururukramaḥ*: 'May Viṣṇu of great strides give us welfare'. (Taitt. Up. 1.1).

महाकर्मा MAHĀKARMĀ: Great are His actions of creation etc., of the world.

महातेजाः MAHĀTEJĀḤ: He by whose brilliance the sun etc., are brilliant, that great brilliance is His. *vide*: *yena sūryastapati tejaseddhaḥ*: 'Illumined by which brilliance the sun shines'. *vide* also the Lord's statement: *yadādityagatam tejaḥ*: 'The light which is in the sun.' (B.G. 15.12).

Or 2. endowed with the great qualities of fierceness, valour, therefore *Mahātejaḥ*.

महोरगः MAHORAGAḤ: A great serpent *vide*: the Lord's statement: *sarpānāmasmi Vāsukiḥ*. 'I am Vāsuki among serpents'. (B.G. 10.12).

महाक्रतुः MAHĀKRATUḤ: The great kratu (the name for a sacrifice). Manu (11.2.60) *yathāśvamedhaḥ kraturāt*: 'As the Asvamedha is the greatest of sacrifices'. That also is He.

महायज्वा MAHĀYAJVĀ: The great Sacrificer (who performs sacrifices strictly according to Vedic rules). He performs sacrifices for the welfare of the world. So, *Mahāyajvā*.

महायज्ञः MAHĀYAJÑAḤ: The great yajna. *vide* the Lord's statement: *yajñānām japayajñosmi*: 'of yajñās, I am the japayajña'. (B.G. 10.25).

महाहविः MAHĀHAVIḤ: The great oblation. The whole universe is offered as an oblation to Brahman as its ātman.

Or *Mahākratuḥ*, etc., may be taken as a *bahuvrīhi samāsa*: For whom big sacrifices are made.

स्तव्यः स्तवप्रियः स्तोत्रं स्तुतिः स्तोता रणप्रियः ।
पूर्णः पूरयिता पुण्यः पुण्यकीर्तिरनामयः ॥ ८६ ॥

Stavyaḥ Stavapriyaḥ Stoṭram Sṭutiḥ Stotā
Raṇapriyaḥ /
Pūrṇaḥ Pūrayitā Puṇyaḥ Puṇyakīrtiḥ
Anāmayaḥ / / 86

स्तव्यः STAVYAḤ: He is praised by all; but none is praised by Him.

स्तवप्रियः STAVAPRIYAḤ: Hence, who delights in praises,

स्तोत्रम् STOTRAM: That by which He is praised. Praise is uttering (His divine) qualities. That is Hari Himself.

स्तुतिः STUTIḤ: The act of praising.

स्तोता STOTĀ: He who praises is He Himself.

रणप्रियः RAṆAPRIYAḤ: He to whom fighting is dear for which He always carries the five great weapons (the conch, the discus, the club, the bow and the lotus).

पूर्णः PŪṚṆAḤ: Fully possessed of all objects of desire and all powers.

पूरयिता: PŪRAYITĀ: Not merely Pūṛṇaḥ (full), but also He who fills all with riches.

पुण्यः PUṆYAḤ: By mere praise (of Him), He destroys all sins.

पुण्यकीर्तिः PUṆYAKĪRTIḤ: Of holy fame, for His fame brings auspiciousness to men (who sing it).

अनामयः ANĀMAYAḤ: He is not afflicted by internal or external ills brought on by karma. (*āmaya* means disease of the body or mind).

मनोजवस्तीर्थकरो वसुरेता वसुप्रदः ।
वसुप्रदो वासुदेवो वसुर्वसुमना हविः ।। ८७ ।।

Manojavaḥ Tīrthakaraḥ Vasuretāḥ
Vasupradaḥ /
Vasupradaḥ Vāsudevaḥ Vasuḥ Vasumanāḥ
Haviḥ / / 87

मनोजवः MANOJAVAḤ: He is swift as the mind as He is everywhere.

तीर्थकरः TĪRTHAKARAḤ: He is the author and also the preceptor of the fourteen vidyās and the auxiliary lores. (The fourteen are: the four Vedas, the six angas, Dharma, Mimāmsa, Tarka or Nyāya and the

Purāṇas). So, Tīrthakara: a sacred preceptor. Paurāṇikas (those who expound the purāṇas) say that, taking the form of Hayagrīva after killing the demons Madhu and Kaitabha at the beginning of creation, He taught Brahma the Vedas and other Vidyās and taught the asuras the non-vedic sciences for deceiving them.

वसुरेता: VASURETĀḤ: His *retas* (vital substance) is gold. So *Vasuretāḥ. vide* Vyāsa's statement: *devaḥ pūrvam apaḥ śrṣṭvā tāsu vīryamapāsṛjat / tat aṇḍam abhavat haimam brahmaṇaḥ kāraṇam param / /* : 'The Lord first created the waters and then deposited vital essence in them. That became the golden egg and was the supreme source of Brahma.'

वसुप्रद: VASUPRADAḤ: *Vasu* is *dhanam*, wealth. He gives it abundantly, i.e., *vasupradah.* He is the lord of wealth in His own right. The other (Kubera) is lord of wealth only by His grace.

वसुप्रद: VASUPRADAḤ: (repeated). 1. *vasu* means the fruit of mokṣa (liberation). He gives it to His devotees. So also *Vasupradaḥ. vide* the śruti: *vijñānam ānandam brahma rāterdātuḥ parāyaṇam tiṣṭhamānasya tadvidaḥ:* Brahman is wisdom and bliss. He is the highest wealth of one who seeks Him. (Bṛ. Up. 5.9.28).

Or 2. He deprives (khaṇḍayati) asuras absolutely of their wealth. So *Vasupradaḥ.* (*do avakhaṇḍane*: da is used in the sense of *avakhaṇḍana*, destroying).

वासुदेव: VĀSUDEVAḤ: Vasudeva's son.

वसु: VASUḤ: All beings reside in Him and He resides in them. Hence *Vasuḥ.*

वसुमना: VASUMANĀḤ: He resides uniformly in all objects, i.e., *vasu* His mind is of that nature. So *Vasumanāḥ.*

हविः HAVIḤ: By the Lord's words *brahmārpaṇam brahmahaviḥ,* Brahman is the offer and also the offering. So *Haviḥ.*

सद्गतिः सत्कृतिः सत्ता सद्भूतिः सत्परायणः ।
शूरसेनो यदुश्रेष्ठः सन्निवासः सुयामुनः ।। ८८ ।।

Sadgatiḥ Satkṛtiḥ Sattā Sadbhūtiḥ
Satparāyaṇaḥ /
Śūrasenaḥ Yaduśreṣṭhaḥ Sannivāsaḥ
Suyāmunaḥ / / 88

सद्गतिः SADGATIḤ: 1. By the śruti (Taitt. Up. 2.6) *asti brahmeti cet veda santam enam tato viduḥ:* 'If one knows that Brahman exists, he is known as *sat,* the existent'. Those that know (realise) that Brahman exists, they are those that are *sat.* The Lord is attained by them; So He is their goal, *Sadgatiḥ.*

Or 2. *Gati* also means buddhi (intellect); *satī buddhiḥ;* He has superior buddhi. So, *Sadgatiḥ.*

सत्कृतिः SATKṚTIḤ: His action of protecting the world is good (*sat*). Hence *Satkṛtiḥ.*

Thus the seventh hundred of the Names has been explained.

सत्ता SATTĀ: The state of existence in which there is no difference of the same kind, of different kind or internal differences is *sattā* (pure existence). For the śruti says: *ekam eva advitīyam.* Reality (Brahman) is 'one only without a second'. (Ch. Up. 6.2.1).

सद्भूतिः SADBHŪTIḤ: *Sat* is Paramātmā of the nature of intelligence not being sublated and as it is shining, it is Sadbhūtiḥ. What is different from *Sat* (Brahman), (the world) is not so as it appears and is sublated. As it appears, it is not *asat* (unreal); as it is sublated, it is not *sat* (Real). It is not *sat* nor is it *asat,*

This has been declared by śruti and by reasoning.

सत्परायणम् SATPARĀYAṆAM: The *param ayanam*, the supreme resting place of those who are *sat*, the knowers of Truth. So, *Satparāyaṇam.*

शूरसेन: ŚŪRASENAḤ: Where valiant commanders like Hanumān exist, that is called *sūrasenā*. He who has got such śūrasenās is *Śūrasenaḥ.*

यदुश्रेष्ठ: YADUŚREṢṬHAḤ: The Chief of the Yadus.

सन्निवास: SANNIVĀSAḤ: The refuge of people who are *sat,* i.e., the learned (*satām-nivāsaḥ*).

सुयामुन: SUYĀMUNAḤ: 1. Surrounded by the handsome *yāmunas,* those connected with (living on the banks of) the Yamunā like Devakī, Vasudeva, Nanda, Balabhadra, Subhadrā and others. So, *Suyāmunaḥ.*

Or 2. In the garb of cowherds He has Brahmā and others on the banks of the Yamunā who surround Him Hence, *Suyāmunaḥ.*

भूतावासो वासुदेवस्त्र सिुनिलयोऽनलः ।
दर्पहा दर्पदो हृप्तो दुर्धरोऽथापराजितः ॥ ८९ ॥

Bhūtāvāsaḥ Vāsudevaḥ Sarvāsunilayaḥ
Analaḥ /
Darpahā Darpadaḥ Dṛptaḥ Durdharaḥ atha
Aparājitaḥ / / 89

भूतावास: BHŪTĀVĀSAḤ: All beings appear before Him (at the time of creation when He thinks of them). In the Harivaṁśa it is said: "*vasanti tvayi bhūtāni bhūtāvāsastato bhavān*: 'All beings live in You; therefore You are *Bhūtāvāsaḥ.*'

वासुदेव: VĀSUDEVAḤ: He conceals or covers the worlds by māyā: therefore *Vāsuḥ*. He is *devaḥ,* too,

Hence *Vāsudevaḥ*. *vide* the Lord's statement (Mahābhārata Śānti Parva 350.41) *chādayāmi jagadviśvam bhūtyā sūrya ivāmsubhiḥ*: 'I envelop the entire world as the sun by his rays'.

सर्वासुनिलयः SARVASUNILAYAḤ: He in whom all *asus* or prāṇas find their abode as the jīvātman is *Sarvaśunilayaḥ*. (He who appears as the jīva is also in essence the Paramātman.)

अनलः ANALAḤ: There is no limit (sufficiency to His power or wealth. So, He is *Analaḥ*. (*alam* signifies limit, *Analaḥ*, unlimited).

दर्पहा DARPAHĀ: He destroys the pride of those who tread the path opposed to righteousness.

दर्पदः DARPADAḤ: He endows those who pursue the path of righteousness with pride.

दृप्तः DṚPTAḤ: By delighting in the nectar of His own ātman, He is proud. Hence *Dṛptaḥ*.

दुर्धरः DURDHARAḤ: As He is free of all limitations (upādhis), concentrated contemplation of Him is not possible. Yet, by His grace, He is held in the mind with effort by meditational practice in thousands of previous lives. So He is *Durdharaḥ*. *vide* the Lord's statement: *kleso'dhikatarasteṣāmavyaktāsaktacetasām / avyaktā hi gatir duḥkham dehavadbhiravāpyate* / / 'Greater is their difficulty whose minds are set on the unmanifested; for the goal of the unmanifested is very hard for the embodied to reach.' (B.G.12.5).

अपराजितः APARĀJITAḤ: Unconquered by the internal enemies of attachment etc., and by the external enemies like the dānavas (asuras) and others.

विश्वमूर्तिर्महामूर्तिर्दीप्तमूर्तिरमूर्तिमान् ।
अनेकमूर्तिरव्यक्तः शतमूर्तिः शताननः ।। ९० ।।

Viśvamūrtiḥ Mahāmurtiḥ
Dīptamūrtiḥ Amūrtimān /
Anekamūrtiḥ Avyaktaḥ
Śatmūrtiḥ Śatānanaḥ / / 90

विश्वमूर्ति: VIŚVAMŪRTIḤ: As He is all pervading, the universe is His form.

महामूर्ति: MAHĀMŪRTIḤ: Big is His form who lies on Adiśeṣa for His bed.

दीप्तमूर्ति: DĪPTAMŪRTIḤ: 1. Resplendant is the nature of His superior knowledge.

Or, 2. He assumed by His own free will His (*taijasa*) bright and flowing form. Hence *Dīptamūrtiḥ*.

अमूर्तिमान् AMŪRTIMĀN: He has no form determined by the bonds of karma.

अनेकमूर्ति: ANEKAMŪRTIḤ: He assumed many forms of His own will in His many incarnations for helping the worlds.

अव्यक्त: AVYAKTAḤ: Though He had many forms, He is not identifiable as being like this or that.

शतमूर्ति: ŚATAMŪRTIḤ: He whose form is pure-consciousness has many forms created by His own thought.

शतानन: ŚATĀNANAḤ: As He is of universal form, He has a thousand faces.

एको नैकः सवः कः किं यत्तत्पदमनुत्तमम् ।
लोकबन्धुर्लोकनाथो माधवो भक्तवत्सलः ॥ ९१ ॥

Ekaḥ Naikaḥ Savaḥ Kaḥ Kiṃ Yat Tat
Padamanuttamam /
Lokabandhuḥ Lokanāthaḥ
Mādhavaḥ Bhaktavatsalaḥ / / 91

एकः EKAH: He is one (only) as in truth He is bereft of any difference of like kind, of different kind or internal differences, *vide* the śruti: *ekamevādvitīyam:* 'one only without a second.' (Chand. Up. 6.2.1).

नैकः NAIKAḤ: (*na ekah*) Not one only. As He is of many forms due to (the action of) māyā. *vide* the śruti: *indro māyābhiḥ pururūpam īyate*: 'The Lord diversifies Himself in many forms by the forces of māyā' (Bṛh.Up.2.5.19).

सवः SAVAḤ: The Soma sacrifice called *Savah* in which the Soma is crushed. (He who is in the form of Soma Yāga.)

कः KAḤ: The sound *ka* stands for sukha, happiness. He is praised by it. Hence kaḥ *vide* the śruti: *kam brahmā:* Happiness is Brahman. (Ch.Up.4.10.5).

किम् KIM: Brahman alone is to be inquired into (as what, *kim*) as It is of the form of all puruṣārthas.

यत् YAT: *Yat* is generally used to indicate what is existent, a *siddhavastu.* By it Brahman is referred to. So *yat* means Brahman (that is, the Lord) *vide* the śruti: *yato vā imāni bhūtani jāyante:* 'That from which these beings are born.' (Taitt.Up.3.1).

तत् TAT: *Tanoti* means pervades; So, Brahman (which envelops the entire universe). *vide* the Lord's statement: *om Tat Sat iti nirdeśo brahmaṇastrividhaḥ smṛtaḥ:* 'The indicatory syllables of Brahman are three-fold as *Om Tat Sat.*' (B. G. 17.23).

पदमनुत्तमम् PADAMANUTTAMAM: The Supreme Abode. *padam* means what is attained by those who desire mokṣa That beyond which there is not a superior is *anuttamam. Padamanuttamam* is one Name wherein the second word is adjective.

लोकबन्धुः LOKABANDHUḤ: 1. All the worlds are bound to Him who is their support. So, *Lokabandhuḥ.*

Or 2. As He is the Father of all the worlds and as there is no *bandhu* comparable to the father.

Or 3. As He does what a *bandhu* does, that is, giving wholesome advice, prescribing the good and prohibiting the evil in the form of śruti and smṛti. So, *Lokabandhuḥ.*

लोकनाथः LOKANĀTHAḤ: Because He is sought by the people of the world, or besought by them or because He torments them or blesses them, or rules over them, He is *Lokanāthaḥ.*

माधवः MĀDHAVAḤ: Born in the family of Madhu, So, *Mādhavaḥ.*

भक्तवत्सलः BHAKTAVATSALAḤ: He has fondness for His devotees. So, Bhaktavatsala.

सुवर्णवर्णो हेमाङ्गो वराङ्गश्चन्दनाङ्गदी ।
वीरहा विषमः शून्यो घृताशीरचलश्चलः ॥ ९२ ॥

Suvarṇavarṇaḥ Hemaṅgaḥ
Varāṅgaḥ Candanāṅgadī /
Vīrdhā Viṣamaḥ Sūnyaḥ
Ghṛtāśiḥ Acalaḥ Calah / / 92

सुवर्णवर्णः SUVARṆAVARṆAḤ: He has the colour of gold. *vide* the śruti: *yadā paśyaḥ paśyate rukmavarṇam;* 'When the seer beholds the red (golden) coloured.' (Muṇḍ. Up.3.5).

हेमाङ्गः HEMĀNGAḤ: His body is like gold. *vide* the śruti: *ya eso'ntarāditye hiraṇmayaḥ puruṣaḥ*: 'The golden Person in the disc of the sun.' (Ch.Up.1.6.6).

वराङ्गः VARĀNGAḤ: His limbs (*aṅgas*) are *vara*, beautiful—excellent.

चन्दनाङ्गदी CANDANĀNGADĪ: His arms are ornamented by *keyūras* (armlets) which are attractive and pleasing.

वीरहा VĪRAHĀ: For the protection of dharma, He kills the *Vīras,* the chief Asuras. So *Vīrahā*.

विषमः VIṢAMAḤ: As He is different from every thing, He has no equal. *vi-samaḥ* (*sa* after *vi* becomes *ṣa*). *vide* the B. G. 11.43. *na tatsamo'sti bhyadhikaḥ kutoya'nyaḥ*: 'there is none equal to You; who is greater than You?'

शून्यः ŚŪNYAḤ: As He is devoid of all qualities, He is *śūnyaḥ*, as it were.

घृताशीः GHṚTĀŚĪḤ: He has no desires. All *āśiṣah prārthanās*, desires, are *ghṛtāḥ,* melted away for Him.

अचलः ACALAḤ: He does not stray from His nature, power, wisdom and other qualities. So *Acalaḥ*.

चलः CALAḤ: Moves in the form of wind. So, *Calaḥ*.

अमानी मानदो मान्यो लोकस्वामी त्रिलोकधृक् ।
सुमेधा मेधजो धन्यः सत्यमेधा धराधरः ॥ ९३ ॥

Amānī Mānadaḥ Mānyah Lokasvāmī
Trilokadhṛk /
Sumedhāḥ Medhajaḥ Dhanyaḥ
Satyamedhāḥ Dharādharaḥ / / 93

अमानी AMĀNĪ: As He is of the form of pure intelligence; He has no leaning towards things which are not the ātman.

मानदः MĀNADAḤ: 1. By the power of His māyā,

He gives to all people attachment as to the ātman to things which are not the ātman.

Or 2. He confers *māna*, prestige, on His devotees.

Or 3. He cuts off from the knowers of the Truth the thought of the ātman in what are not the ātman (The root *da* means both to give and to cut.)

मान्यः MĀNYAḤ: As He is the Lord of all, He is worthy of universal worship, *(mānanīyaḥ: pūjanīyaḥ)*.

लोकस्वामी LOKASVĀMĪ: As He is the Lord of the fourteen worlds, He is *Lokasvāmī*.

त्रिलोकधृक् TRILOKADHṚK: He supports (*dhārayati*) the three worlds. So, He is *Trilokadhṛk*.

सुमेधाः SUMEDHĀḤ: His *medhā*—intelligence—is *śobhanā*: bright, auspicious. Hence *Sumedhāḥ*.

मेधजः MEDHAJAḤ: Born in *medhā* i.e., sacrifice.

धन्यः DHANYAḤ: Of realised purpose.

सत्यमेधाः SATYAMEDHĀḤ: His intelligence is never falsified, is always true.

धराधरः DHARĀDHARAḤ: Supporting the earth by His *aṁśas*, manifestations like Adiśeṣa and others, He is *Dharādharaḥ*.

तेजोवृषो द्युतिधरः सर्वशस्त्रभृतां वरः ।
प्रग्रहो निग्रहो व्यग्रो नैकशृङ्गो गदाग्रजः ।। ९४ ।।

Tejovṛṣaḥ Dyutidharaḥ Sarvaśastrabhṛtām varaḥ /
Pragrahaḥ Nigrahaḥ Vyagraḥ Naikaśṛngaḥ Gadāgrajaḥ / / 94

तेजोवृषः TEJOVṚṢAḤ: In the form of the sun He rains the *tejas* (radiance) which takes the form of waters. So, *Tejovṛṣaḥ*.

द्युतिधरः DYUTIDHARAḤ: He bears the radiance of His limbs.

सर्वशस्त्रभृतांवरः SARVAŚASTRABHṚTĀMVARAḤ: The best of all who wield weapons.

प्रग्रहः PRAGRAHAḤ: 1. He receives the leaf, flower etc., offered by the devotees.

Or 2. He controls, by the reins dowered by His grace, the horses that are the sense organs which caper in the forest of sense objects.

निग्रहः NIGRAHAḤ: He brings everything under His control. So, Nigrahaḥ.

व्यग्रः VYAGRAḤ: 1. *agra,* the end or destruction for whom has vanished.

Or 2. In the matter of fulfilling the desires of devotees, ever intent.

नैकशृङ्गः NAIKAŚṚNGAḤ: Four-horned. *vide* the mantra *catvāri śṛṇgā* 'He having four horns. (Taitt. Āraṇ 1.10.17).

गदाग्रजः GADĀGRAJAḤ: 1. By the Nigada mantra, born ahead (*agraja*), the letter *ni* in *Nigadāgraja* is dropped and it becomes *Gadāgrajaḥ* (instead of *Nigadāgrajaḥ*).

Or 2. Vāsudeva's younger brother is Gada. Born prior to him is Gadāgrajaḥ.

चतुर्मूर्तिश्चतुर्बाहुश्चतुर्व्यूहश्चतुर्गतिः ।
चतुरात्मा चतुर्भावश्चतुर्वेदविदेकपात् ।। ९५ ।।

Caturmūrtiḥ Caturbāhuḥ
Caturvyūhaḥ Caturgatiḥ /
Caturātmā Caturbhāvaḥ Caturvedaviṭ
Ekapāṭ / / 95

चतुर्मूर्तिः CATURMŪRTIḤ: 1. Virāt, Sūtra, Avyākṛta and Turīya are the names of His four bodies.

Or 2. White, red, yellow and black are His four forms.

चतुर्बाहु: CATUṚBĀHUḤ. He has four arms. So *Caturbāhuḥ*. This is well known for Vāsudeva.

चतुर्व्यूह: CATUṚVYŪHAH: As mentioned in the Bahvṛcopaniṣad, Śarīra Puruṣa, Chandaḥ Puruṣa, Veda Puruṣa and Mahā Puruṣa are His four vyūha forms. Therefore, He is Caturvyūhaḥ.

चतुर्गति: CATUṚGATIḤ: The goal of those who observe the four āśramas and varṇas in the ordained way. So *Caturgatiḥ*.

चतुरात्मा CATURĀTMĀ: 1. As He is free of attachment and aversion, His ātmā, that is manas is clear and quick *(caturaḥ)*.

Or 2. His antaḥkaraṇa is fourfold as manas, buddhi, ahankāra and citta. So *Caturātmā*.

चतुर्भाव: CATUṚBHĀVAḤ: From Him arise the four puruṣārthas, namely, dharma, artha, kāma and mokṣa.

चतुर्वेदवित् CATUṚVEDAVIT: He knows correctly the meaning of the four Vedas.

एकपात EKAPĀT: His foot is one. Hence *Ekapat. vide the śruti: pādosya viśvābhūtāni*: 'All beings are one foot of Him,' and the Lord's statement *viṣṭabhyāhamidam kṛtsnam ekāmśena sthito jagat:* 'I stand supporting the whole universe with a single fragment of Myself.' (B. G. 10.42)

समावर्तोऽनिवृत्तात्मा दुर्जयो दुरतिक्रमः ।
दुर्लभो दुर्गमो दुर्गो दुरावासो दुरारिहा ॥ ९६ ॥

Samāvartaḥ Anivṛttātmā Durjayaḥ
Duratikramaḥ

Duṛlabhaḥ Duṛgamaḥ Duṛgaḥ
Durāvasaḥ Durārihā / / 96

समावर्तः SAMĀVAṚTAH: One who rotates well the wheel of samsāra.

अनिवृत्तात्मा ANIVṚTTĀTMĀ: Being omnipresent, His ātmā (mind) does not withdraw from objects.

दुर्जयः DURJAYAḤ: unconquerable.

दुरतिक्रमः On account of fear, the sun etc., do not transgress Him. *vide* the mantra: *bhayādasyāgnistapati bhayāt tapati sūryaḥ / bhayādindraśca vāyusca mṛtyuṛ dhāvati pañcamaḥ / /* 'By fear of Him, fire burns and the sun shines, through fear of Him run Indra and Vāyu, and Death as the fifth.' (Kaṭha Up. 2.3.3.) and also *mahadbhayam vajramudyatam*: 'It is a great fear like an uplifted thunderbolt.' (Kaṭha Up. 2.3.2).

दुर्लभः DURLABHAḤ: As He can be attained only by devotion, which is difficult to practise, *Durlabhaḥ*. *vide Vyāsa: janmāntara sahasreṣu tapojnānasamādhibhiḥ / narāṇām kṣīṇapāpānām kṛṣṇe bhaktiḥ prjāyate / /* : 'Devotion to Kṛṣṇa arises only to men whose sins have died out by tapas, jnāna and samādhi in thousands of other lives' and also the Lord's words: *bhaktyā labhyastvananyayā*: 'I can be obtained only by devotion to Me alone.' (B.G.8.22).

दुर्गमः DURGAMAḤ: Is attained, known, with difficulty. So, *Durgamaḥ*.

दुर्गः DURGAḤ: Is attained with difficulty by those who have overcome impediments.

दुरावासः DURĀVĀSAḤ: In samādhi He is retained in the mind by yogis with difficulty.

दुरारिहा DURĀRIHĀ: He kills the vile enemies like asuras and others. So, *Durārihā.*

शुभाङ्गो लोकसारङ्गः सुतन्तुस्तन्तुवर्धनः ।
इन्द्रकर्मा महाकर्मा कृतकर्मा कृतागमः ॥ ९७ ॥

Śubhāṅgaḥ Lokasāraṅgaḥ
Sutantuḥ Tantuvardhanaḥ /
Indrakarmā Mahākarmā Kṛtakarmā
Kṛtāgamaḥ / / 97

शुभाङ्गः ŚUBHĀNGAḤ: As He has to be meditated on as having beatutiful limbs, He is *Śubhāngaḥ.*

लोकसारङ्गः LOKASĀRANGAḤ: 1. Like the saranga (the honey bee), He acquires the essence of the worlds. So *Lokasārangaḥ. vide* the śruti. *prajāpatiḥ lokān abhyatapat:* 'Prajapati reflected on mankind." (Ch.Up.2.23.3).

Or 2. The essence of the universe (loka sāra) is Omkara. He is to be attained by it.

सुतन्तुः SUTANTUḤ: His universe is expanded as a beautiful thread. So *Sutantuḥ.*

तन्तुवर्धनः TANTUVARDHANAḤ: He makes that thread to grow or cuts it. (He protects or destroys the universe).

इन्द्रकर्मा INDRAKARMĀ: His action is like that of Indra, glorious in nature.

महाकर्मा MAHĀKARMĀ: The great elements like the sky are His actions. So *Mahākarmā.*

कृतकर्मा KṚTAKARMĀ: As He is kṛtārtha, of realised purpose, there is no action left to be done by Him. Hence *Kṛtakarmā.*

Or 2. He is one who has performed actions characterised by dharma.

कृतागमः KṚTĀGAMAḤ: He by whom the Āgamas of the form of Vedas were created. He from whom the Vedas came is *Kṛtāgamaḥ*. *vide* the śrutis like *asya mahato bhūtasya niśśvasitametat*: 'This (the Vedas) is the breath of this mighty Being.' (Brh. Up.4.4.10).

उद्भवः सुन्दरः सुन्दो रत्ननाभः सुलोचनः ।
अर्को वाजसनः शृङ्गी जयन्तः सर्वविज्जयी ॥ ९८ ॥

Udbhavaḥ Sundaraḥ Sundaḥ Ratnanābhaḥ
Sulocanaḥ /
Arkaḥ Vājasanaḥ Śṛngī Jayantaḥ
Sarvavit Jayī / / 98

उद्भवः UDBHAVAḤ: 1. He assumes a superior janma of His own free Will.

Or 2. As He is the cause of all, there can be no birth for Him.

सुन्दरः SUNDARAḤ: Of beauty which is the wonder of the world. Hence *Sundaraḥ*.

सुन्दः SUNDAḤ: He gets well moistened in the mind. It means the Merciful.

रत्ननाभः RATNANĀBHAḤ: By the word *ratna* splendour is indicated. His navel is beautiful as *ratna*. So, *Ratnanābhaḥ*.

सुलोचनः SULOCANAḤ: His eyes or jñāna is good (auspicious). *Śobhanalocanaḥ*.

अर्कः ARKAḤ: As He is worshipped even by Brahma and others who themselves deserve to be worshipped.

वाजसनः VĀJASANAḤ: To those who ask for it, He gives (*sanoti vājam*) annam, food. Hence *Vājasanaḥ*.

शृङ्गी: SṚNGĪ: In the waters of the great deluge, Pralaya, He is of form of a kind of fish with horn.

जयन्तः JAYANTAḤ: He wonderfully vanquishes His enemies, or He is the cause of victory. So, *Jayantaḥ*.

सर्ववित् SARVAVIT: He has encyclopaedic knowledge.

जयी JAYĪ: He has the capacity to conquer the internal enemies like attachment and the external ones like Hiraṇyākṣa who are difficult to conquer.

सर्वविज्जयी SARVAVIJJAYĪ: Is one Name, He being both *Sarvavit* and *Jayī*, knows everything and is victorious.

सुवर्णबिन्दुरक्षोभ्यः सर्ववागीश्वरेश्वरः ।
महाह्रदो महागर्तो महाभूतो महानिधिः ॥ ९९ ॥

Suvarṇabinduḥ Akṣobhyaḥ
Sarvavāgīśvareśvaraḥ /
Mahāhradaḥ Mahāgartaḥ
Mahābhūtaḥ Mahānidhiḥ / / 99

सुवर्णबिन्दुः SUVARṆABINDUḤ: 1. His limbs (bindavaḥ) are gold. *vide* the śruti: *ānakhāt sarva eva suvarṇaḥ;* having a golden body up to the nails (Ch.Up. 1.6.6).

Or 2. He in whose *mantra* the letters and *bindu* are auspicious. So, *Svarṇabinduḥ*.

Thus the eighth hundred of Names has been explained.

अक्षोभ्यः AKṢOBHYAḤ: Not liable to be agitated by attachment, aversion, etc., by sound and other external objects and by enemies of the devas.

सर्ववागीश्वरेश्वरः SARVAVĀGĪŚVAREŚVARAḤ: He is the Lord of even all the Lords, of speech, Brahmā and others.

महाह्रदः MAHĀHRADAḤ: The yogins remain peaceful and happy plunging in the refreshing waters of His bliss. So, He is *Mahāhradaḥ* like a big pond of cool water.

महागर्तः MAHĀGARTAḤ: 1. Like a great chasm *(garta)* His maya is difficult to get over. So, He is *Mahāgartaḥ. vide* the Lord's assertion: *mama māyā duratyayā'* My māyā is difficult to get over. (B.G.7.14).

Or 2. Lexicographers say that *garta* is a synonym of *ratha* (chariot). So *Mahāgartaḥ* means *Mahārathaḥ.* That He is a Mahāratha is celebrated in Mahābhārata and other works. (*Mahāratha* is the highest distinction of the general of an army.)

महाभूतः MAHĀBHŪTAḤ: As His form is not subject to limitations of three periods of time, He is Mahabhūtaḥ.

महानिधिः MAHĀNIDHIḤ: All beings are deposited (find rest) in Him, so *nidhiḥ* and it (the nidhi) is great. So Mahānidhiḥ.

कुमुदः कुन्दरः कुन्दः पर्जन्यः पावनोऽनिलः ।
अमृताशोऽमृतवपुः सर्वज्ञः सर्वतोमुखः ॥ १०० ॥

Kumudaḥ Kundaraḥ Kundaḥ
Parjanyaḥ Pāvanaḥ Anilaḥ /
Amṛtāśaḥ Amṛtavapuḥ
Sarvajñaḥ Sarvatomukhaḥ // 100

कुमुदः KUMUDAḤ: 1. He makes *Ku* the earth happy by decreasing its burden (bhūbhāra of evil men). So, *Ku-mudaḥ.*

कुन्दरः KUNDARAḤ: He bestows fruits of (actions) which are pure as a kunda flower. *Kunda-rah, rāti* means *dadāti,* gives.

Or 2. *Lāti* meaning *ādatte*: receives (the kunda flower) *ralayorabhedaḥ. ra* and *la* are interchangeable.

Or 3. Pierced or clove the earth, *kum-darah* taking the form of a boar to kill Hiraṇyākṣa. So, *Kundaraḥ.*

कुन्दः KUNDAḤ: 1. He has handsome limbs like a kunda flower. Being spotlessly white as a crystal, He is *Kundaḥ.*

Or 2. He gave the earth *ku* to Kāsyapa, *kum-adāt.* The Harivamśa says: 'Bhṛgu's son (Parasurāma) performed a horse sacrifice to absolve himself of the sin (of killing the Kṣatriya kings). In that sacrifice, he gladly made a great gift of the earth to Kāsyapa.'

Or 3. He who brings the earth under subjection. *kum:* the earth, *dyati khaṇdayati:* brings under subjection.

Or 4. *Ku* stands for the kings of the earth. As the Viṣṇu Dharma has it: "May that chief of the Bhārgavas who rid the earth of kṣatriyas and also cut off the forest of hands of Kārtavīrya increase my prosperity."

पर्जन्यः PARJANYAḤ: 1. Like the rain cloud He allays the afflictions of the body etc., (ādhyātmika, ādhibhautika, ādhidaivika).

Or 2. He rains the fruition of all desires. So, *Parjanyaḥ.*

पावनः PĀVANAḤ: He purifies by mere thought of Him.

अनिलः ANILAḤ: 1. *ilati* means induces or orders. As He is without it, as He is not subject to the inducement or command of another, He is *An-ilaḥ.*

Or 2. *ilati* may mean *svapiti* sleeps. So, *one who* is ignorant (sleeps to knowledge) is *ilah.* He is the opposite of it as He is eternally awake in wisdom. So *Anilaḥ.*

Or 3. The root *nila* is used in the sense of dense or inaccessible. He is not inaccessible to devotees. So, *Anilaḥ.*

अमृताशः AMṚTĀŚAḤ: 1. He drinks the nectar of His own Ātman *amṛtam aśnāti.*

Or 2. Making the devas drink the nectar obtained by churning the ocean, drinks it Himself. So *Amṛtāsah.*

Or 3. His desires (*āsāḥ*) yield undying amrtāḥ fruits: amṛtāḥ āsāḥ. So, *Amṛtāsaḥ.*

अमृतवपुः AMṚTAVAPUḤ: *mṛtam* is *maraṇam:* death. He has a body which is not subject to death. So *Amṛtavapuḥ.*

सर्वज्ञः SARVAJÑAḤ: *yaḥ sarvajñaḥ sarvavit:* He who is omniscient and knows all. (Mund. Up.1.1.9). He knows everything, omniscient. So, *Sarvajñaḥ.*

सर्वतोमुखः SARVATOMUKHAḤ: By virtue of the Lord's assertion: *sarvatokṣi śiromukham:* With eyes, heads and faces all round (B.G.13.13).

सुलभः सुव्रतः सिद्धः शत्रुजिच्छत्रुतापनः ।
न्यग्रोधोदुम्बरोऽश्वत्थश्चाणूरान्ध्रनिषूदनः ॥ १०१ ॥

Sulabhaḥ Suvrataḥ Siddhaḥ
Satrujit Satrutāpanaḥ /
Nyagrodhaḥ Udumbaraḥ Asvatthaḥ
Cānūrāndhranisūdanaḥ / / 101

सुलभः SULABHAḤ: He is easily attained by leaf, flower and fruit offered with pure devotion alone. *vide* the Mahābhārata: patreṣu puṣpeṣu phaleṣu toyesvakrī talabhyeṣu sadaiva satsu / bhaktyekalabhye puruṣe purāṇe muktau katham na kriyate prayatnaḥ // 'When leaves, flowers and fruits are always available, without any cost, why is not endeavour made for mokṣa by propitiating with them the ancient Puruṣa who can be attained by devotion alone?'

सुव्रत: SUVRATAḤ: He who is of excellent vows or enjoys eminently or ceases from enjoyment (as the occasion may demand) *Su-vrataḥ*.

सिद्ध: SIDDHAḤ: Ever existent without dependence on others.

शत्रुजित् ŚATRUJIT: The enemies of the devas alone are His enemies. He vanquishes them. So, *Śatrujit*.

शत्रुतापन: ŚATRUTĀPANAḤ: The afflictor of the enemies of the devas.

न्यग्रोध: NYAGRODHAḤ: *Nyak* means *arvāk:* downward *rohati* grows (downward) (*ha* in *roha* becomes *dha*) He (the root) is standing above all beings who are below. Or He conceals His māyā or controls them by it, by using root *rudh*.

उदुम्बर: UDUMBARAḤ: 1. Issued out from the sky as the cause, *ut-ambaraḥ,* by special rule *a* becomes *u*.

Or 2. *Udumbara* means food etc., He nourishes the universe with it. So *Udumbaraḥ. vide* the śruti ūrgvā *annādyam udumbaram*: '*udumbara* means food etc.'

अश्वत्थ: AŚVATTHAH: *Śvaḥ tiṣṭati iti śvaṣthaḥ.* What stands tomorrow is *śvasthah.* What is not *śvasthaḥ* i.e., that of which it cannot be said as 'staying tomorrow' is *aśvasthaḥ.* That is, that whose existence is not determined by time, as today, tomorrow, being ever present without demarcation of time is *aśvatthaḥ.* By special rule *aśvasthaḥ* becomes *aśvatthaḥ. vide* śruti: *ūrdhvamūlo'vākśākhaḥ eṣo'śvatthaḥ sanātanaḥ.* 'the eternal tree with roots above and branches below.' (Kaṭha Up. 6.1) and the smṛti (B.G. 15.1) *ūrdhvamulam adhaśśākham aśvattham prāhuravyayam*: 'they speak of a deathless tree with roots above and branches below'.

चाणूरान्ध्रनिषूदनः CĀNŪRĀNDHRANIṢŪDANAḤ: The killer of the wrestler from Andhra deśa of the name of *Cāṇūra*. (*āndhra* also means a man of low caste).

सहस्रार्चिः सप्तजिह्वः सप्तैधाः सप्तवाहनः ।
अमूर्तिरनघोऽचिन्त्यो भयकृद्भयनाशनः ॥ १०२ ॥

Sahasrārciḥ Saptajihvaḥ
Saptaidhāḥ Saptavāhanaḥ /
Amūrtiḥ Anaghaḥ Acintyaḥ
Bhayakṛt Bhayanāśanaḥ // 102

सहस्रार्चिः SAHASRĀRCIH: He who has thousand, endless rays. *vide* the *Gīta* statement: *divi sūryasahasrasya*: 'of the splendour of a thousand suns in the sky' (15.1). (11·12)

सप्तजिह्वः SAPTAJIHVAḤ: He is seven-tongued. *vide* the śruti: kālī *karālī ca manojavā ca sulohitā yā ca sudhūmravarnā / sphulinginī viśvaruciśca devī lolāyamānā iti sapta jihvāh*. The seven flickering tongues are Kāḷī (the black), *Karālī* (the terrific) *Manojavā* (fleet as the mind) Sulohitā (the very red) Sudhūmravarṇā (of purple colour) *Sphulinginī* (sparkling) and *Viśvaruciḥ* (of universal form (Mund. Up. 2.4).

सप्तैधाः SAPTAIDHĀḤ: He, *agni*, has seven flames, *vide* the *śruti sapta te agne samidhaḥ sapta jihvāḥ*: 'O' Agni, thou hast seven flames, seven tongues'. (Taitt. Sam. 1.5.2).

सप्तवाहन: SAPTAVĀHANAḤ: 1. Seven horses are His vehicles.

Or 2. A horse called *Sapta* is His vehicle. *vide* the śruti. *eko'śvo vahati saptanāmā*: the horse named *Sapta* is carrying (Him) (Taitt. Ar. 3.11).[22]

अमूर्ति: AMŪRTIḤ: 1. *Mūrti* (figure) is what is weighty and which can support, of the nature of the moveable and immoveable. *vide* the śruti: *tābhyo'bhitaptābhyo mūrtirajāyata*: 'from them agitated, the form was born' (Ai. Up. 3.2). He who is devoid of it is *A-mūrtiḥ*.

Or 2. *Mūrti* means what is compacted of the body and limbs capable of perception and feelings. As He is without them He is *A-mūrtiḥ*.

अनघ: ANAGHAḤ: *Agham* is sorrow or sin. Being without it, *An-aghaḥ*.

अचिन्त्य: ACINTYAḤ: 1. Being the witness of the knower etc., He cannot be thought of by any canon of knowledge.

Or 2. Being different from the universe, He cannot be thought of in the form: He is like this. So, *Acintyaḥ*.

भयकृत् BHAYAKṚT: 1. He causes fear to those who pursue the path of unrighteousness (*bhayam karoti*).

Or 2. He removes the fear of the devotees (*bhayam-kṛintati*). So, *Bhayakṛt*.

भयनाशन: BHAYANĀŚANAḤ: He destroys the fear of those who are steadfast in the duties of their *varṇa* and *āśrama*. *vide* the words of *Parāśara: varṇāśramācāravatā puruṣena paraḥ pumān / viṣṇorārādh-*

22. In these, as in similar Names, the Lord is identified with these devatas. Agni, Vāyu, Varuṇa and others who are instinct with Him.

yate panthāh nanyastattoṣakārakaḥ / / : 'The path of supreme Puruṣa is worshipped by those who practise varṇa and āśrama. There is no other way to please Him.' (Viṣṇu Purāṇa 3.8.9).

अणुर्बृहत्कृशः स्थूलो गुणभृन्निर्गुणो महान् ।
अधृतः स्वधृतः स्वास्यः प्राग्वंशो वंशवर्धनः ।। १०३ ।।

Aṇuḥ Bṛhat Kraśaḥ Sthūlaḥ
Guṇabhṛt Nirguṇaḥ Mahān /
Adhṛtaḥ Svadhṛtaḥ Svāsyah
Prāgvamśaḥ Vamśavardhanaḥ / / 103

अणुः ANUḤ: As He is extremely subtle, *Aṇuḥ*. *vide* the śruti: *eṣo'ṇurātmā cetasā veditavyaḥ*: This minute Ātman is to be known by the mind. (Muṇd. Up. 3.1.9).

बृहत् BṚHAT: Being big and growing (to infinitude) Brahman is *Bṛhat*. vide the śruti *mahato mahīyān*: 'greater than the great'. (Kaṭha 1.20.20).

कृशः KṚŚAḤ: By the expression *asthūlam,* not gross, His being material is denied. So, *Kṛṣaḥ,* thin.

स्थूलः STHŪLAḤ: Being stout is used figuratively He being everything.

गुणभृत् GUṆABHṚT: Presiding over creation, preservation and dissolution (*sṛṣṭi, sthiti* and *laya*) by virtue of the qualities (guṇas) of *sattva, rajas* and *tamas,* the Lord is *Guṇabhṛt,* the bearer of guṇas.

निर्गुणः NIRGUṆAḤ: But, really He is without qualities, *Nirguṇaḥ, vide* the śruti: *kevalo nirguṇasca:* One only and qualitiless (Sve. Up. 6.11).

महान् MAHĀN: It is impossible to speak of Him as possessing any quality even for the sake of argument as He is devoid of the qualities of sound etc., as He is extremely subtle, as He is ever pure and omnipresent, etc. Therefore only He is *Mahān*. Āpastamba says: *anango' śabdo' śarīro' sparśaśca mahān śuciḥ*: 'Partless, bodiless, devoid of touch and mahān, pure.' (Dharma Sūtra 1.22.7).

अधृत: ADHṚTAḤ: Being the supporter of all supports like the earth, He is not supported by anything else. So, *Adhṛtaḥ*.

स्वधृत: SVADHṚTAḤ: By way of removing the doubt as to by whom then He is supported, it is said: He is supported by His own glory. So, *Sva-dhṛtaḥ. vide the śruti sa bhagavaḥ kasmin pratiṣṭhita iti sve mahimni:* 'O lord! where does He abide? In His own eminence'. (Ch.Up.7.24.1).

स्वास्य: SVĀSYAḤ: 1. His face is beautiful, handsome as the red colour inside a lotus flower. So, *Su-āsyaḥ.*

Or 2. The upadeśa of the great store of Vedas which can give the puruṣārthas came out of His mouth. So, *Su-āsyaḥ. vide* the śruti *asya mahato bhūtasya:* "From this great Being emanated'. (Rg. Veda, Yejur Veda etc. (Bṛh. Up.4.4.10).

प्राग्वंश: PRĀGVAMŚAḤ: The race of others are later. His race, namely the universe has been in existence before all that, not later. So *Prāk-vamśaḥ.*

वंशवर्धन: VAMŚAVARDHANAḤ: As expanding or cutting the Universe (*Vamśam*) He is *Vamśavardhanaḥ.*

भारभृत्कथितो योगी योगीशः सर्वकामदः ।
आश्रमः श्रमणः क्षामः सुपर्णो वायुवाहनः ॥ १०४ ॥

Bhārabhṛt Kathitaḥ Yogī Yogīśaḥ Sarvakāmadaḥ
Āśramaḥ Śramaṇaḥ Kṣāmah Suparṇah
Vāyuvāhanaḥ / / 104

भारभृत् BHĀRABHṚT: In the form of *Ananta* or *Ādiśeṣa,* He carries the weight of the earth. So, *Bhārabhṛt.*

कथित: KATHITAḤ: 1. By the Vedas, He alone is declared to be the Supreme.

Or 2. He is celebrated by all Vedas. *vide* the śruti and smṛti texts: *sarve vedā yatpadamāmananti*: 'He who is celebrated by all the Vedas.' (Kaṭha Up. 2.15); *vedaisca sarvairahameva vedyaḥ*: 'I alone am to be known by all the Vedas'. (B.G. 15.15). *vede rāmāyane puṇye bhārate bharatarṣabha / ādau madhye tathā cānte viṣṇuḥ sarvatra gīyate / /* : 'In the holy Vedas, the Rāmāyaṇa, Bhārata, at the beginning and at the end Viṣṇu is sung everywhere'. (Harivamśa 323.93). It is said: *so' dhvanaḥ paramāpnoti tadviṣṇoḥ paramam padam*: 'he attains the goal of the road; the Supreme abode of Viṣṇu' (Kaṭha. Up. 3.9). In reply to the question: What is the supreme abode of Viṣṇu who is all-pervading, it is said to be beyond all the senses etc., beginning with *indriyebhyaḥ parā hyarthāḥ* (Kaṭha Up. 3.10) and ending with *puruṣānna param kincit sā kāṣṭha sā parā gatiḥ,* (Kaṭha Up. 3.11): 'the objects are beyond the senses: there is nothing beyond Puruṣa, that is ultimate, the final goal. As so celebrated, *Kathitaḥ.*

योगी YOGĪ: 1. Yoga stands for *jñānam.* As He is attained by it alone, He is *Yogī.*

Or 2. Yoga is samādhi. As He stabilises His Ātman in His Ātman, He is *Yogī.*

योगीश: YOGĪŚAḤ: Other yogis are obstructed by impediments; they fall away from their status. As He is devoid of that condition, He is the Lord of the yogīs: *Yogīśah.*

सर्वकामद: SARVAKĀMADAḤ: He ever fulfils all

desires. As Vyāsa said in the Brahmasūtras, *phalamata upapatteh:* 'From Him (the Lord) the fruit (of works) arises; for that stands to reasoning'. So, *Sarvakāmadaḥ.*

आश्रम: ĀŚRAMAḤ: As the resting place like a hermitage of those who wander in the forest of samsāra, *Āśramaḥ.*

श्रमण: ŚRAMAṆAḤ: He causes grief to the ignorant people.

क्षाम: KṢĀMAḤ: He causes all beings to decay.

सुपर्ण: SUPARṆAḤ: Of Him who is in the form of the tree of samsāra, the Vedas are the beautiful leaves. So. *Suparṇaḥ vide* Bhagvān's statement: *chandāmsi yasya parṇāni:* The Vedas (*chandāṁsi*) are His leaves (B.G. 15.1).

वायुवाहन: VĀYUVĀHANAḤ: He by fear of whom the wind carries beings is *Vāyuvāhanaḥ. vide* the śruti: *bhīṣā' smāt vātaḥ pavate*: 'by fear of Him the wind blows'. (Taitt. Up. 2.8).

धनुर्धरो धनुर्वेदो दण्डो दमयिता दमः ।

अपराजितः सर्वसहो नियन्ता नियमोऽयमः ॥ १०५ ॥

Dhanurdharaḥ Dhanurvedaḥ

Daṇḍaḥ Damayitā Damaḥ /

Aparājitaḥ Sarvaśahaḥ

Niyantā Niyamaḥ Ayamaḥ / / 105

धनुर्धर: DHANURDHARAḤ: Śrīmān Rāma wielded the great bow. So Dhanurdharaḥ (in His incarnation as Rāma).

धनुर्वेद: DHANURVEDAḤ: He (Dāsarathī) also knows the science of archery—*dhanurveda.*

दण्ड: DAṆḌAḤ: The daṇda of those who punish. The Lord said: *daṇḍo damayatām asmi*: 'I am the *daṇḍa* of those who inflict punishment.' (B.G. 10.33).

दमयिता DAMAYITĀ: In the form of *Vaivaśvata* (Yama or the God of death) or in the form of kings, He is the punisher of people.

दमः DAMAḤ: Of those who deserve to be punished, punishment is the fruit. That too is the Lord. So *Damaḥ*.

अपराजितः APARĀJITAḤ: Unconquered by enemies.

सर्वसहः SARVASAHAḤ: 1. Skilful in all actions. Or 2. Withstands all enemies.

नियन्ता NIYANTĀ: He establishes (ordains) all people in their respective functions.

नियमः / अनियमः NIYAMAḤ/ANIYAMAH: He is not bound by any code: for to Him who is the ordainer of all, there is no other ordainer. So, *Aniyamaḥ*. Or niyama being limb of yoga and hence possessed by Him, He himself is *Niyamaḥ*.

यमः / अयमः YAMAḤ/AYAMAH: There is no Yama, *mṛtyu,* death for Him. Hence *Ayamaḥ*. Or yama being limb of yoga and hence possessed by Him, He himself is *Yamaḥ*.

सत्त्ववान्सात्त्विकः सत्यः सत्यधर्मपरायणः।
अभिप्रायः प्रियार्होऽर्हः प्रियकृत्प्रीतिवर्धनः॥ १०६॥

Sattvavān Sāttvikaḥ Satyaḥ
Satyadharmaparāyaṇaḥ /
Abhiprāyaḥ Priyārhaḥ Arhaḥ
Priyakṛt Prītivardhanaḥ / / 106

सत्त्ववान् SATTVAVĀN: He has *Sattva,* strength compacted of courage and valour.

सात्त्विकः SĀTTVIKAḤ: Is established predominantly in sattva guṇa. So *Sāttvikaḥ*.

सत्यः SATYAḤ: As He is good to good people, He is *Satyaḥ.*

सत्यधर्मपरायण: SATYADHARMA PARĀYAṆAH: He is constant to truth which is expressing a thing as it is and Dharma based on commands. So He is *Satyadharmaparāyaṇaḥ.*

अभिप्राय: ABHIPRĀYAḤ: 1. Desired or sought by those who are after the puruṣārthas.

Or 2. During pralaya, the world goes towards Him. *abhi praiti (jagat).*

प्रियार्हः PRIYĀRHAḤ: He deserves (*arhati*) whatever is *priya, iṣṭa* or dear. The Smṛti says: *yadyadiṣṭatamam loke yaccāsya dayitam gṛhe / tattat guṇavate deyam tadevākṣayamicchatā / /* 'Whatever is superlatively dear in the world, the most beloved at home, that must be given to the worthy by one who desires the Imperishable.' (Viṣṇu Dharma 55.3).

अर्हः ARHAḤ: One who deserves to be worshipped by words of welcome, offer of a seat, water to wash the hands and feet, praise, prostration and other instruments of worship.

प्रियकृत् PRIYAKṚT: Not merely deserves to be loved, but He also fulfils the desires of those who worship Him by praise etc.

प्रीतिवर्धनः PRĪTIVARDHANAḤ: He increases their endearment (to Him) or His endearment to them.

विहायसगतिर्ज्योतिः सुरुचिर्हुतभुग्विभुः ।
रविर्विरोचनः सूर्यः सविता रविलोचनः ।। १०७ ।।

Vihāyasagtiḥ Jyotiḥ Suruciḥ Hutabhuk Vibhuh /
Raviḥ Virocanaḥ Sūryaḥ Savitā
Ravilocanaḥ // 107

विहायसगति: VIHĀYASAGATĪḤ: The sky (*vihayasam*) is His abode (*gatih*), *Viṣṇupadam,* or, himself the Sun (moving through sky).

ज्योति: JYOTIḤ: He shines by Himself, So *Jyotiḥ* *vide* the mantra *nārāyaṇaḥ param jyotiḥ*: 'Nārāyaṇa is the Supreme Light'. (Maha U.13).

सुरुचि: SURUCIḤ: Of splendrous light or of good tastes. So, *Suruciḥ.*

हुतभुक् HUTABHUK: In all sacrificial acts dedicated to whatever god, He enjoys the oblation or protects it.

विभु: VIBHUḤ: Because He is omnipresent or because He is the Lord of the three worlds, He is *Vibhuḥ.*

रवि: RAVIḤ: He draws the juices, *rasan ādatte;* So He is *Raviḥ,* of the form of Āditya the Sun.

विरोचन: VIROCANAḤ: Has various tastes: *vividham rocate.*

सूर्य: SŪRYAḤ: *sūte śriyam,* giver of wealth. Or, *sūte* or *suvati* brings (the world) to birth or induces to work. By Panini's dictum *rājasūya sūrya...,* the word *surya* in different senses is obtained. He is verily the sun, *surya.*

सविता SAVITĀ: He that brings to birth the entire universe. *vide* the Viṣṇu Dharmottara: *rasānam ca tathādānāt ravirityabhidhīyate / prajānām tu prasavanāt saviteti nigadyate / /* : 'As He takes away all the juices, He is called Ravi. He is called Savitā from issuing the beings out of Himself'.

रविलोचन: RAVILOCANAḤ: *Ravi* the sun is His *locanam,* eye. *vide* the śruti: *agnirmūrdhā cakṣuṣī candrasūryau:* 'Fire is (His) head and the moon and the sun are (His) eyes' (Mund Up.3.4.).

अनन्तो हुतभुग्भोक्ता सुखदो नैकजोऽग्रजः ।
अनिर्विण्णः सदामर्षी लोकाधिष्ठानमद्भुतः ॥ १०८ ॥

Anantaḥ Hutabhuk Bhoktā Sukhadaḥ
Naikajaḥ Agrajaḥ /
Anirviṇṇaḥ Sadāmarṣī Lokādhiṣṭhānam
Adbhutaḥ / / 108

अनन्तः ANANTAḤ: 1. Endless (*Ananta*) as He is eternal, as He is omnipresent, and unlimited by time and space.

Or 2. Of the form of Ādiseṣa who is called *Ananta.*

हुतभुक् HUTABHUK: As He protects *bhunakti* what is *hutam* offered in *oblation.*

भोक्ता BHOKTĀ: 1. He eats (enjoys) *bhunkte* the enjoyable things which constitute *prakrti* or nature

Or 2. He protects the universe.

सुखदः SUKHADAḤ: 1. Gives *sukha* or bliss of mokṣa to (His) devotees. So, *Sukhadaḥ.*

Or 2. Spelt as *ASUKHADAḤ*, He cuts (removes) (*dyati, khandayati*) the *asukham* the miseries (of His devotees).

नैकजः NAIKAJAḤ: Being born (incarnated) many times for the preservation of dharma, He is *Naikajaḥ* (*ekajaḥ* means born once; *na ekajaḥ* not born only once; born many times).

अग्रजः AGRAJAḤ: Born first: *agre jāyate,* i.e., Hiraṇyagarbha who is the first born. *vide* the śruti: *hiraṇyagarbhaḥ samavartatāgre:* 'Hiraṇyagarbha appeared first' (Taitt.Sam.4.1.8).

अनिर्विण्णः ANIRVIṆṆAḤ: He has no grief as He is of all realised desires. (There can be no desire unrealised for Him or as He has no want to desire its realisation). So *Anirviṇṇaḥ.*

सदामर्षी SADĀMARṢĪ: He is good to good people, or forgives or bears with them. *Sataḥ mṛṣyate kṣamate.*

लोकाधिष्ठानम् LOKĀDHIṢṬHĀNAM: All worlds remain in position standing on Him, who has no support, as their support, i.e. Brahma.

अद्भुत: ADBHUTAḤ: Because He is wonderful *vide* the *śruti: sravaṇāyāpi bahubhiryo na labhyaḥ sṛṇvanto' pi bahavo yam na vidyuḥ / āścaryo vaktā kuśalo sya labdhā āscaryo jñāta kuśalānuśiṣṭaḥ / /* 'Who cannot be obtained by many even for hearing about Him, Whom many do not attain though they hear of Him; the expounder of Him is a wonder, and able is he who obtains Him; wonderful is the knower and he who attains Him is able.' (Kaṭh. Up. 2.7) and the Lord's statement: *āscaryavat paśyati kaścidenam*: 'one sees Him as wonderful. (B.G. 2.29).

सनात्सनातनतमः कपिलः कपिरप्ययः ।
स्वस्तिदः स्वस्तिकृत्स्वस्ति स्वस्तिभुक्स्वस्तिदक्षिणः ।। १०९ ।।

Sanāt Sanātanatamaḥ Kapilaḥ Kapiḥ Apyayaḥ /
Svastidaḥ Svastikṛt Svasti Svastibhuk
Svastidakṣiṇaḥ // 109

सनात् SANĀT: The participle *sanāt* conveys the meaning of long duration. Time or *kāla* is a manifestation of the Supreme. The Viṣṇu Purāṇa says: *parasya brahmaṇo rūpam puruṣaḥ prathamam dvija / vyaktāvyakte tathaivanye rūpe kālastathā param / /* 'O twice born! Puruṣa is the first form of Parabrahman, *vyakta* and *avyakta* the manifested and the unmanifested are the next forms; the next is *kāla* or Time'. (1.2.15)

सनातनतम: SANĀTANATAMAḤ: Being the cause of everything and being more ancient than *Viriñci* (Brahma) and others who are ancient, He is most ancient.

कपिल: KAPILAḤ: 1. The colour of the *badabānala,* the submarine fire is dark blue (*kapila*). The Lord is of that form. So, He is *Kapilaḥ.*

कपि: KAPIḤ: 1. *Kam* stands for water. *pi* stands for drinking it with his rays. So Kapiḥ is Sūrya. Being of the form of the Sun; He is *Kapiḥ.*

Or 2. *Kapiḥ* means *Varāha,* the boar-incarnation. *vide* the statement *kapirvarāhah śreṣthaśca*: 'Kapi is Varāha and the eminent.' (Mahā Bhārata Śānti 352.25).

अप्यय: APYAYAḤ: The worlds go unto Him even at the time of praḷaya (universal deluge) So, *Apyayaḥ.*

Thus the ninth hundred of Names has been explained.

स्वस्तिद: SVASTIDAḤ. He confers *mangaḷam (svasti)* auspiciousness on devotees. So, *Svasti-daḥ.*

स्वस्तिकृत् SVASTIKṚT: He does that, mangalam, itself.

स्वस्ति SVASTI: His nature is auspiciousness characterised by supreme bliss.

स्वस्तिभुक् SVASTIBHUK: 1. The enjoyer of that *svasti* or auspiciousness *(bhunkte).*

2. He makes His devotees enjoy that svasti (*bhunakti*).

स्वस्तिदक्षिण: SVASTIDAKṢIṆAḤ. 1. He grows in the form of svasti (*daksate* means *vardhate* grows).

Or 2. He is efficient in conferring *svasti.* So, *Svastīdakṣiṇaḥ.*

Or 3. The word dakṣinaḥ is applied to one who does action quickly. He alone is able to confer *svasti* quickly. For by mere devout thought of Him are realised all *siddhis. vide* the statements: *smṛte sakalakalyāṇa bhājanam yatra jayate / puruṣastamajam nityam vrajāmi śaraṇam harim / /* : 'I always seek refuge in Hari the unborn who, when remembered, becomes the source from which all auspiciousness flows,' and *smaraṇādeva kṛṣṅasya papaṣanghātapanjaram / śatadhā bhedamāyāti girirvajrahato yathā / /*: 'By remembrance alone of Kṛṣṇa the totality of sins is split hundredfold like a mountain blown by vajra, Indra's thunderbolt.'

अरौद्रः कुण्डली चक्री विक्रम्यूर्जितशासनः ।
शब्दातिगः शब्दसहः शिशिरः शर्वरीकरः ॥ ११० ॥

Araudraḥ Kuṇḍalī Cakrī Vikramī Ūrjitaśasanaḥ /
Śabdātigaḥ Śabdasahaḥ
Śiśiraḥ Śarvarīkaraḥ // 110

अरौद्रः ARAUDRAḤ: Action is wild; attachment is passionate; anger is violent; He in whom these three kinds of fierceness (*raudratrayam*) do not exist by reason of His being of all fulfilled desires (as, by reason of His fullness, He has no wants) and as He is not moved by attachment, aversion etc., He is *Araudraḥ.*

कुण्डली KUṆDALĪ: 1. Being of the form of a serpent, śeṣa (which lies on the ground in a circle, *kuṇḍala*), He is *Kuṇḍalī.*

Or 2. He has ear ornaments like the sun, the *sahasrāmśu.*

Or 3. His ear ornaments are Sānkhya and Yoga, shaped as a fish. So *Kuṇḍali;-*

चक्री CAKRĪ: He wields the discus known as Sudarśana of the nature of (fleet as) the mind (*manastatva*) for the protection of all the worlds. *vide*, the Viṣṇu Purāna statesment: *calasvarūpam atyantajavenāntaritānilam / cakrasvarūpam ca mano dhatte viṣṇuḥ kare sthitam* / / Viṣṇu holds in His hand the Cakra (discus) representing the unsteady mind, swifter than the wind.' (1.22.71).

विक्रमी VIKRAMĪ: *Vikrama* is foot, step; or, valour. Both are different in Him from other people. So, *Vikramī*.

ऊर्जितशासनः ŪRJITAŚASANAḤ: His commands are powerful of the nature of Śruti and Smṛti. The Lord said *śrutismṛtī mamaivājne yaste ullanghya vartate / ājñācchedī mama dveṣī madbhaktopi na vaiṣṇavah* / /: 'Śruti and Smṛti are in truth My commands. Whoever transgresses them, disobeys Me and is a hater of Me. Though a devotee, he is not a votary of Viṣṇu.'

शब्दातिगः ŚABDĀTIGAḤ: He is inexpressible as the elements that enable being spoken of in words like class quality and action—jāti, guṇa and karma—cannot apply to Him. So, He is *Śabdātigaḥ*. *vide* the śruti: *yato vāco nivartante aprāpya manasā saha:* 'from Whom speech returns along with the mind without attaining Him.' (Taitt. Up. 2.4) and the smṛti: *na śabdagocaro yasya yogidhyeyam param padam*: 'Whose supreme abode is to be meditated on by yogins and is not within the reach of words.' (Viṣṇu Purāṇa 17.22).

शब्दसहः ŚABDASAHAḤ: He Who is declared by the Vedas, Sabda as their import: *vide* the śruti: *sarve vedā yat padam āmananti:* 'that supreme state proclaimed by all the Vedas' and the smrti: *vedaisca sarvaira-*

hameva vedyaḥ: 'By the several Vedas I alone am to be known.' (B.G.15.65).

शिशिर: ŚIŚIRAḤ: Being the place of repose for those afflicted by the three kinds of pain (*adhyātmika, adhibhautika* and and *adhidaivika*) He is cool, *Śiśiraḥ*.

शर्वरीकर: ŚARVARĪKARAḤ: The Maker of night. For those caught in samsāra, the ātman is dark as the night (as they have no light of knowledge of the ātman) But to the jñāni samsāra is night (as they ever dwell in the light of ātmajñāna) The Lord creates the two nights. So, He is *Śarvarīkaraḥ (śarvarī* means night). *vide* the Lord's statement: *yā niśā sarvabhūtānām tasyām jāgarti samyamī / yasyām jāgrati bhutāni sā niśā paśyato muneḥ / /*: 'That which is night for all beings, then wakes the wise man. When the beings are awake, that is the night for the perceiving sage.' (B.G.2.69).

अक्रूरः पेशलो दक्षो दक्षिणः क्षमिणां वरः ।
विद्वत्तमो वीतभयः पुण्यश्रवणकीर्तनः ।। १११ ।।

Akrūraḥ Peśalaḥ Dakṣaḥ Dakṣinaḥ
Kṣamināmvaraḥ /
Vidvattamaḥ Vītabhayaḥ
Puṇyaśravaṇakīrtanaḥ // 111

अक्रूर: AKRŪRAḤ: Not-cruel, Cruelty is a quality of the mind. It is born of excess of anger. It is internal and leads to anguish and excitement. The Lord has no wants to cause desire. Being without desire, there is no frustration and no consequent anger. So there is no cruelty in Him. So *Akrūraḥ*.

पेशल: PEŚALAḤ: Charming by action, by mind and by speech and in body He is handsome.

दक्ष: DAKŚAḤ: One who has grown up, able,

quick in execution is called *dakṣa.* All these are always associated with the Lord, so He is *Dakṣaḥ.*

दक्षिण: DAKṢIṆAḤ: Dakṣiṇaḥ has the same meaning as Dakṣaḥ. Yet it is not a tautology, as the word is different. Or, dakṣate means goes or kills i.e. killer of the wicked: Confer *dakṣa gatihimsanayoḥ.*

क्षमिणांवर: KṢAMIṆĀMVARAḤ: 1. The most eminent of forgiving persons like yogis and carriers of burden like the earth etc., *vide* Vālmiki's description: of Śrī Rāma: *kṣamayā pṛthivīsamaḥ*: in forgiveness like the earth.'

Or 2. Carrying the entire Brahmāṇḍa like the earth with all things on it, the Lord is not afflicted by it and so is greater than the earth.

Or 3. Kṣaminaḥ stands for persons who are able. Being All powerful, the Lord is able to do all actions. with superlative efficiency. So, *Kṣamiṇāmvaraḥ.*

विद्वत्तम: VIDVATTAMAḤ: He has always the most wonderful knowledge about everything, none else. So, *Vidvattamaḥ.*

वीतभय: VĪTABHAYAḤ: He has no fear of samsāra or pertaining to samsāra as He is the Lord of all or ever free (*mukta*).

पुण्यश्रवणकीर्तन: PUṆYAŚRAVAṆAKĪRTANAḤ: To hear or sing His praise begets merit. *vide* at the end of this stotra: *ya idam śṛṇuyāt nityam yascāpi parikīrtayet / nāśubham propynuyāt kincit so' mutreha ca mānavaḥ / /* : 'Whoever hears this every day and whoever utters it will not experience anything that is inauspicious here and hereafter.'

उत्तारणो दुष्कृतिहा पुण्यो दुःस्वप्ननाशनः ।
वीरहा रक्षणः सन्तो जीवनः पर्यवस्थितः ।। ११२ ।।

Uttāraṇaḥ Duṣkṛtihā Puṇyaḥ Dussvapnanāśanaḥ /
Vīrahā Rakṣaṇaḥ Santaḥ
Jīvanaḥ Paryavasthitaḥ // 112

उत्तारण: UTTĀRAṆAḤ: He rescues (mortals) from the ocean of samsāra. So, *Uttāraṇaḥ*.

दुष्कृतिहा DUṢKṚTIHĀ:1. He destroys evil actions called *pāpas*.

Or 2. The word *duṣkrti* may apply to the evil-doers He kills evil-doers. So, *Duṣkṛtihā*.

पुण्य: PUṆYAḤ: 1. He confers merit on all who do *śravaṇa* (hearing) etc., of His Name and other forms of devotion. So, *Puṇyaḥ*.

Or 2. By His commands in the form of śruti and smṛti, He enables all to do meritorious deeds.

दु:स्वप्ननाशन: DUSSVAPNANĀŚANAḤ: When meditated on, praised, sung about and worshipped, He wards off the dreams ominous of future evil happenings.

वीरहा VĪRAHĀ: By conferring liberation, He destroys the different ways of life of samsārins. *vividhāḥ īrāḥ hanti* (Īrā is gati: way of life) — *vīrahā*.

रक्षण: RAKṢAṆAḤ: Taking His stand on the *sattva* guṇa, He protects the three worlds.

शान्त: ŚĀNTAḤ: Śāntas are those who pursue the path of righteousness. In their form, for the promotion of knowledge and humility, He himself stands as an embodiment.

जीवन: JĪVANAḤ: In the form of breath, He makes all creatures live. So, *Jīvanaḥ*.

पर्यवस्थित: PARYAVASTHITAḤ: He envelops the universe pervading it everywhere.

अनन्तरूपोऽनन्तश्रीर्जितमन्युर्भयापहः ।
चतुरस्रो गभीरात्मा विदिशो व्यादिशो दिशः ।। ११३ ।।

Anantarūpaḥ Anantaśrīḥ Jitamanyuḥ
Bhayāpahaḥ /
Caturasraḥ Gabhīrātmā Vidiśaḥ
Vyadiśaḥ Diśaḥ // 113

अनन्तरूप: ANANTARŪPAḤ: Endless are His forms who is of the form of the vast universe.

अनन्तश्री: ANANTAŚRĪḤ: His supreme power (*parā śakti*) is endless and inexhaustible. *vide* the śruti: *parāsya śaktiḥ vividhaiva śrūyate:* 'His supreme śakti is pronounced to be various.' (Svet.Up.6.8).

जितमन्यु: JITAMANYUḤ: He by whom anger has been conquered is *Jitamanyuḥ*.

भयापह: BHAYĀPAHAḤ: He destroys the fear born of samsāra.

चतुरस्र: CATURASRAḤ: One who acts by rule is Caturasraḥ. He deals the effects of men's actions according to their karmas.

गभीरात्मा GABHĪRĀTMĀ: His ātmā or mind (*citta*) cannot be measured. (*gabhira* means deep).

विदिश: VIDIŚAḤ: He gives various effects of actions especially to their respective *adhikārins*.

व्यादिश: VYĀDIŚAḤ: Giving various commands to Indra and others.

दिश: DIŚAḤ: In the form of the Vedas, He gives the fruits of all actions.

अनादिर्भूर्भुवोलक्ष्मीः सुवीरो रुचिराङ्गदः ।
जननो जनजन्मादिर्भीमो भीमपराक्रमः ।। ११४ ।।

Anādiḥ Bhuṛbhuvolakṣmīḥ
Suvīraḥ Rucirāngadaḥ /

Jananaḥ Janajanmādiḥ

Bhīmaḥ Bhīmaparākramaḥ // 114

अनादि: ANĀDIḤ: There is no *adi* or cause for Him as He is the cause of all. So, *Anādiḥ*.

भूर्भुवोलक्ष्मी: BHŪRBHUVOLAKSMIḤ: 1. *Bhūḥ* means support. *bhuvaḥ* of the earth which is well known as the support of all beings; He is also splendour while being support of even the earth.

Or 2. Not only is He splendour of the earth, but also splendour of *bhuvaḥ loka*.

Or 3. *bhūḥ* is *bhūloka,* bhuvaḥ is *bhuvarloka, lakshmīḥ* is *ātmavidyā, vide* the śruti: *ātmavidyā ca devi tvam.* 'Devi. You are *ātmavidyā.*'

Or 4. He is the splendour *(sobhā)* of the earth and the sky. So, *Bhurbhuvo lakṣmīḥ.*

सुवीर: SUVĪRAḤ: 2. He whose various *īrāḥ, gatayaḥ,* movements are śobhana auspicious. So *Suvīraḥ.*

रुचिराङ्गद: RUCIRĀNGADAḤ: He whose armlets *angade* are handsome, *rucire, kalyaṇe.*

जनन: JANANAḤ: He creates all beings. So, *Jananaḥ.*

जनजन्मादि: JANAJANMĀDIḤ: The primeval cause of birth of creatures. (*janma* is birth, *adi* is cause).

भीम: BHĪMAḤ: Being the cause of fear, *Bhīmaḥ. vide* the śruti: *mahadbhayam vajramivodyatam*: 'A great fear has arisen like a thunderbolt.' (Kaṭha Up. 2.3.2).

भीमपराक्रम: BHĪMAPARĀKRAMAḤ: The valour in all His incarnations is the cause of great fear to asuras and others.

आधारनिलयोऽधाता पुष्पहासः प्रजागरः ।
ऊर्ध्वगः सत्पथाचारः प्राणदः प्रणवः पणः ॥ ११५ ॥

Ādhāranilayaḥ Adhāta Puṣpahāsaḥ Prajāgaraḥ /
Ūrdhvagaḥ Satpathācāraḥ Prāṇadaḥ
Praṇavaḥ Paṇaḥ // 115

आधारनिलयः ĀDHĀRANILAYAḤ: Being the support of the supports of the earth and *pañcabhūtas,* He is *Ādhāranilayaḥ,* (the resting place of supports).

अधाता ADHĀTĀ: Being supported by Himself, He has no outside support.

Or DHĀTĀ: At the time of samhāra, He *dhārayati* carries or *dhayati* drinks or consumes (causes *laya* of) all beings.

पुष्पहासः PUṢPAHĀSAḤ: He blossoms as the world like buds blossom.

प्रजागरः PRAJĀGARAḤ: Being ever of the nature knowledge, He is exceedingly awake.

ऊर्ध्वगः ŪRDHVAGAḤ: He stands above all.

सत्पथाचारः SATPATHĀCĀRAḤ: The actions of the good are *satpathāḥ.* He observes them. So, *Satpathācāraḥ.*

प्राणदः PRĀṆADAḤ: He brought back to life Parīkṣit and others who died. (He gave them life). Hence *Prānadaḥ.*

प्रणवः PRAṆAVAḤ: *Praṇava* is Omkara signifying the Paramātman. Being non-different from it, He is *Praṇavaḥ.*

पणः PAṆAH: 1. *Paṇati* is used in the sense of worldly dealings. He does them (causes the worldly activities to take place) So, *Paṇaḥ. vide:* the śruti: *sarvāṇi rūpaṇi vicintya dhīraḥ nāmāni kṛtvābhivadan yad āste:* "He, the wise One remains creating the various forms and giving names to them." (Taitt. Āraṇ. 3.12).

Or 2. All meritorious actions are *paṇam*: He who collectively confers the fruits to their *adhikārins*, is, by a figure of speech, called *Paṇaḥ*.

प्रमाणं प्राणनिलयः प्राणभृत्प्राणजीवनः ।
तत्त्वं तत्त्वविदेकात्मा जन्ममृत्युजरातिगः ॥ ११६ ॥

Pramāṇam Prāṇanilayaḥ Prāṇabhṛt
Prāṇajīvanaḥ /
Tattvam Tattvavit Ekātmā
Janmamṛtyujarātigaḥ / / 116

प्रमाणम् PRAMĀṆAM: *Pramiti* is samvit or knowledge. It is self-effulgent (self-certifying). It is *Pramāṇam. vide* the śruti: *prajñānam brahma*: "Wisdom is Brahman". (Ai.Up.3.3). The Viṣṇu Purāṇa (1.2.6) *says: jnānasvarūpam atyantanirmalam paramārthataḥ / tadevārthasvarūpeṇa bhrāntidarśanataḥ- sthitam / / :* 'In reality, the nature of knowledge is unblemished. By illusory sight, it takes form as (various) objects.'

प्राणनिलयः PRĀNAṆILAYAḤ: 1. Prāṇas are the senses. They merge in the jīva as they are extra-dependent (In the ultimate analysis, the jīva is identical with Brahman). So, He is Prāṇanilayaḥ.

Or 2. *prāṇa, apana* etc., are the supports of the body. They merge in Him. So *Prāṇanilayaḥ*.

Or 3. Breathes (*prāṇiti*) stands for prāṇa, the jīva. That merges in the supreme Person.

Or 4. He destroys the prāṇas and jīvas. So, *Prāṇanilayaḥ*.

प्राणभृत् PRĀṆABHṚT: Through food He sustains the prāṇas. i.e. life. So, *Prāṇabhṛt*.

प्राणजीवनः PRĀṆAJĪVANAḤ: By the winds called prāṇas, He makes creatures live. *vide* the mantra:

na prāṇena nāpānena martyo jīvati kascana / itareṇa tu jīvanti yasminnetāvupāśritau / / : 'Not by prāṇa, not by apāna does a mortal live; but he lives by another on which these two depend.' (Kaṭha Up.5.5).

तत्त्वम् TATTVAM : Of Brahma who is the transcendental Existence *tathyam amṛtam satyam paramārthasat tattvam* are synonyms for Brahman.

तत्त्ववित् TATTVAVIT: He knows Truth, His svarūpa as it is. So, *Tattvavit.*

एकात्मा EKĀTMĀ: He is one and Ātmā. *vide* the śruti: *ātmā vā idameka evāgra āsīt: 'this ātmā* was one only at the beginning.' *yaccāpnoti yadādatte yaccatti viṣayāniha / yaccāsya santato bhāvaḥ taṣmāt ātmeti gīyate / /* : 'that which pervades, that which receives, that which enjoys the objects and that which exists always is called the Ātman'.

जन्ममृत्युजरातिग: JANMAMṚTYUJARĀTIGAḤ: He who transcends the six modifications indicated by the words 'is born' 'exists' 'grows' 'changes' 'declines' and 'dies' is He who goes beyond birth and death (and the intervening states) *vide* the mantra: *na jāyate mriyate vā vipascit:* 'The intelligent Ātma is not born nor does He die'. (nor undergoes the intervening changes). Kaṭha. Up. 2.18).

भूर्भुवःस्वस्तरुस्तारः सपिता प्रपितामहः ।
यज्ञो यज्ञपतिर्यज्वा यज्ञाङ्गो यज्ञवाहनः ।। ११७ ।।

Bhurbhuvassvastaruḥ Tāraḥ Sapitā
Prapitāmhaḥ /
Yajñah Yajñapatiḥ Yajvā Yajñāngaḥ
Yajñavāhanaḥ / / 117

भूर्भुवःस्वस्तरु: BHŪRBHUVASSVASTARUḤ: 1. Bhūh, Bhuvah, Svah, are known as three *vyāhṛtis.* They are pure and the essence of the Vedas. By means of these and the oblations in the fires, one crosses the three worlds. Manu says (3.76) *agnau nyastāhutiḥ samyagādityamupatiṣṭhate / ādityājjāyate vṛṣṭiḥ vṛṣṭerannam tatah prajāh / /* 'the oblation devoutly made into the fire reaches the sun, from the sun arises rain; from the rain food and from food all beings'.

Or 2. He is as the threefold samsāra vṛkṣa of the three worlds *bhūḥ, bhuvaḥ* and *svaḥ*.

Or 3. He envelops like a tree the three worlds *bhūh, bhuvaḥ* and *svaḥ*.

तार: TĀRAḤ: 1. He helps to cross the ocean of samsāra. So *Tāraḥ*.

Or 2. The praṇava.

सपिता SAPITĀ: The progenitor of all worlds.

प्रपितामहः PRAPITĀMAHAḤ: The father of Brahma also who is known as pitāmahaḥ (*pitāmahasya pitā* the g and-sire).

यज्ञ: YAJÑAḤ: Samgantā. He who unites yajñas with their fruits is called *Yajñaḥ*.

यज्ञपति: YAJÑAPATIḤ: The protector of the sacrifice or the lord of it. *vide* the Lord's statement: *aham hi sarvayajñānām bhoktā ca prabhureva ca:* 'I am the enjoyer and the lord of all sacrifices'. (B.G.9.24).

यज्वा YAJVĀ: Being in the form of *yajamāna* in a sacrifice, He is *Yajvā*.

यज्ञाङ्ग: YAJÑANGAḤ: Sacrifices are His limbs in His incarnation as Varāha. The Harivamsa says: (42 Ch).

> The Vedas are His feet; the sacrificial post His jaws; the sacrifices His hands; the *citi* His face; the fire His tongue; the darbha grass His hair; Brahma

is the head of the great One.

Day and night are His eyes; the Vedāngas are His ear ornaments; the clarified butter is His nose; the ladle is His neck; the Sāma chant is His loud talk. His body is made of dharma and satya, and all good actions are movements of His feet; His nails are the expiation ceremonies. The *paśu* or the sacrificial animal is His knee and mighty arm.

The *Udgāta* is His bowels, *homa* is His generative organ; the seeds and herbs are His outward body. Wind is His mind or spirit. The mantras are His buttocks. The *vikṛta soma* is His blood.

The altar is His upper arm; the oblation is His smell; Havya and Kavya are His bones and urges Prāgvamsa is His body. Thus the Shining One is worshipped by many vows. *Dakṣiṇa* is the heart of the great Yogin, and the yāgas are made for Him. The upākarma is His lips and the pravargya, His naval.

His paths are the many metres (chandaṣ) the secret upaniṣads are His seat; He has *Chāyā Devi* as His consort and He is lofty like the Meru peak.[22]

यज्ञवाहनः YAJÑAVĀHANAḤ: He directs the performance of the yajñas which are fruitful.

यज्ञभृद्यज्ञकृद्यज्ञी यज्ञभुग्यज्ञसाधनः ।
यज्ञान्तकृद्यज्ञगुह्यमन्नमन्नाद एव च ।। ११८ ।।

Yajñabhṛt Yajñakṛt Yajñī Yajñabhuk
Yajñasādhanaḥ /
Yajñāntakṛt Yajñaguhyam Annam Annādaḥ
eva ca / / 118

22. I have adopted here the translation of Śrī R. Anantakṛṣna Śāstri: Theosophical Publishing House edition.

यज्ञभृत् YAJÑABHṚT: He supports the yajña or protects it. So, *Yajñabhṛt.*

यज्ञकृत् YAJÑAKṚT: At the beginning of the world and at the end of it, He performs yajña or destroys it (kṛntati). So *Yajñakṛt.*

यज्ञी YAJÑĪ: Yajñas are to please Him. He is the whole of which the yajñas are parts.

यज्ञभुक् YAJÑABHUK: He enjoys the sacrifice or protects it.

यज्ञसाधनः YAJÑASĀDHANAḤ: Yajñas are the means to attain Him.

यज्ञान्तकृत् YAJÑĀNTAKṚT: 1. He gives the fruit of the sacrifice at the end.

Or 2. By uttering the Vaiṣṇavī Ṛk. in the final oblation, He concludes the sacrifice.

यज्ञगुह्यम् YAJÑAGUHYAM: The secret of sacrifices is jñanayajña or the sacrifice performed without attachment to result. Brahman is considered as non-different from it and is said to be Yajñaguhyam.

अन्नम् ANNAM: He causes all beings to eat or Himself eats them.

अन्नादः ANNĀDAḤ: He eats *annam.* So, *Annādaḥ.* *Eva* is used to show that the whole world is constituted of food in the form of the eater and the eaten.

ca is used to show that all words can be applied together to one Supreme Person.

आत्मयोनिः स्वयंजातो वैखानः सामगायनः ।
देवकीनन्दनः स्रष्टा क्षितीशः पापनाशनः ।। ११९ ।।

Ātmayoniḥ Svayamjātaḥ
Vaikhānaḥ Sāmagāyanaḥ /
Devakīnandanaḥ Sraṣṭā
Kṣitīśaḥ Pāpanāśanaḥ / / 119

आत्मयोनि: ĀTMAYONIḤ: He Himself is *yoni* or the material cause, *upādāna kāraṇa,* of the universe, not anything else. So, *Ātmayoniḥ*.

स्वयंजात: SVAYAMJĀTAḤ: To show that He is also the efficient cause, *nimitta kāraṇa,* it is said *Svayam jātaḥ.*

That Hari is both the material and the efficient cause is established by the Vedānta Sūtra *prakṛtiśca pratijñā-dṛṣṭāntānuparodhāt*: 'Brahman must be the twofold cause so as not to contradict the proposition and the illustration.'

वैखान: VAIKHĀNAḤ: As He digs especially. It is well-known in the Purāṇa that the Lord dug especially into the earth and assuming the form of the boar, killed Hiraṇyākṣa who had his abode in the nether world.

सामगायन: SĀMAGĀYANAḤ: He sings the sāmans.

देवकीनन्दन: DEVAKĪNANDANAḤ: Devakī's son. The Mahābhārata says: *jyotīṃṣi śukrāṇi ca yāni loke trayo lokā lokapālāstrayī ca / trayo' gnayaścāhutayaśca pañca sarve devā devakīputra eva / /* 'All the luminaries in the world, the three worlds, the protectors of the worlds, the three Vedas, the three sacred fires, the five oblations and all the devas are the son of Devakī (Kṛṣṇa).'

स्रष्टा SRAṢṬA: The Creator of the entire world.

क्षितीश: KṢITĪŚAḤ: The lord of the earth. Dasaratha's son, Rama.

पापनाशन: PĀPANĀŚANAḤ: Praised, worshipped, meditated on, remembered, destroys the load of sins. So, *Pāpanāśanaḥ. pakṣopavāsād yatpāpam puruṣasya praṇaśyati / prāṇāyāmaśatenaiva tatpāpam naśyate nṛṇām / / prāṇāyāmasahasreṇa yat pāpam naśyate nṛṇām /*

kṣaṇamātreṇa tatpāpam harerdhyānāt praṇaśyati / /
'That sin of men which is destroyed by fasting fortnightly, is destroyed by performance of hundred prāṇayāmas. That sin of men which is destroyed by performance of a thousand prāṇāyāmas dies out by thinking of Hari for a moment.' (Vṛddhaśatātapa Smṛti)

शङ्खभृन्नन्दकी चक्री शार्ङ्गधन्वा गदाधरः।
रथाङ्गपाणिरक्षोभ्यः सर्वप्रहरणायुधः
सर्वप्रहरणायुधः ॐ नम इति ॥ १२० ॥

Śaṅkhabhṛt Nandakī Cakrī Śarṅgadhanvā Gadādharaḥ /
Rathāṅgapāṇiḥ Akṣobhyaḥ Sarvapraharaṇāyudhaḥ
Sarvapraharaṇāyudhaḥ Om nama iti / / 120

शङ्खभृत् ŚANKHABHṚT: The bearer of the conch called *Pāncajanya* of the form of the five elements and the *ahamkāra*.

नन्दकी NANDAKĪ: His sword is called Nandaka, of the nature of knowledge.

चक्री CAKRĪ: 1. His is the discus, *cakra,* called *Sudarśana* of the form of the *manastattva*.

Or 2. He sets the wheel of samsāra in motion. So, *Cakrī.*

शाङ्र्गधन्वा ŚARNGADHANVĀ: He has the bow called *Śārṅga* of the form of the sense organs and the *ahamkāra.*

गदाधरः GADĀDHARAḤ: He bears the club, *gadā,* called *Kaumodakī* of the form of the buddhitattva.

रथाङ्गपाणि: RATHĀNGAPĀṆIḤ: In His hand is the wheel which is the part of a chariot.

अक्षोभ्यः AKṢOBHYAḤ: Therefore it is (as He

has all these weapons) that He cannot be discomfited.

सर्वप्रहरणायुध: SARVAPRAHARAṆĀYUDHAḤ: There is no rule that these only are His weapons. He has all kinds of offensive weapons. Even finger nails that are not famous as weapons are also included. So, He has all kinds of weapons of offence. *Sarvapraharaṇāyudhaḥ.*

The reference to Sarvapraharaṇāyudhaḥ at the end is intended to indicate that He is the Lord of all, to fulfil His purposes. *vide* the Śruti: *eṣa sarveśvaraḥ:* 'He is the Lord of all.' (Br. Up.6.4.22).

Repetition of the last Name shows the completion of the Sahasranāma.

ॐ नम: OM NAMAḤ: *Omkara* has the meaning of auspiciousness. *mangalārthaḥ. vide Omkāraśca atha śabdaśca dvāvetau brahmaṇah purā / kaṇṭham bhittvā viniryātau tasmāt māngalikāvubhau:* '*Om* and *atha,* both these came out of the throat of Brahman at the beginning. Therefore they both stand for auspiciousness.'

By traditionally saying *namaḥ* at the end, prostration is done. *vide* the mantra: *bhūyiṣṭhānte namauktim vidhema:* "To Thee we submit our word 'prostration' at the end." Also: *dhanyam tadeva lagnam tannakṣatram tadeva puṇyamahaḥ / karaṇasya ca sā siddhiryatra hariḥ prāk namaskriyate / / :* 'When Hari is prostrated to, that alone is auspicious lagna, auspicious nakṣatra holy day and the proper karaṇa', *prāk:* in the beginning, is only indicative as namaskāra at the end also is observed by the good. The fruit of *namaskāra,* prostration, was shown at the beginning itself.

'One prostration to Kṛṣṇa properly done is equal to the final baths of ten horse sacrifices. The man who has performed ten horse sacrifices is born again; but, he who has made prostration to Kṛṣṇa is not born again.

'Those who bow to Govinda who is of the colour *atasī* flower (hemp) who is clad in yellow and is called *Acyuta,* have no fear.

'By bowing a little with the head to the Lord of the three worlds, of matchless glory, the Supreme Ruler, a man's accumulated sins of thousands of previous lives are quickly liquidated.'

Thus the tenth hundred Names has been explained.

इतीदं कीर्तनीयस्य केशवस्य महात्मनः ।
नाम्नां सहस्रं दिव्यानामशेषेण प्रकीर्तितम् ।। १२१ ।।

itīdam kīrtanīyasya keśavasya mahātmanaḥ /
nāmnām sahasram divyānām aśeṣeṇa
prakīrtitam // 121

Thus are declared thousand divine Names of Keśava of superlative glory who is celebrated in the string of Names without omitting any.

By the words *itidam* it is shown that the Names are exactly a thousand, no more and no less. The Names include different ways of expressing the same meaning. In the beginning it was asked *kimjapan mucyate jantuḥ:* 'by muttering which is a person liberated?' By saying *kīrtayan* uttering; three kinds of *japa,* loud, low and silent are indicated.

PHALA ŚRUTI

य इदं शृणुयान्नित्यं यश्चापि परिकीर्तयेत् ।
नाशुभं प्राप्नुयात्किञ्चित्सोऽमुत्रेह च मानवः ।। १२२ ।।

ya idam śṛṇuyāt nityam yaścāpi parikīrtayet /
nāśubham prāpnuyāt kiñcit so' mutreha
ca mānavaḥ // 122

Whoever hears this daily, whoever utters it does not experience anything inauspicious both here and hereafter.

The meaning is clear. Even for him who has attained the other world, no evil will befall as in the case of Nahuṣa and Yayāti. Hence the word *amutra*, hereafter.

वेदान्तगो ब्राह्मणः स्यात्क्षत्रियो विजयी भवेत् ।
वैश्यो धनसमृद्धः स्याच्छूद्रः सुखमवाप्नुयात् ।। १२३ ।।

vedāntago brāhmaṇah syāt kṣatriyo vijayībhavet /
vaiśyo dhanasamṛddhaḥ syāt śūdraḥ sukham
avāpnuyāt / / 123

(By reciting this Stotra) a Brāhmana will attain the end of Vedānta, a Kṣatriya will be victorious, a Vaiśya will come by much wealth and a Śudra will attain his welfare.

Vedāntagah: He understands Brahman Who is the purport of Vedānta or the upaniṣads. It was said *kim japanmucyate jantuh;* 'by making japa of which is a person liberated?' It may be doubted if liberation is attained directly by japa. It was said *vedāntago brāhmaṇaḥ syāt* to show that karma cannot directly cause liberation, but it can only be by jñāna. Karma is the cause of mokṣa through purification of the internal organ (*antaḥkaraṇa*).

'The good actions remove the impurities from the mind and then jñāna leads to the supreme goal. When the impurities are removed by actions, then jñāna arises.

'By getting eternal knowledge a man is released from bondage. By dharma, he gets happiness and knowledge. By jñāna mokṣa is realised.

'Yogis perform karma abandoning attachment for the purification of the mind. A man is bound by karma and freed by knowledge alone.

'Therefore yatis who have seen the goal of Brahmasākṣātkāra do not engage in karma. The best of the twice-born give up even the prescribed karmas and make an effort for ātmajñāna (knowledge of the Self) and equanimity. By austerity he removes impurity and by knowledge he attains immortality. Jñāna arises for man by the decline of sinful actions as clearly as he sees himself in a mirror.'

These smṛtis are in support of this view. And the following smṛtis also:

tametam vedānuvacanena brāhmaṇā vividiṣanti yajñena dānena tapasā nāśakena: 'In accordance with the teaching of the Veda, the Brāhmaṇas desire to know Him by yajña, dāna, tapas.'

yena kenachid yajatāpi yajnenāpi darvīhomenānupahatamanā eva bhavati: 'by whatever one may perform a yajña by ladle or homa, his mind becomes unclouded.' (Bṛh. Up. 6.4.22).

The following texts support the position that Mokṣa is by jñāna only:

jñānādeva tu kaivalyam prāpyate tena mucyate: 'By jñāna alone is kaivalya attained. One is released (from Samsara) by it.'

brahmavid āpnoti param: 'The knower of Brahman attains the Highest." (Taitt.Up.2.1).

tarati śokam ātmavit: The knower of the Ātman transcends the sorrow (of samsāra), (Ch. Up.7.1.3).

brahma veda brahmaiva bhavati: 'He who knows Brahman (*ipso facto*) becomes Brahman only.'

brahmaiva san brahmāpyeti: 'Becoming Brahman, one attains Brahman.' (Taitt.Aran.2.2).

tameva viditvā atimṛtyumeti nānyaḥ panthā vidyate

'yanāya. 'By knowing Him (Brahman) alone, one gets over death; there is no other path for reaching the Supreme Goal.' (Śvet. Up.2.6.15).

ānandam brahmaṇo vidvān na bibheti kutaścana: 'The knower of the bliss of Brahman is not afraid of anything.' (Tait. Up. 2.9).

iha cedavedīt atha satyamasti nacedavedīn mahatī vinaṣṭiḥ: 'If here (in this world) a man knows (the ātman, the Truth is attained. If he does not know here, great is the loss.' (Kena Up.2.13).

yadā carmavadākāśam veṣṭayiṣyanti mānavāḥ / tadā devam avijñāya duhkhasyānto bhaviṣyati / / 'When men roll up the sky like a piece of leather, then the end of sorrow will arise without knowing Brahman.' (In other words, the latter is as impossible as the former.)

na karmaṇā na prajayā dhanena tyāgenaike amṛtatvamānaśuh: 'Not by action, not by progeny, not by wealth, but only by renunciation can one attain immortality.' (Kaivalya Up. 3).

vedānta vijñāna suniścitārthāḥ sannyāsayogād yatayaḥ śuddhasattvāḥ / te brahmaloke tu parāntakāle parāmṛtāt parimucyanti sarve / / 'Those who have grasped the meaning of Vedāntic knowledge, who have become pure in mind by yoga and are striving for emancipation, on their death, enjoy the highest immortality in the world of Brahman.' (Kaivalya Up.4).

The Sūdra will attain happiness by mere hearing, not by japa or yajña, *vide* the śruti: *tasmāt śūdro yajne anavakḷptaḥ.:* Therefore, the Śūdra is not ordained to perform yajñas'. (Tait. Samhita. 7.1.6) By the Mahabhārata text: *śrāvayet caturo varṇān kṛtvā brāhmaṇam agrataḥ:* 'One should teach all castes keeping the brāhmaṇa at the head (Śānti Parva 335.48).' The Harivamśa says: *sugatimiyāt śravaṇāt ca śudrayoniḥ*: 'One born a sūdra attains good by listening.' It is distinctly said: *yaḥ śūdraḥ śṛṇuyāt sa sukham avāpnuyāt*: 'If the śūdra hears, he will attain happiness;' for the other varṇas the word used is *kīrtayet,* who utters'.

धमर्थी प्राप्नुयाद्धर्ममर्थार्थी चार्थमाप्नुयात् ।
कामानवाप्नुयात्कामी प्रजार्थी प्राप्नुयात्प्रजाम् ।। १२४ ।।

dharmārthī prāpnuyāt dharmam
arthārthī ca artham āpnuyāt /
kāmānavāpnuyāt kāmī
prajārthī ca āpnuyāt prājam / / 124

He who aims at dharma will get it by reciting this stotra; he who seeks wealth will get it, he who wants the fulfilment of his desires will have them fulfilled; he who wants progeny will get it.

Kāma or desire is the mind's activity backed by the ātman through the senses in relation to their respective objects. *praja* is so called as he is born *prajāyate; prajā* is progeny.

By the following verse begining with *bhaktimān,* it is shown what extraordinary merit will accrue to a superior qualified person who has devotion, is pure, is ever intent, of concentrated mind and who is earnest.

भक्तिमान् यः सदोत्थाय शुचिस्तद्गतमानसः ।
सहस्रं वासुदेवस्य नाम्नामेतत् प्रकीर्तयेत् ।। १२५ ।।
यशः प्राप्नोति विपुलं याति प्राधान्यमेव च ।
अचलां श्रियमाप्नोति श्रेयः प्राप्नोत्यनुत्तमम् ।। १२६ ।।

bhaktimānyaḥ sadotthāya
śuciḥ tadgatamānasaḥ /
sahasram vāsudevasya
nāmnāmetat prakīrtayet / / 125
yaśaḥ prāpnoti vipulam yāti prādhānyam eva ca /

acalām śriyamāpnoti śreyaḥ prāpnoti
anuttamam // 126

He who has devotion, being ever alert, pure and with a mind oriented to the Lord utters these thousand Names of Vasudeva, gets wide fame, attains pre-eminence, attains unswerving prosperity and gets supreme spiritual glory.

न भयं क्वचिदाप्नोति वीर्यं तेजश्च विन्दति ।
भवत्यरोगो द्युतिमान् बलरूपगुणान्वितः ।। १२७ ।।

na bhayam kvacidāpnoti vīryam tejaśca vindati /
bhavatyarogo dyutimān
balarūpaguṇānvitaḥ / / 127

He is never subject to fear; he gets valour and excellence. He is not afflicted by disease and he is endowed with strength and comely form.

रोगार्तो मुच्यते रोगाद्बद्धो मुच्येत बन्धनात् ।
भयान्मुच्येत भीतस्तु मुच्येतापन्न आपदः ।। १२८ ।।

rogārto mucyate rogāt baddho mucyeta bandhanāt /
bhayāt mucyeta bhītastu mucyeta āpannaḥ
āpadaḥ / / 128

The sick is relieved of his sickness, the bound, of his bonds. He who is afraid gets over his fear, he subject to danger gets rid of his danger.

दुर्गाण्यतितरत्याशु पुरुषः पुरुषोत्तमम् ।
स्तुवन्नामसहस्रेण नित्यं भक्तिसमन्वितः ।। १२९ ।।

durgāṇyatitaratyāśu puruṣaḥ puruṣottamam /
stuvan nāmasahasreṇa nityam bhakti-
samanvitaḥ / / 129

He quickly overcomes obstacles who praises Puruṣottama with devotion by these thousand Names.

वासुदेवाश्रयो मर्त्यो वासुदेवपरायणः ।
सर्वपापविशुद्धात्मा याति ब्रह्म सनातनम् ।। १३० ।।

vāsudevāśrayo martyaḥ vāsudevaparāyaṇaḥ /
sarvapāpaviśuddhātmā yāti
brahma sanātanam / / 130

That mortal who takes refuge in Vāsudeva and is devoted to Him is freed of all sins and attains the eternal Brahman.

न वासुदेवभक्तानामशुभं विद्यते क्वचित् ।
जन्ममृत्युजराव्याधिभयं नैवोपजायते ।। १३१ ।।

na vāsudevabhaktānām aśubham vidyate kvacit /
janmamṛtyujarāvyādhibhayam
naivopajāyate / / 131

No evil arises to the devotees of Vāsudeva and they do not have to suffer from the effects of birth, death, old age and disease.

इमं स्तवमधीयानः श्रद्धाभक्तिसमन्वितः ।
युज्येतात्मसुखक्षान्तिश्रीधृतिस्मृतिकीर्तिभिः ।। १३२ ।।

imam stavamadhīyānaḥ śraddhābhaktisamanvitaḥ
yujyetātmasukhakṣānti śrīdhṛti smṛti
kīrtibhiḥ / / 132

He who recites this praise with earnestness and devotion is endowed with mental happiness, forgiveness, wealth, courage, memory and fame.

śraddhā means belief in the existence of God. *āstikyabuddhiḥ; bhaktiḥ* refers to worship. *ātmasukham* is the happiness of the mind. With them and with forgiveness etc., he is endowed.

न क्रोधो न च मात्सर्यं न लोभो नाशुभा मतिः ।
भवन्ति कृतपुण्यानां भक्तानां पुरुषोत्तमे ।। १३३।।

na krodhah na ca mātsaryam
na lobhaḥ na aśubhā matiḥ /
bhavanti kṛta puṇyānām bhaktānām
puruṣottame / / 133

In the virtuous devotees of Puruṣottama, there is no anger or jealousy, no covetousness or evil thought.

द्यौः सचन्द्रार्कनक्षत्रा खं दिशो भूर्महोदधिः ।
वासुदेवस्य वीर्येण विधृतानि महात्मनः ।। १३४ ।।

dyauḥ sacandrārka nakṣatrā kham diśo
bhūrmahodadhiḥ /
vāsudevasya vīryeṇa vidhṛtāni
mahātmanaḥ / / 134

The sky with the moon and the stars, the firmament, the directions, the earth and the ocean are held in position by the great Vāsudeva.

ससुरासुरगन्धर्वं सयक्षोरगराक्षसम् ।
जगद्वशे वर्ततेदं कृष्णस्य सचराचरम् ।। १३५ ।।

sasurāsuragandharvam sayakṣoragarākṣasam /
jagadvaśe vartatedam kṛṣṇasya
sacarācaram / / 135

The world of moving and unmoving things made up of devas and asuras, gandharvas, yakṣas; uragas and rākṣasas is under the control of Kṛṣṇa.

इन्द्रियाणि मनो बुद्धिः सत्त्वं तेजो बलं धृतिः ।
वासुदेवात्मकान्याहुः क्षेत्रं क्षेत्रज्ञ एव च ।। १३६ ।।

indriyāṇi mano buddhiḥ sattvam tejo balam dhṛtiḥ /
vāsudevātmakānyāhuḥ kṣetram kṣetrajña eva
ca / / 136

The senses, the mind, the intellect, life, energy, strength and courage have Vāsudeva as their soul, as also the body and the knower of the body.

सर्वागमानामाचारः प्रथमं परिकल्प्यते ।
आचारप्रभवो धर्मो धर्मस्य प्रभुरच्युतः ।। १३७ ।।

sarvāgamānām ācāraḥ prathamam parikalpyate /
ācāraprabhavo dharmaḥ dharmasya
prabhuracyutaḥ / / 137

Discipline is stated foremost in all scriptures; dharma is the basis for discipline. The Lord of dharma is Acyuta.

ऋषयः पितरो देवा महाभूतानि धातवः ।
जङ्गमाजङ्गमं चेदं जगन्नारायणोद्भवम् ।। १३७ ।।

ṛṣayaḥ pitaro devāḥ mahābhutāni
dhātavaḥ /
jangamājangamam cedam
jagannārāyaṇodbhavam / / 138

Ṛṣis, pitṛs, devas, mahābhutas, the great elements, whatever is moving and stationary—have all sprung from Nārāyaṇa.

योगो ज्ञानं तथा सांख्यं विद्याः शिल्पादि कर्म च ।
वेदाः शास्त्राणि विज्ञानमेतत्सर्वं जनार्दनात् ।। १३९ ।।

yogo jñānam tatha sānkhyam vidyāḥ śilpādi
karma ca /
vedāh śāstrāṇi vijñānam etat sarvam
janārdanāt / / 139

Yoga, Sankhya, the sciences, the Vedas, Knowledge, arts like sculpture, śāstras—all are from Janārdana.

एको विष्णुर्महद्भूतं पृथग्भूतान्यनेकशः ।
त्रींल्लोकान्व्याप्य भूतात्मा भुङ्क्ते विश्वभुगव्ययः ।। १४० ।।

eko viṣṇur mahat bhūtam pṛthak bhūtāni
anekaśaḥ /
trīn lokān vyāpya bhūtātmā bhunkte
visvabhugavyayaḥ / / 140

Viṣṇu is the one Supreme, the Great Being, the rest are diversely separate. He envelops the three worlds, and, as the universal undecaying eater, enjoys all.

It is shown that the fruit of the recital of the glory of Vāsudeva in the verses beginning with *dyauḥ sacandrārka nakṣatrā* is not mere laudatory, but the bare truth. By the interposition of *sarvāgamānām' ācāraḥ* etc., it is shown that one who observes a disciplined life is alone qualified.

इमं स्तवं भगवतो विष्णोर्व्यासेन कीर्तितम् ।
पठेद्य इच्छेत्पुरुषः श्रेयः प्राप्तुं सुखानि च ।। १४१ ।।

imam stavam bhagavataḥ viṣṇorvyāsena kīrtitam
paṭhet ya icchet puruṣaḥ śreyaḥ prāptum
sukhāni ca / / 141

A person who seeks spiritual merit and happiness must read this stotra of Bhagavān Viṣṇu spoken by Vyāsa.

By saying *imam stavam* etc., it is shown that all seekers must read with fervour for the fruition of their desire this work written by the omniscient Bhagavān Kṛṣṇa Dvaipāyana Vyāsa who knows all branches of the Vedas and who is God Nārāyaṇa Himself.

विश्वेश्वरमजं देवं जगतः प्रभवाप्ययम् ।
भजन्ति ये पुष्कराक्षं न ते यान्ति पराभवम् ।। १४२ ।।

viśveśvaramajam devam jagataḥ prabhavāpyayam /
bhajanti ye puṣkarākṣam na te yānti
parābhavam / / 142

Those who worship the Lord of the Universe, the cause of the origination and dissolution of the world who Himself is unborn who is lotus-eyed are never discomfited.

Thus ends the 149th chapter called Viṣṇudivya Sahasranāma Stotra in the discourse between Bhīṣma and Yudhiṣṭhira in the Ānuśasanika Parva of Śri Mahābhārata.

By 'viśveśara' it is shown that only by worship of Viśveśvara those who recite this stotra become virtuous, have their purposes fulfilled and of accomplished actions.

Vyāsa says:

'The śruti declares any act done negligently, whatever has been omitted in a sacrifice becomes complete by remembering the name of Viṣṇu.

'If one praises the Lord of the Universe with the same ardour with which one praises a rich man to get money, would he not be released from bondage?'

This Commentary on Sahasranāma supported by śruti, smṛti and reasoning which will be productive of good to all is placed at the feet of Hari.

Thus ends the Sahasranāma Stotrabhāṣyam
among the works of Sri Śaṅkarācārya
the disciple of Sri Govinda
Bhagavat Pūjyapāda

॥ ओम् तत् सत् ॥

Om Tat Sat

APPENDIX I

Explanation of grammatical forms of certain Nāmas in the text of the Viṣṇusahasranāma Stotra as given by Śrī Śankara in the course of his Bhāṣya.
(The Translator is indebted to Dr. M. Narasimhachari, Reader in Sanskrit in the University of Madras, who kindly wrote this part of the book).

(1) Śl. 15. पुरुषः *Puruṣaḥ,* second meaning:

अस्तेः व्यत्यस्ताक्षरयोगात् आसीत् पुरा पूर्वमपीति विग्रहं कृत्वा व्युत्पादितः 'पुरुषः' ।

The word 'puruṣa' is derived from the root 'as' (अस् =to be), by explaining the components as "one that existed before", i.e., "even before" (आसीत् पुरा i.e. पूर्वमपि) and reading them in the reverse direction (i.e., पुरा आसीत् पुरुषः)

(2) Śl. 15. साक्षी *Sākṣī*

साक्षाद्द्रष्टरि संज्ञायाम् (V.2.91) इति पाणिनिवचनादिनिप्रत्ययः ।

Suffix "ini" is added to the indeclinable "sākṣāt", when it indicates a name, in the sense of "one who sees".

[Sākṣāt+ini=Sākṣ+in=Sākṣin.]

(3) Śl. 15. क्षेत्रज्ञः *Kṣetrajñaḥ*:

आतो ऽनुपसर्गे कः इति कप्रत्ययः ।

The affix 'ka'(क) is added as per the above aphorism to the long 'ā'-ending root 'jñā' (without a prefix whereby ज्ञा becomes ज्ञः (in Masculine).

[*Note:* In suffix 'ka', only 'a' (अ) remains, 'k' (क् being elided.]

(4) Śl. 15. अक्षरः *Akṣaraḥ*:

अश्नातेर्वा सरप्रत्ययान्तस्य रूपमक्षर इति ।

Or, the form 'akṣara' can be derived from the root "aśū" (to pervade) (V conjugation) by adding suffix "sara" to it.

(5) Śl. 16. केशवः *Keśavaḥ,* second meaning:

'केशाद्वोऽन्यतरस्याम्' इति वप्रत्ययः प्रशंसायाम् ।

The affix 'va' (व) is added in the sense of praise, according to the rule: "*Va* is optional after the word *keśa*" (meaning one who possesses).

(6) Śl. 16. केशव : *Keśavaḥ:*

केशिवधाद्वा केशवः । पृषोदरादित्वात् शब्दसाधुत्वकल्पना ।

Or, he is called Keśava since he killed a demon by name Keśin. The form "Keśava" can be justified by including it in the Pṛṣodara-group of words.

[*Note*: pṛṣat+udara=pṛṣodara. Here the final त् of पृषत् is dropped for which there is no authority in Grammar. Such words are listed and treated as correct. Cf. Pāṇini: पृषोदरादीनि यथोपदिष्टम् (VI.3.109). The words read in this list are: पृषोदरम्, बलाहकः, हंसः, सिंहः, गूढोत्मा, बृसी etc. This list is not exhaustive. Other words exhibiting similar features can also be included. (This is therefore called an ākṛtigaṇa.) Thus we may add कर्तुकामः, कर्तुमनाः etc. in the pṛṣodarādi-list.]

(7) Śl. 16. पुरुषोत्तमः *Puruṣottamaḥ:*

'न निर्धारणे' इति षष्ठीसमासप्रतिषेधो न भवति, जात्याद्यनपेक्षया समर्थत्वात् ।

The sixth-case (Genitive) compound cannot be prohibited here by the rule: "A word in the genitive case is not compounded with another, when the sixth case implies specification" (II.2-10); because, the words here (puruṣa and uttama) are connected in sense, and have no reference to genus (*jāti*) etc.

(8) Śl. 17. निधिः *Nidhiḥ:*

'कर्मण्यधिकरणे च' इति किप्रत्ययः ।

Affix *ki* is added by the rule: "The affix *ki* comes after a '*ghu*' verb when a word in the second case is in composition with it, and when the relation of the word thus formed is one of 'location'." (III-3-99)

[*Note*: (1) In the affix (*ki*), 'i' (इ) alone remains.

(2) '*Ghu*' is the technical name given to verbs having the form of *dā* (to give) and *dhā* (to place), excepting दाप् (to cut) and दैप् (to clean).]

(9) Śl. 18. महास्वनः *Mahāsvanaḥ:*

'सन्महत्' इत्यादिना समासे कृते 'आन्महतः समानाधिकरणजातीययोः' इत्यादिना आत्वम् ।

First the compound (in महास्वनः) is formed by the rule: "The words *sat* (good), *mahat* (great)" etc.,

(II.1.61) and then long ā is substituted (i.e., महत् > महा) by the aphorism: "For the final of *mahat*, *āt* (long ā) is substituted before a word which is in apposition with it, and before the word jātīya (जातीय) (VI.3.46).

(10) Śl. 19. त्वष्टा ।

त्वक्षतेः तनूकरणार्थात् तृच् प्रत्ययः ।

The word "tvaṣṭā" is derived from the root "tvakṣ" meaning, "to chisel" or "to pare", by adding the suffix "tṛc".

[*Note*: Tvakṣ is a Parasmaipadi root belonging to the I Conjugation.

The suffix 'tṛc' expresses the sense of agent and is ordained by the rule: "ṇvultṛcau (III.1.133)". In tṛc, "c" is an indicatory letter and is dropped; only tṛ remains.

Thus tvakṣ+tṛ=tvaṣṭṛ and, in rom. sing., tvaṣṭā.]

(11) Śl. 19. हृषीकेशः *Hṛṣīkeśaḥ*:

यस्य वा सूर्यरूपस्य चन्द्ररूपस्य च जगत्प्रीतिकरा हृष्टाः केशा रश्मयः सः हृषीकेशः ।

पृषोदरादित्वात् साधुत्वम् ।

Or, Hṛṣīkeśa is one Who in the form of the sun and the moon possesses rays which delight the world. The word Hṛṣīkeśa can be justified by including it in the Pṛṣodara-group.

(12) Śl. 20. पवित्रम् *Pavitram:*

"पुवः संज्ञायाम् '(III-2-185), "कर्तरि चर्षिदेवतयोः" (III-2-186) इति पाणिनिस्मरणात् इत्रप्रत्ययः ।

The word "pavitra" is obtained by adding the suffix "itra" to the root "pū" to purify, according to the following rules of Pāṇini:

1. "The affix *itra* is added to *pū*, 'to purify', in the sense of the agent, so expressed being the instrument, when the word is an appellation but not descriptive."

2. "The affix *itra* is added to *pū* 'to purify' in the sense of the agent or the instrument when it is used in connection with a sage or deity respectively."

(13) Śl. 21. ज्येष्ठः *Jyeṣṭhaḥ*:

"ज्य च" इत्यधिकारे 'वृद्धस्य च' इति वृद्धशब्दस्य ज्यादेशविधानात् । प्रशस्यतमः श्रेष्ठः, 'प्रशास्यस्य श्रः' इति श्रादेशविधानात् ।

['The eldest one' is called jyeṣṭha.' Because suffix *jya* is ordained as the substitute for the word *vṛddha* by the rule: "[Jya] It also substitutes *vṛddha* when followed by the suffixes *iṣṭha* (इष्ठ) and *īyasun* (ईयसुन्)" (V.3.62) which comes under the governing rule "*Jya* also" (is the substitute for *praśasya* when it is followed by *iṣṭha* and *īyasun*)." (V.3.61)

The word *śreṣṭha* means 'the most praiseworthy'. It is ordained by the rule: "*Śra* is substituted for the word *praśasya*, when followed by *iṣṭha* (superlative degree) and īyasun (comparative degree) suffixes." (V.3.60)

(14) Śl. 21. श्रेष्ठः *Śreṣṭhaḥ:*

'प्राणो वाव ज्येष्ठश्च श्रेष्ठश्च' इति श्रुतेः (छा० 5-1-1) मुख्यप्राणो वा, "श्रेष्ठश्च" (ब्र.सू. II-4-8) इत्यधिकरणसिद्धत्वात् ।

Or the word "śreṣṭha" may mean the chief or vital air, as stated in the text "Prāṇa is the supreme and the, best" (Chāndogya V.i.1). This meaning is obtained from the section constituting the aphorism "śreṣṭhaśca" (Brahmasūtra II.iv.8).

(15) Śl. 22. मेधावी *Medhāvī:*

'अस्मायामेधास्रजो विनिः' इति विनिप्रत्ययः ।

Suffix *vini* is ordained by the rule: "*Vini* is added after words ending in *as* (as *yaśas*) and after the words *māyā, medhā* and *srak.*" (V-2-121)

(16) Śl. 23. सुरेशः *Sureśaḥ,* second meaning:

सूपपदो वा राधातुः । शोभनदातॄणाम् ईशः सुरेशः ।

Or, the root *rā* (to give) has '*su*' as a dependant word (*upapada*). Thus *Sureśa* is the lord of those who confer all good things.

[सु + रा + ईशः]

(17) Śl. 34. हंसः *Haṁsaḥ,* first meaning:

"अहं सः" इति तादात्म्यभाविनः संसारभयं हन्तीति हंसः । पृषोदरादित्वात् शब्दसाधुत्वम् ।

Haṁsa denotes One who dispels the fear of transmigratory existence for one who feels the identity thus "I am (the same as) He." The word can be justified by including it in the pṛṣodara-list.

[अहं + सः = हंसः]

(18) Śl. 34. पद्मनाभः *Padmanābhaḥ*:

पृषोदरादित्वात् साधुत्वम्।

The word *Padmanābha* (from Padma+nābhi) may be justified by including it in the *Pṛṣodarādi*-group.

(19) Śl. 35. सिंहः *Simhaḥ*:

हिनस्तीति सिंहः। पृषोदरादित्वात् साधुत्वम्।

He who harms is *Simha* (from हिंसि हिंसायाम्). This is correct as it is included in the *Pṛṣodarādi*-list.

(20) Śl. 39. विश्वधृक् *Viśvadhṛk*:

विश्वं धृष्णोति इति विश्वधृक्, ञिधृषा प्रागल्भ्ये।

The word *viśvadhṛk* means he who overpowers or surpasses the universe. It is derived from the root "*ñi dhṛṣā*", meaning, to overcome, or surpass.

[*Note*: In ञिधृषा, ञि and the final आ are इत् letters and are dropped.]

(21) Śl. 40. शिष्टकृत् *Śiṣṭakṛt*:

शिष्टान् करोति पालयतीति वा। सामान्यवचनो धातुः विशेषवचनो दृष्टः, कुरु काष्ठानि इत्याहरणे यथा।

He who 'makes' or "protects" good people is called "Śiṣṭakṛt". A verbal root which conveys a general sense sometimes conveys a specific sense. Thus the expression "make the faggot" means "bring the faggot".

[Śaṅkara's point is that the root 'कृ' (करोति) should be taken as 'पाल्' (पालयति) in this case.]

(22) Śl. 41. वृषाही *Vṛṣāhī*:

वृषाह इत्यत्र 'राजाहः सखिभ्यः टच्' इति टच् प्रत्ययः समासान्तः।

In the word *vṛṣāha,* the affix "*ṭac*" [i.e., अ] is added at the end of a [Tatpuruṣa] compound, according to the following aphorism: "The affix "*ṭac*" is added to the words *rājan, ahan* and *sakhi,* at the end of a Tatpuruṣa compound." (V.4.91).

[*Note*: The affix टच् (i.e., अ) substitutes the finals (of compound words) and thus we have राजन् + टच् = राज् अ = राजः; अहन् + टच् = अहः ; सखि + टच् = सखः]

(23) Śl. 45. अनलः *Analaḥ,* second meaning:

(अनलः) णलतेः गन्धवाचिनो नञ्पूर्वाद्वा।

Or, the word (*anala*) is from the root *ṇal*, to smell, preceded by the negative particle nañ (नञ्).

[*Note*: In णल्, the initial cerebral (ण) is replaced by the dental न]

(24) Śl. 46. नैकमाय: *Naikamāyaḥ*:

नलोपो नञः इति नकारलोपो न भवति, ञकारानुबन्धरहितस्यापि नकारस्य प्रतिषेधवाचिनो विद्यमानत्वात्।

[In the word नैकमाय:] The letter *na* is not dropped according to the rule "The न् (*n*) of the Negative Particle नञ् is elided, when it is the first member of a compound", (VI.3.73) because there is also the letter *na* in the sense of negation, without the indicatory letter ञ् (ñ).

[In Sanskrit, both न and नञ् convey 'negation'. In नैकमाय: the particle न but not नञ् is used.]

(25) Śl. 49. पुरंदर: *Puramdaraḥ*:

'वाचंयमपुरंदरौ च' इति पाणिनिना निपातनात्।

The word *Puramdara* is irregularly formed, as indicated by Pāṇini's rule "*vācamyama* and *puramdara* are irregularly formed." (VI.3.69) [The irregularity is the non-elision of the Accusative case.]

(26) Śl. 52. भीम: *Bhīmaḥ*:

बिभेत्यस्मात् सर्वमिति भीमः। 'भीमादयोऽपादाने' इति पाणिनिस्मृतेः।

Bhīma is one, of whom, everything else is afraid, as stated in the following aphorism of Pāṇini: "The words *bhīma* etc. are irregularly formed and denote ablation." (III.4.74).

(27) Śl. 55. व्यवस्थान: *Vyavasthānaḥ*

कृत्यल्युटो बहुलम् (III-3-113) इति बहुलग्रहणात् कर्तरि ल्युट्प्रत्ययः।

The word vyavasthāna is got by adding lyuṭ (to vyava+sthā). This is by the rule: "The affix called kṛtya and the affix called lyuṭ are diversely applicable." Lyuṭ can be added in the sense of the agent by the force of the expression "diversely applicable" (*bahula*) used in the aphorism.

[*Note*: In lyuṭ, the initial "l" and the final "ṭ" are indicatory and hence dropped; "yu" is then replaced by "ana".

Thus we have—

vyava+sthā+lyuṭ=vyavasthā+yu=vyavasthāna.]

(28) Śl. 60. अभूः *Abhūḥ,* second meaning:

अथवा 'भू सत्तायाम्' इत्यस्य संपदादित्वात् क्विप् ।

Or, *Kvip* is the affix added after the root *bhū* 'to be' since it belongs to the *sampadādi* group.

[Thus भू + क्विप्. In क्विप् all syllables are to be elided (सर्वलोप) भू + O = भू: ; न + भू: = अभू:]

(29) Śl. 60. क्षामः *Kṣāmaḥ:*

'क्षायो मः' इति निष्ठातकारस्य मकारादेशः ।

[In the word *kṣāma*] *Ma* is substituted for the *Niṣṭhā* 'ta' after the root क्षै (VIII.2.53)

[*Note*: The past passive participle *'kta'* (i.e., *ta*) and the Active participle affix *ktavatu* (i.e. *tavat*) are technically called *Niṣṭhā*.]

(30) Śl. 63. वत्सलः *Vatsalaḥ:*

'वत्सांसाभ्यां कामबले' इति लच्प्रत्ययः ।

Affix "*lac*" लच्, is added by the following rule: "Affix '*lac*' is added after the words *vatsa* and *aṁsa* in the sense of 'affectionate' and 'strong', respectively." (V.2.98)

[*Note*: In लच्, ल alone remains, च् being an इत् letter (to be elided).]

(31) Śl. 67. सात्वतां पतिः *Śattvatām patiḥ:*

सात्वतं नाम तन्त्रम् । 'तत्करोति तदाचष्टे' इति णिचि कृते क्विप् प्रत्यये णिलोपे च कृते पदं सात्वत् । तेषां पतिः योगक्षेमकरः इति सात्वतां पतिः ।

Sāttvata is the name of a religious text.

When causal *ṇic* is added (in the sense of he who does or speak about or follow) and then *kvip* after the word सात्वत्, *'ṇi'* (of ṇic) gets completely elided, leaving the form सात्वत् as it is. सात्वतां पतिः therefore means the master, who looks after the welfare of those people (i.e., the followers of the Sāttvata school.)

(32) Śl. 68. मुकुन्दः *Mukundaḥ:*

मुक्तिं ददाति इति मुकुन्दः । पृषोदरादित्वात् साधुत्वम् । अक्षरसाम्यान्निरुक्तिवचनात् मुकुन्द इति निरुक्तिः ।

One who bestows *mukti* (liberation) is called *muk-*

unda. This word is correct, since it can be included in the *Pṛṣodarādi* list.

The word *mukunda* is derived in the above way (i.e., one who bestows *mukti*) by the Etymologists since it has been stated (by Yāska) that etymological derivation should be given for words, even on the basis of similarity of letters.

[From *muktim+dadāti,* we can thus form the word *muk* (un) *da,* since there are some letters in common.]

(33) Śl. 68. अन्तकः *Antakaḥ*:

अन्तं करोति भूतानामिति अन्तकः। तत्करोति तदाचष्टे इति णिचि ण्वुलि अकादेशः।

He who brings about the end of the beings is called *Antaka* (*Anta+ka*). Here suffix *ṇic* is added in the sense of 'he who performs or speaks of', and then ण्वुल् (ṇvul) is added (in the sense of the agent). *Aka* is the substitute for (*vu* of) *ṇvul.*

[*Note*: ण्वुल् is added in the sense of agency by the rule: ण्वुल्तृचौ (II-1-133). In ण्वुल् the initial ण् and the final ल् are इत् letters and are dropped. वु is then replaced by अक by the rule: युवोरनाकौ (VII-1-1).]

(34) Śl. 75. शम : *Śamaḥ*:

'तत्करोति तदाचष्टे इति णिचि पचाद्यचि कृते रूपं शम इति।

The form *Śama* is obtained by adding *ṇic* and then '*ac*' of the *pacādi* group, to the root शम्. *ṇic* is added in the sense of 'he who does, or speaks of' (agency).

[Thus शम् + णिच् + अच्
शम् + अ = शमः

अच् is added to *Pacādi*-roots by the rule: नन्दिग्रहिपचादिभ्यो ल्युणिन्यच: (III-1-134).]

(35) Śl. 75. परायणम् *Parāyaṇam*:

परमुत्कृष्टमयनं स्थानं पुनरावृत्तिशङ्कारहितमिति परायणम्। पुंलिङ्गपक्षे बहुव्रीहिः।

Parāyaṇam means the supreme, or the highest abode, being free from suspicion (fear) of return. If the word is taken in masculine gender (as *Parāyaṇaḥ*), it will be a *Bahuvrīhi*-compound (Epithetised, meaning, he whose abode is free from fear of return).

(36) Śl. 76. कुवलेशयः *Kuvaleśayaḥ*, second meaning:
'शयवासवासिष्वकालात्' इति अलुक् सप्तम्याः ।

The locative case is not elided according to the following aphorism: "There is no elision of the seventh case after words which do not indicate time, provided those words are followed by *śaya, vāsa* and *vāsin*." (VI.3.18)

(37) Śl. 76. वृषप्रियः *Vṛṣapriyaḥ*, first meaning:
वृषो धर्मः प्रियो यस्य सः वृषप्रियः; 'वा प्रियस्य' इति पूर्वनिपातविकल्पविधानात् परनिपातः ।

He who likes *vṛṣa* or *dharma* is called *vṛṣapriya*. Here the word (*priya*) is placed next to the word *vṛṣa*, since its being ordained as the first member is optional according to the following: [Vārtika of Vararuci under II.2.35:] "In a Bahuvrīhi compound the word *priya* may optionally be placed as the first member."

(38) Śl. 83. वीरः *Vīraḥ*:
गत्यादिमत्वात् वीरः ; 'वी गति (व्याप्ति) प्रजनकान्त्यसनखादनेषु' इति धातुपाठात् ।

The word *vīra* is from root *vī*, (2nd conjugation) denoting one who possesses qualities like movement. This is read in the list of verbs thus: "*vī* is used to denote going (pervading), bringing forth (conceiving), shining, throwing and eating."

(39) Śl. 93. सुमेधाः *Sumedhāḥ*:
'नित्यमसिच् प्रजामेधयोः' इति समासान्तोऽसिच् ।

[In *sumedhas*] Affix *asic* (असिच्) is added as the final of a Taddhita compound, according to the following rule: "Affix *asic* is obligatory after the words *prajā* and *medhā* prefixed by *nañ* (नञ्) *dus* (दुस्) and *su* (सु) (V.4.122)."

(40) Śl. 94. प्रग्रहः *Pragrahaḥ*:
'रश्मौ च' इति पाणिनिवचनात् प्रग्रहशब्दस्य साधुत्वम् ।

The word *Pragraha* (reins) is justified on the authority of Pāṇini: The affix घञ् (ghañ) comes optionally after the verb 'grah' in composition with 'pra', when the word so formed, means "reins". (III.3.53)

[In घञ् only अ remains; the optional form is प्रग्राहः]

(41) Śl. 98. सुन्दः *Sundaḥ*:

'सुष्ठु उनत्तीति सुन्दः', उदी क्लेदने इत्यस्मात् धातोः पचाद्यच् ; आर्द्रीभावस्य वाचकः करुणाकर इत्यर्थः ; पृषोदरादित्वात् पररूपत्वम् ।

Sunda is one who becomes extremely wet (melted). This is from the root उन्द् to wet (moisten, bathe), to which affix *ac* (*a*) of the *Pacādi*-group is added. It then denotes 'becoming wet' and means 'one who is an abode of compassion'. Here in the combination [su+und+a=su+undaḥ], the second vowel [*u* of undaḥ] alone remains in the place of both the preceding and the following vowels, because it can be included in the *pṛṣodarādi*-list. Hence no सवर्णदीर्घसन्धि.

(42) Śl. 98. जयी *Jayī*:

आभ्यन्तरान् रागादीन् बाह्यान् हिरण्याक्षादींश्च दुर्जयान् जेतुं शीलमस्येति जयी । तच्छीलाधिकारे 'जिदृक्षि' इत्यादिपाणिनीयवचनात् इनि-प्रत्ययः ।

Jayī is one who is in the habit of conquering the internal as well as external enemies like undue attachment and Hiraṇyākṣa respectively, difficult to vanquish.

Affix *ini* (i.e., *in*) is added to root *ji* by the rule of Pāṇini: "The affix *ini* is added to roots *ji*—to conquer, *dṛ*—to respect, *kṣi*—to waste, to dwell, to go, etc." in the sense of "the agent having such a habit" etc. This sūtra comes under the governing rule ordaining habit etc.

[*Note*: The full sūtra of Pāṇini (III.2.157) is: जिदृक्षिविश्रीण्वमाव्यथाभ्यमपरिभूप्रसूभ्यश्च ।

"Affix इनि comes, in the sense of 'the agent having such a habit etc.', after the verbs जि (to conquer), दृ (to respect), क्षि (to waste, to dwell, to go), विश्रि (to shelter), इ (to go), वम् (to vomit), अव्यथ (not to give pain), अभ्यम (to injure), परिभू (to insult) and प्रसू (to give birth to)."

The governing rule referred to above is "आ क्वेः तच्छीलतद्धर्मतत्साधुकारिषु" (III-2-134) [From this sūtra as far as क्विप् (III-2-177) inclusive, the affixes that are ordained are to be understood in the sense of 'agents having such a habit', or 'nature', or 'having skill in such and such action'.]

(43) Śl. 100. अनिलः *Anilaḥ*, third meaning:

अथवा निलतेर्गहनार्थात् कप्रत्ययान्ताद्रूपम् । अगहनः अनिलः । भक्तेभ्यः सुलभः इति ।

Or, the form *anila* can be derived from the root *nila* (VI Conjugation) meaning 'to become grave, hard' etc., to which suffix ka (i.e., अ) is added. One who is not hard to approach, is *anila*. It means one who is of easy access to his devotees.

(44) Śl. 101. न्यग्रोध : *Nyagrodhaḥ:*

न्यक् अर्वाक् रोहति, सर्वेषामुपरि वर्तत इति न्यग्रोधः पृषोदरादित्वात् हकारस्य धकारादेशः ।

'Nyagrodha' (banyan tree) is that which grows (roh) downwards (nyak); in other words it is on the top of all things. The "h" [of *roh*] is replaced by "dh" since this word can be included in the Pṛṣodarādi-list.

[nyag+roh=nyag+rodh=nyagrodhaḥ.]

(45) Śl. 101. उदुम्बर: *Udumbaraḥ:*

न्यग्रोधोदुम्बर इत्यत्र विसर्गलोपे संधिरार्षः ।

In the expression "nyagrodhodumbara", the coalescence which takes place after dropping the visarga, has to be traced to the Ṛṣi (Vyāsa) (i.e., archaic, and hence unquestionable).

[nyagrodhaḥ + udumbaraḥ = nyagrodha + udumbaraḥ=nyagrodhodumbaraḥ, by the Guṇa-rule आद् गुणः (VI.1.87).]

(46) Śl. 101. अश्वत्थः । *Aśvatthaḥ:*

श्वोऽपि न स्थातेति अश्वत्थः । पृषोदरादित्वादेव सकारस्य तकारादेशः ।

'Aśvattha' [the peepal tree] is that which will not last [na sthātā] even till 'tomorrow' (śvaḥ). The letter "s" (of sthā) is replaced by "t", only by reading this in the Pṛṣodara-list.

[Thus न + श्वः + स्था = न + श्व + त्थ = अश्वत्थः]

(47) Śl. 104. क्षाम : *Kṣāmaḥ:*

क्षामाः क्षीणाः सर्वाः प्रजाः करोतीति क्षामः । 'तत्करोति तदाचष्टे' इति णिचि पचाद्यचि कृते संपन्नः क्षाम इति ।

One who makes all beings waste away, (during pralaya) is *kṣāma*. The word *kṣāma* is obtained by adding *ṇic* to the root *kṣi* (to waste away) in the sense of 'he who does, or speaks of', and also by adding *ac* (*a*) of the *Pacādi*-group.

(48) Śl. 107. सूर्यः *Sūryaḥ*:

सूतेः सुवतेर्वा सूर्यशब्दो निपात्यते । 'राजसूयसूर्य' इति पाणिनिवचनात् सूर्यः ।

The word 'sūrya' is an irregular form derived from either the root षङ् (to give birth to, to produce) (II conjugation) or from षू (to stir into activity) (VI conjugation). The word 'sūrya' has been ordained by Pāṇini in the rule "rājasūya-sūrya" etc.

[The full Sūtra is "राजसूय-सूर्य-मृषोद्य-रुच्य-कुप्य-कृष्टपच्य-अव्यथ्याः" (III-1-114). All these words end in the suffix क्यप् (i.e., य) and are to be taken for granted.]

(49) Śl. 111. दक्षिणः *Dakṣiṇaḥ*:

दक्षते गच्छति हिनस्तीति वा दक्षिणः । 'दक्ष गतिहिंसनयो :' इति धातुपाठात् ।

He who goes or injures is *dakṣiṇa.* The list of verbal roots reads thus: "*Dakṣ* is used in the sense of going and harming."

(50) Śl. 114. जननः *Jananaḥ*:

जन्तून् जनयन् जननः ; ल्युड्विधौ बहुलग्रहणात् कर्तरि ल्युट् प्रत्ययः प्रयोगवचनादिवत् ।

He who procreates people is called *janana.* This is formed by adding suffix *lyuṭ* (i.e., *yu,* replaced by *ana*), in the sense of agency because the word *bahula* "diversely applicable" is used in the rule ordaining lyuṭ. The word *janana* is thus formed like the words *prayoga* and *vacana.*

[Note: The rule referred to is कृत्यल्युटो बहुलम् (III-3-133). "The affixes called *Kṛtya* (III-1-95) and the affix lyuṭ' are diversely applicable."]

(51) Śl. 114. भीमः *Bhīmaḥ*:

भयहेतुत्वात् भीमः । 'भीमादयः अपादाने' इति निपातनात् ।

He who is the cause of fear is called *bhīma.* It is ordained by the rule: "The words *bhīma* etc. are irregularly formed and denote ablation." (III.4.74)

[Same as भीमः in Śl. 52.]

(52) Śl. 115. अधाता *Adhātā*:

स्वात्मना धृतस्यान्यो धाता नास्तीति अधाता । 'नञ्सुतश्च' इति समासान्तविधिरनित्यः' इति कप्प्रत्ययाभावः ।

The word *adhātā* means He who does not have another supporter for the world which is already supported by Himself.

It does not take the affix *kap* (*ka*) by the rule: "Suffix *kap* comes after a Bahuvrīhi compound having the word *nadī* and also a word ending in short ṛ, as the second members." (V.4.153)

This is so because a rule pertaining to the finals of compounds is not obligatory. [It may or may not operate.]

(53) Śl. 115. धाता *Dhātā*:

संहारसमये सर्वाः प्रजाः धयति पिबतीति वा धाता; धेट् पाने इति धातुः ।

Dhātā is He who drinks in (takes in) all the beings at the time of cosmic destruction. Here the root is '*dheṭ* (I Conjugation) to drink'.

[*Note*: In धेट् the final ट् is an इत् letter and hence is dropped. So, धे + अ + ति = धयति (III pers. singular form, present tense).]

(54) Śl. 120. शार्ङ्गधन्वा *Śārṅgadhanvā*:

'धनुषश्च' इति अनङ् समासान्तः ।

[In the word *śārṅgadhanvan*], Anaṅ (i.e. *an*) is the affix substituted at the end of a compound according to the rule: "*Anaṅ* is the substitute for the final of a Bahuvrīhi compound, ending in the word *dhanus*." (V.4.132)

[*Note*: Thus, शार्ङ्ग + धनुस् > शार्ङ्ग + धनु (स्) + अनङ् > शार्ङ्ग + धनु + अन् > शार्ङ्गधन्वन्]

———:*:———

APPENDIX II

Index of Nāmas which occur more than once in the Viṣṇusahasranāma Stotra but with different meanings.

Nāma	Śl
अ	
अक्षोभ्यः ..	99,120
अच्युतः ..	24,48
अजः ..	24,35,69
अनघः ..	29,102
अनन्तः ..	83,108
अनलः ..	45,89
अनिरुद्धः ..	33,81
अनिर्देश्यवपुः ..	32,83
अनिर्विण्णः ..	60,108
अपराजितः ..	89,105
अमितविक्रमः ..	68,81
अमेयात्मा ..	24,32
अमोघः ...	25,30
अव्ययः ..	15,17
आदित्यः ..	[illegible],73
आदिदेवः ..	49,65
ई	
ईश्वरः ..	17,22
उ	
उद्भवः ..	54,98
ऋ	
ऋद्धः ..	43,57
क	
कर्ता ..	47,54
कान्तः ..	45,83
कुमुदः ..	76,100
कृतज्ञः ..	22,70
कृतागमः ..	83,97
कृष्णः ..	20,72
केशवः ..	16,82
क्षामः ..	60,104
ग	
गहनः ..	54,71
गुरुः ..	36,65
गोपतिः ..	66,76
गोप्ता ..	66,76
गोविन्दः ..	33,71
च	
चक्री ..	110,120
चतुरात्मा ..	28,95
चतर्व्यूहः ..	28,95
ज	
ज्योतिः ..	73,79,107
त	
तारः ..	50,117
द	
दक्षः ..	58,111
दुर्धरः ..	42,89
द्युतिधरः ..	43,94
ध	
धाता ..	18,115

॥ श्रीः ॥

॥ नामानुक्रमणिका ॥

Index of Nāmas.